Cognitive Behavioural Therapy
with Older People

Cognitive Behavioural Therapy with Older People

INTERVENTIONS FOR THOSE WITH AND WITHOUT DEMENTIA

IAN ANDREW JAMES

Jessica Kingsley Publishers
London and Philadelphia

First published in 2010
by Jessica Kingsley Publishers
116 Pentonville Road
London N1 9JB, UK
and
400 Market Street, Suite 400
Philadelphia, PA 19106, USA

www.jkp.com

Library of Congress Cataloging in Publication Data
A CIP catalog record for this book is available from the Library of Congress

British Library Cataloguing in Publication Data
A CIP catalogue record for this book is available from the British Library

ISBN 978 1 84905 100 2

Printed and bound in Great Britain by the MPG Books Group

Contents

PART 2

PART 3

LIST OF FIGURES AND TABLES

Chapter 1

Introduction

1.1: INTRODUCTION

The literature on treating older people informs us that they can not only benefit from psychotherapy (Hartman-Stein 2005; Zalaquett and Stens 2006), but in some situations may show better outcomes than their younger counterparts (Walker and Clarke 2001). This book provides a review of the use of cognitive behavioural therapy (CBT) for people with and without cognitive difficulties. The book is in three parts. The first orientates the reader to the topic, examines potential adaptations, and discusses CBT from a practical and conceptual perspective. Part 2 reviews older people's therapy in terms of the key stages of assessment, formulation and interventions. Finally, Part 3 provides practical advice, using both case examples and observations taken from trainees' therapy to help improve therapeutic competence.

1.2: PARTITIONING – PARTS 1 TO 3

Part 1

Following this introductory chapter, the first three chapters (2–4) orientate the reader to both the topic and population. Chapter 2 is entitled 'Patients' Presentations and How CBT Helps'. It provides a general overview of patients' experience of negative affect, discussing their difficulties across a range of domains (neurological, behavioural, cognitive, interpersonal, etc.). The initial section attempts to demonstrate the sorts of basic challenges that a therapist will encounter when working with someone with depression or anxiety. The next part of this chapter outlines the manner in which CBT is structured to deal with such difficulties.

Chapter 3 specifically addresses working with older people and is entitled 'Adapting Therapy for Older People'. It criticises the tendency to discuss older people as if they are a homogenous, well-defined population. An attempt to capture the heterogeneity is made by representing older people's issues within four distinct quadrants along the two dimensions of cognitive versus physical abilities. It is suggested that within these quadrants, one will have differing patient profiles and treatments.

The fourth chapter 'Cognitive Changes, Executive Functioning, Working Memory and Scripts' aims to link the first chapters with the subsequent one on 'Assessment'. Once again the nature of mood disorders is discussed, but this time solely from a neurological and cognitive perspective. Particular emphasis is placed on the important roles that executive functioning and working memory play in patients' abilities to engage well in therapy. Some of the typical problems associated with deficits in these areas are discussed.

Part 2

Chapters 5–7 discuss the classic stages of therapy: assessment, case formulation, and change techniques respectively. It is emphasised throughout this part of the book that it is rather artificial to make clear distinctions between these three therapy phases because they share many common structures and processes. For example, good interpersonal skills, pacing and collaborating are required throughout, and diaries, questionnaires, etc. may be used (with different functions) as both assessment and intervention tools.

The discussion sections of these chapters emphasise that the aim of therapy is to develop effective interventions to change people's mood states. With respect to CBT, the above aims are achieved through the development of idiosyncratic formulations. Chapter 6 gives an overview of the numerous formulations that have been used with older people, examining their utility and suitability with respect to the various presentations therapists encounter when working with older people. Chapter 7 on 'Change Techniques' pays attention to the need for therapists to have a good understanding of the change mechanisms underpinning their change strategies. It is argued that without such awareness, there is the possibility that one might intervene inappropriately, lowering patients' mood further and inadvertently reinforcing negative cognitions. Such scenarios are most likely to occur when therapists are operating at the level of core beliefs.

Part 3

Chapters 8–10 are practical in nature, with Chapter 8 and 10 each discussing a case. The first case study concerns a woman, Mary, with recurrent depression who is treated with a diathesis-stress formulation approach. The material used in her treatment is designed to illustrate those features discussed in the preceding chapters (Part 2) regarding assessment, conceptual work and change strategies.

Chapter 9, entitled 'Assessing and Developing Clinical Competence', presents an adaptation of a competency scale used to assess therapists' abilities to use CBT. The original scale was called the Cognitive Therapy Scale-Revised (CTS-R), which I was involved in developing (Blackburn *et al.* 2001). The version presented here has been adapted for use with older people. It describes 12 core items associated with CBT, providing details of their rationale and practical guidance regarding their performance.

Chapter 10 presents a case of a man with dementia, Donald, who is displaying a challenging behaviour. The approach used to treat him is a form of psychotherapy used over the last ten years by a specialist team in Newcastle-upon-Tyne, UK. The approach borrows heavily from group CBT formats. The chapter shows how CBT principles can be used with care staff working in 24-hour care environments.

The final chapter of the book, Chapter 11, briefly considers important topics that could not be discussed in detail in the main sections of the text. The three main topics are 'Working with carers', 'Alternative models to CBT in the treatment of depression' and 'Improving access to psychological therapies: provision of mental health services of older people'. This chapter ends with some reflections on the book and on my personal journey over the last 20 years as a clinician using and adapting CBT.

The book ends with two appendices. In Appendix I a number of the disorder-specific conceptual frameworks are discussed in relation to the anxiety disorders (panic, generalised anxiety disorder, obsessive compulsive disorder and social phobia). They have been included in support of Chapters 3 and 6 (adapting therapy and case formulation respectively). The material provides the reader with an overview of how generic formulations need to be changed to accommodate the features of each diagnosis. Appendix II presents an unpublished manuscript designed to aid teaching of the CST-R. The content enhances the material presented in Chapter 9, providing the reader with specific examples of good and poor practice taken from my clinical and supervisory work over the last ten years.

PART I

Chapter 2

Patients' Presentations and How CBT Helps

2.1: INTRODUCTION

In this chapter the reader is first provided with a description of mood disorders as experienced by patients and is then given a summary of standard CBT. The former aims to highlight the difficulties faced by both patients and therapists during treatment. The latter describes how CBT is designed to deal with such problems.

This chapter aims to illustrate the following:

1. Mood disorders can be conceptualised from many different perspectives (neuropsychological, chemical, behavioural, cognitive, etc.).

2. People suffering from mood disorders experience their distress within many of the above domains.

3. When patients attend therapy, they bring their amotivation, avoidance, poor memory, concentration and attention with them. Hence, therapy must factor these features in, requiring the therapeutic framework to be simple and conducted very slowly.

4. CBT is a therapy that attempts to impose simple structures around people's experiences, making their difficulties less overwhelming and more manageable.

5. The acronym KISS (Keep It Simple and Slow...very slow) can be used as a reminder for clinicians, regarding their therapeutic approach.

6. The principles of CBT can be used in non-standard forms in numerous other settings (e.g. working with people with dementia and their carers).

2.2: NATURE OF THE MOOD DISORDERS

The nature of depression and anxiety may be conceptualised in terms of a number of domains. For example, they can be described in terms of: the actions of neurotransmitters, brain changes, hormones, information processing biases, intrapsychic features, and interpersonal changes. Neurotransmitters are generally the targets of psychotropic medication, and will not be discussed in detail in this text. Structural alterations to the brain are associated with low mood, with some form of late-onset depression linked to arteriosclerotic, inflammatory and immune changes (Alexopoulos 2005). A great deal of debate has occurred about whether such changes indicate that this type of depression is 'untreatable' via medication. In contrast to this hotly debated issue, less attention has been paid to the changes frequently found in brain functioning as observed by scanning techniques (Drevets and Raichle 1995). Of particular interest to therapists (James, Reichelt, Carlsson and McAnaney 2008) are the changes occurring within the frontal lobes because these have a direct influence on therapeutic processes (see Chapter 4). Psychometric studies of people experiencing low mood also reveal marked information processing deficits. Some of these deficits can be related directly to frontal lobe dysfunction, but others, such as marked memory problems, demonstrate the more diffuse impact of the psychiatric disorders (Cassens, Wolfe and Zola 1990; Williams 1992). Behavioural changes are also common when someone is experiencing poor mood. Indeed, depending on the nature of the difficulties, the person may become either more agitated or increasingly withdrawn. Further, low mood often leads to changes in people's self image, and both their view of the world and their future. Beck has described the latter in terms of the triadic model (aka the content specificity model, Beck 1976, Figure 2.1). As outlined in the diagram, when all three self-views are negative, the belief formed is associated with a negative mood state. The specific views and themes associated with these mood states are outlined in the table.

The belief systems become the engine room of negative patterns of thinking, and a positive feedback loop is set up with the thinking reinforcing the person's belief systems. Thus over time, dysfunctional cycles become established, resulting in a reduction in the threshold of activation of the belief systems. This leads to negative styles of thinking becoming the default

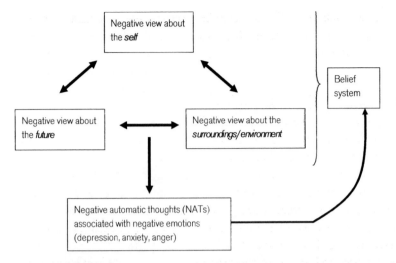

Cognitive themes in triads (self, future, surroundings)		Emotions
Triads	Sense of self as worthless or inadequate, with negative view of world and viewing the future as being hopeless	Depression
	Sense of vulnerability, perception of the environment as chaotic, and the future as unpredictable	Anxiety
	Sense of personal injustice, perception of the environment as hostile, a need to act to protect self from future harm	Anger

Figure 2.1: Triadic models and cognitive themes

way of interpreting the world for the individual. Beck labelled the products of this style of thinking 'negative automatic thoughts' (NATs). Cognitive therapists are particularly interested in NATs as they are the verbalised form of patients' experiences. However, it is important to note that the thoughts are merely the tip of the iceberg in relation to the person's difficulties, and if one solely dealt with them it is unlikely that one would obtain lasting benefits (James, Southam and Blackburn 2004). Indeed, below the level of the NATs is an inter-connected, symbiotic network of chemical, neurological, behavioural, intrapsychic processes. And because these processes reinforce each other, their collective actions work to maintain the negative homeostasis. For example, consider a depressed person who has just received some 'good' news about a part-time job in a local charity shop. Rather than this serving to improve her mood, the success may actually make her feel worse! First, her cortisol levels may begin to rise. She may start to experience physical tension across the shoulders and stomach. Her stress may lead to mouth ulcers, making it difficult to eat. With respect to the achievement of getting the job, she may perceive herself to have been lucky, rather than accomplished. She may even start focusing on the negative consequences of gaining the new role. Figure 2.2, the fragile egg (James 2001a), outlines how patients can reassess information, even positive stimuli, in negative ways.

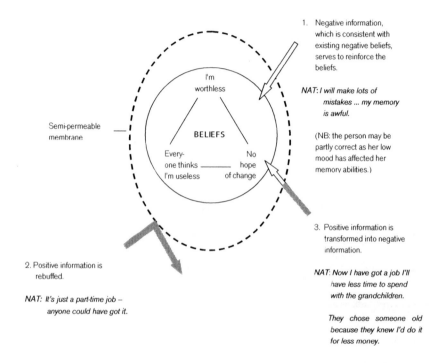

Figure 2.2: Representation of information processing in depression – the fragile egg

Table 2.1 outlines some of the common information biases found in depression.

In addition to these reinterpretations, there may be interpersonal worries too. For example, she may worry about how she will cope with meeting new people. This is because low mood typically interferes with people's abilities to maintain interpersonal relationships. Indeed, those suffering often avoid others or fail to find pleasure in others' company. The person may also worry about how she is going to cope with her recent intellectual changes, probably being aware of her slowed speed of thinking and impaired problem solving.

Table 2.1: Common information biases found in affective disorders (adapted from Westbrook et al. 2007)

Type of bias	Comment	Example
a. Extreme thinking		
Black and white (dichotomous) thinking	Seeing the world only in terms of the extremes – an 'all or nothing' thinking style.	He's dead, and so no-one will ever want me again. I am unattractive.
Unrealistic expectations	A person with dysfunctionally high standards, which are not adjusted for changes in health status.	If I can't do all my housework perfectly, then I'm useless.
Catastrophisation	Predicting the worst in situations that do not warrant such pessimism.	I lost my car keys again, I'm positive I've got dementia.
b. Selective attention		
Over-generalisation	Seeing a single negative event as an indication that everything is bad.	Driving into the ditch means I'm no longer a safe driver.
Magnification of negative and minimisation of the positive	Exaggerating the importance of negative events and playing down the relevance of positive ones.	In my seventies I got another degree, but unlike before I wasn't top of the class.
c. Relying on intuition		
Jumping to conclusions	Making negative judgements without sufficient evidence.	Joan has not phoned me since Tuesday; she must be seriously ill.
Emotional reasoning	Assuming feelings reflect facts.	I can just feel that something really bad is going to happen if I go out today.
d. Self-reproach		
Taking things personally	Taking a negative personal interpretation in a neutral situation.	They asked the neighbour to baby-sit my grandchild; they mustn't trust me.
Self-blame	Unfairly blaming oneself for events and situations.	I was too soft on John when he was young. That's why he's left his wife and kids.

The utility of conceptualising mood disorders in this rather broad fashion is that it helps one to appreciate some of the experiences a patient is coping with when she comes for treatment. It highlights the fact that when someone is either depressed or anxious it is not just their cognitions that become negative, but a whole host of other features. Further, these other features will be having a very real impact on the person's physiology, memory, behaviour, etc. Hence, when engaged in therapy, the patient's poor attention, amotivation, distractability, etc. are not signs of laziness (or reasons to discharge her), rather they are the characteristic features of the disorders. An overview of patients' experiences is presented in Table 2.2. Thus, from a therapist's perspective, it is important to appreciate that any therapy offered must take account of the executive and memory difficulties, the poor motivation, and limited attentional capacity of the individual. In short, one must choose a therapeutic model that has the appropriate rationale, structure and process features to deal with the symptoms. It is my view that CBT provides an appropriate model and theoretical framework to accommodate such issues. Nevertheless, it is also important to remember that if CBT is applied inappropriately it can further decrease mood, increasing the risk of self-harm (James 2001b). Indeed, in contrast to Andrews' views (Andrews 1996), CBT is *not* 'a safe alternative to medication', rather it is a powerful psychotherapy that can potentially reinforce dysfunctionality, and even create new dysfunctional core beliefs, when misapplied (James 2001b). Owing to these concerns, some of the later material in this text addresses issues of therapeutic competence (see Chapter and Appendix II).

Table 2.2: The experience of depression: features that need to be acknowledged during treatment

low mood	sleep disturbance
co-morbid anxiety	concrete thinking
negative thinking	lack of motivation
hopelessness	negative information biases (catastrophising,
withdrawal/avoidance	magnifying)
low sense of worth	interpersonal difficulties
agitation	behavioural features (withdrawal)
poor concentration	
poor attention	
poor problem solving	
other executive problems	

2.3: NATURE OF STANDARD CBT

There is a comprehensive description of CBT in *A Clinician's Guide to Mind Over Mood* (Greenberger and Padesky 1995), and it is noteworthy that one of their four main case studies is an older person. From an older people's perspective a helpful pair of manuals (a patient's and therapist's version) have been produced by Thompson *et al.* (2009) and Gallagher-Thompson and Thompson (2009), respectively. In Chapter 9 of the present text, an account of the structural and process components that make up the cognitive approach are discussed in detail. However, the purpose of the present section is to provide a basic overview of CBT's rationale, and how it attempts to deal with some of the difficulties raised in Table 2.2. The section is written under three headings, mirroring the therapy format: socialisation to CBT and assessment; formulation and intervention stages; termination and relapse management work. It is important for the therapist to be working collaboratively with the patient throughout these phases. Indeed, the working alliance is the bedrock on which the therapy is based. Thus the therapist must work hard at establishing and maintaining a good interpersonal relationship, moving deftly between the roles of collaborator, supporter, advocate, trainer, supervisor, and consultant (Ungar 2006). In her role as collaborator it is vital that the patient understands the nature of her disorder and understands how CBT is going to help. Thus a partial knowledge of CBT is insufficient because this will not permit the establishment of a true therapeutic partnership. Owing to the relevance of the former, the therapist is required to progress slowly at the start of the therapy, spending a great deal of time socialising his patients to CBT and giving them an understanding of their disorder within a cognitive framework (depression, panic, generalised anxiety disorder (GAD)). Such psycho-education can be greatly facilitated through the use of appropriate bibliotherapy (Floyd 1999; Scogin, Jamison and Gochneaur 1989). Indeed, Mohlman and Gorman's (2005) study examining the treatment of older people with GAD is an excellent example of a treatment package using psychoeducation enhanced through workbooks.

i. Socialisation to CBT and assessment

As described above, people who are depressed and/or anxious often experience difficulties across many domains. There is a mixture of physical, social, chemical and cognitive sensations to deal with, leading to patients having a rather chaotic experience of themselves and their surroundings. Owing to the amorphous nature of the problems patients deal with, they often find it difficult to know where to begin tackling difficulties. CBT helps with this by placing a structure around the problem. Hence, a patient's problem is first given a name (i.e. a diagnosis – depression, panic, obsessive compulsive disorder (OCD), GAD, social phobia, etc.). A diagnosis alone does not help to understand the complexity of an individual's problems, yet it helps to direct the therapist towards 'condition-specific' models of the disorders (e.g. CBT model of panic – see Appendix I). Such idiosyncratic models are usually introduced once the patient's suitability for CBT has been assessed (Safran and Segal 1990, see Chapter 5), and also after the basic generic CBT cycle has been introduced. The four key structural units of the generic model are: feeling states, cognitions, behaviours and physical sensations. These units are a pretty comprehensive way of describing both people's experiences and their responses to them. Indeed, from discussions with patients it seems the simplicity yet comprehensiveness of the four-unit structure is a reason why people relate well to the therapy.

Figure 2.3 outlines the basic cycle that patients are introduced to early on in therapy. The representation is sometimes referred to as the 'hot-cross bun' model or, if the 'trigger' component is added, it is termed the five-element conceptualisation. It is essential that patients clearly understand this cycle and are able to differentiate the units from each other. They must also become articulate in describing their experiences in terms of these units. Initially, patients often find it difficult to describe their disorder in these rather artificial terms, but with a great deal of slow and deliberate practice, people often become skilled and articulate with respect to the cycle. A common error of many therapists is to rush this stage, resulting in the patient never truly understanding the fundamentals of the therapy. Appendix II outlines some of the other frequent errors made by therapists when initially using the model with patients. In my supervisory work, I emphasise the importance of steady patient progress via the acronym KISS: 'Keep It Simple and Slow'.

The basic cycle forms the core of CBT, and its structure guides many of the therapeutic processes. Indeed, many of the assessment sheets used contain the four units of the cycle (e.g. Figure 2.4 – Daily monitoring sheet). The figure shows how a carer of someone with dementia is reacting to her husband's repeated attempts to leave for work. Through reflection the carer begins to recognise that he is not really doing this on purpose, although the behaviour is still annoying. By removing this arm of the anger triad (i.e. the intentionality component), the level of the anger is reduced. It is relevant to note that it is only once the patient has become completely socialised to expressing their distress in terms of the features of the cycle that one should encourage the patient to re-evaluate the cognitions in the 'Thoughts*' column in the table. There are a number of versions of these sheets; for example, there is one specifically designed for people with poor memory,

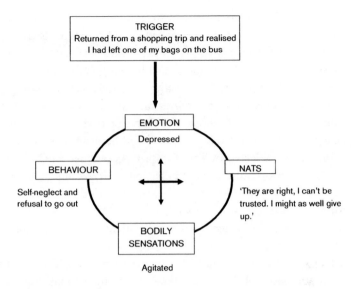

Figure 2.3: Generic CBT cycle (hot-cross bun model)

which contains three columns (Coon, Thompson and Gallagher-Thompson 2007). Coon provides a helpful discussion of their use in a case study of an older person with cognitive impairment.

Triggering situation	Your feelings	Bodily sensations	Your thoughts*	Your behaviour	Re-evaluation of thoughts*
He got up again this morning, insisting he was late for work.	Angry	Tense and wound up	He never listens to me. I've told him a hundred times he's retired. He's winding me up on purpose.	I shouted at him to go back to bed.	This dementia means he's got a memory like a goldfish. He's not trying to wind me up; he can't help it.

This column is only completed when the patient has become competent using the rest of the sheet to describe her experiences to do with the emotion.

Figure 2.4: Daily monitoring sheet for a carer of someone with dementia

Measures of severity are used early in the assessment stage to obtain a baseline against which progress of therapy can be measured. A discussion of the various measures used with older people is provided in Chapter 5. By the end of the assessment phase the therapist will have a good idea of how suitable the patient is with respect to CBT. Safran and Segal (1990) have produced a ten-item suitability scale to assist with such an assessment (see Chapter 5). Based on the 'suitability' findings, the therapist is able to determine what treatment approach to take. The approach will be determined by the nature of the formulation selected by the therapist. As outlined in Chapter 6, this can take the form of either a basic behavioural or a complex idiosyncratic formulation; the latter taking account of the patient's diagnosis and his early life history (i.e. diathesis-stress model).

As part of the assessment phase the patient will be informed of the structure and nature of the therapy arrangements, and this will often be affirmed in the form of a contract. The contract is likely to indicate the number of sessions, their frequency, timings, and the various responsibilities within the relationship, including an agreement by the patient to undertake homework assignments. The contract will also highlight the therapeutic goals jointly set by the therapist and patient. Such goals need to be Specific, Measurable, Achievable, Relevant, Timely (SMART, Chapter 5).

ii. Formulation and intervention stages

In developing the formulation, the therapist and patient are essentially pattern detectors, examining the patient's difficulties looking for the links between feeling states, behaviours and thinking styles during everyday activities. If deemed appropriate, the therapist may also choose to make links with the patient's earlier life, and possibly her childhood. Chapter 6 examines the various types of formulation approaches that are used with older people. It is important to remember that the function of the formulation is to guide the interventions; thus the production of the formulation should not become the main goal of the therapy. Some therapists are very concerned about the validity of formulations – whether they are truly accurate representations of the people's difficulties. In truth the veracity is less important than the 'workability' of the formulation. Hence, the development of an incorrect formulation, which presents a helpful therapeutic pathway, is often better than a more accurate one that has less strategic value.

As mentioned above, the formulation guides the interventions, and so it is important that the therapist and patient have a shared view about how they relate to each other. In other words the therapist needs to ensure that the patient has an understanding of the 'mechanism of change' with respect to the CBT processes employed. For example, Figure 2.5 is a diagrammatic representation of the 'mechanism of change' used in Chapter 8 with the case study of Mary. As you will see, she was socialised to the view that the negative beliefs established in her past were generating negative automatic thoughts (NATs). Such thoughts were helping to maintain her depressive cycle and, as such, her treatment needed to disrupt this self-reinforcing system. Through the use of experiential exercises she soon discovered that disruption could be achieved by monitoring her NATs, because such monitoring served both to (i) make her thoughts less automatic and more open to conscious awareness, and (ii) slow down the whole process, making the patterns more explicit and accordingly open to problem-solving strategies. Further, she was able to understand that focusing on the cognitions helped clarify the exact content of the NATs and negative beliefs, enabling her to assess their validity and the evidence she was using to support them. In this case study, once the contents of her cognitions were established, work began on making them more *flexible* (e.g. moving from beliefs like 'no-one likes me' to a slightly healthier belief of 'some people don't like me, but some *do*') and more *refined* (e.g. from 'I am totally stupid' to 'After spending time with my husband's friends, I often think I'm stupid'). It is important to remember that despite there being a lot of focus on the cognitive features of CBT, the behavioural components

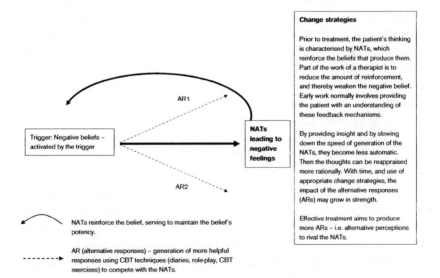

Figure 2.5: Change mechanisms in CBT

are crucial in both the assessment and intervention phases (Thompson *et al.* 2009). Indeed, the importance of regular, well-planned experiential work both in-session (experiments, role-play, etc.) and out-of-session (homework assignments) cannot be over-stated.

iii Termination and relapse management work

The label 'termination' is most frequently used in the interpersonal psychotherapy (IPT) literature (Hinrichsen and Clougherty 2006), but is also seen as a relevant feature of CBT with older people (Scholey and Woods 2003). Its relevance stems from the fact that over the preceding weeks the therapist will have been working hard to maintain a good therapeutic alliance with the patient. Hence, towards the end of therapy, careful consideration needs to be given about how to bring the collaboration to an end. Part of this work will also involve engaging the patient in a relapse management plan. Such plans are described well by Westbrook, Kennerley and Kirk (2007) in terms of treating 'working aged adults'. Of note, they view it important to introduce the notion of relapse management early on in therapy, emphasising the notion that throughout the therapy the patient is moving towards greater independence from the therapist. Their goal is to help the patient to deal effectively with the inevitable set-backs that are likely to occur post-discharge when she is operating autonomously. In order to promote such independence, and help people deal with future set-backs, Westbrook *et al.* (2007) suggest socialising patients to apply the following three questions when problems arise during the course of treatment, prior to discharge:

1. How can I make sense of this set-back?

2. What can I learn from this?

3. With hindsight, what could I do differently?

It is suggested that if these questions are applied with difficulties arising from homework tasks then the skills of using them can be honed by the time therapy finishes.

It is relevant to note that relapse management can often be different for older people compared to their younger counterparts, owing to issues of poor health. Hence, for some patients, full independence may not be possible. As such, in many situations the relapse management plan may require the support of carers, and/or other services and organisations (social services, etc.). For example, one may facilitate the patient's attendance at a day-centre, carer's group, Alzheimer's Society group, etc. as part of the relapse plan.

2.4: WORKING WITH PEOPLE IN NON-STANDARDISED CBT FORMATS

The previous discussion has provided a description of a rather standard evidence-based CBT approach. However, CBT principles can be applied in less standardised forms when working with other patient presentations. This is a particularly important issue with older people, as many older patients do not perform well against the suitability criteria set for CBT (Safran and Segal 1990), and thus there is the risk of them being excluded. This issue is of particular relevance to my work, as it involves applying therapy to people with dementia. Hence, the following short section outlines why it is appropriate to use CBT in this speciality, and introduces some of the concepts underpinning treatment.

Chapter 3 outlines some of the CBT literature regarding people with dementia. A number of studies have shown that formulation-led therapy can be effective with people with dementia (CBT – Scholey and Woods 2003; Teri and Gallagher-Thompson 1991; IPT – Hinrichsen and Clougherty 2006; Miller 2009). Despite such evidence, on the whole, many therapists are sceptical about using a cognitive approach owing to the 'chaotic' nature of some patients' thinking. Yet it is my belief that the application of cognitive therapy is essential to working with people with dementia. Indeed, the principles used in standard CBT illuminate the experience of people with dementia, and help target our treatments. For example, consider the scenario of John, a 74-year-old man with dementia, who is staying overnight in his son's house. Let us reflect on the nature of his thinking, in this self-report of a distressing incident.

Box 2.1: John's experience

'I wake up, and I think I'm going to be late for work. I have a sense that something is not quite right, so I guess I've got something really important to do today.

I go downstairs, it's very dark. I can't remember where the light switch is; I stumble, hurting my wrist. Fortunately, the moonlight through the window guides me into the kitchen. But that's strange, this isn't my kitchen!

Where am I? Whose home is this? Am I on holiday, or maybe staying with one of my family? I'll take a look outside because that'll give me a clue. BLAAAR...BLAAAR. Oh no, an alarm's gone off. The next minute I see my son standing beside me, looking very angry. He says: "Dad, what are you doing? You've gone and set the alarm off again. Don't you know what time it is? Come on, Dad...get back to bed."'

In this extract one sees that far from John's thoughts being chaotic, or irrelevant, they are extremely coherent and logical. In his situation it is evident that he is disoriented by the unfamiliar surroundings, and thus he sensibly engages in a problem-solving exercise. Unfortunately, his search strategy sets off the alarm and makes his son angry. So, in truth, this is not a confused old man, rather this is a man with memory problems, who requires help with his orientation. Hence, instead of excluding him from therapy, a careful examination of his thinking processes would be very helpful. It would reveal his weaknesses and strengths (e.g. his intact problem-solving skills), and suggest some treatment strategies (the use of orientation signs and notepaper placed around the house).

Having spent a lot of time listening to such scenarios in my clinics, and examining the thoughts of people with dementia, it is evident that these patients are in a double-bind. First, they have memory and processing difficulties due to their organic changes. Second, they are in constant problem-solving mode due to the fact they are often trying to remember things, or orientate themselves to time and place (Where am I? What was I going to do next?). Indeed, people with dementia appear to be 'superthinkers', engaged in continual processing of information in situations that others would deal with without any difficulties at all. The excessive thinking adds to the difficulties as their information processing system becomes over-burdened, further reducing problem-solving capacities. From my perspective, many therapists fail to listen carefully to their patients with dementia, and do not try to disentangle the important thought patterns in their speech. Instead, they pay little attention to their patients' thoughts. Indeed, many clinicians often tend to dismiss their thinking as a by-product of a confused mind. Despite my enthusiasm about using CBT principles in developing interventions, it is important not to 'fool' ourselves into thinking that we can undertake conventional CBT with everyone with dementia. It is my belief that CBT cannot be performed with people who are unable to collaborate with the contents of the session, nor with those who cannot be socialised to the CBT framework. If the person is unable to comply with these conditions, as is the case for many people with dementia, the therapy is normally done with the support of the patients' caregivers. As such there is a strong argument for labelling such work as a 'CBT carer intervention'. The latter views are examined further in Chapter 10, where I discuss the use of the CBT principles with older people with dementia.

2.5: CONCLUSION

This chapter has provided a quick review of patients' experiences of depression and anxiety in order to examine what therapy needs to accommodate and address when treating these disorders. It is evident from empirical findings that CBT is one of the most effective approaches to use (Chapter 3), and some of the reasons for this success have been outlined above. A brief overview of the format of the standardised CBT approach has also been outlined. The subsequent chapters will unpack some of the details discussed, focusing specifically on work conducted with older adults. Although much of the content of the book will describe the application of standardised CBT, there are also chapters that show how cognitive concepts have been used in other settings. Particular focus is given to the use of cognitive concepts in work conducted with staff who are caring for people with dementia.

Chapter 3

Adapting Therapy for Older People

3.1: INTRODUCTION

A number of texts have been written on how to adapt therapies for older people (Dick, Gallagher-Thompson and Thompson 1996; Glantz 1989; Koder, Brodaty and Anstey 1996; Zalaquett and Stens 2006; Zarit and Knight 1996). Such guides generally suggest using slower paced approaches, shorter sessions, a more concrete communication style, repeated presentation of key materials/concepts, use of multiple modalities, and use of life-review material. They also often advise that therapists should employ strategies to support people's sensory impairment and memory deficits (tape recordings, bibliotherapy, cue cards and pictures), and encourage the assistance of families and advocates in the treatment programmes (Dick, Gallagher-Thompson and Thompson 1999; Teri and Gallagher-Thompson 1991). Further, Koder *et al.* (1996) suggest the gradual termination of therapy, with a need for follow-up sessions to consolidate progress. Miller (2009) stresses the importance of undertaking a medical review of the patient's health status because he notes that many of the common physical conditions associated with ageing (e.g. hypothyroidism, cardiac conditions) and their pharmacological treatments can lower affect (see Kupfer *et al.* 2008).

Despite broadly acknowledging the helpfulness of some of these suggestions, care must be taken not to overgeneralise their relevance, because of the heterogeneity within this group. The elderly group is composed of a number of different cohorts, within an age range of 65 to 100+. To stop ourselves from becoming too generic in providing advice about adapting therapies, this chapter provides a simple framework to capture some of the diversity in the population (see Figure 3.1).

This chapter aims to illustrate the following:

1. The single label 'older people' does not do justice to the heterogeneity in this group of people.

2. Discussions about the application of therapy are aided by categorising the population into relevant groups along the axes of cognitive and physical health status.

3. Older people with few cognitive and physical health problems perform well with CBT.

4. When working with people with physical problems, the therapist requires a good understanding of the limits set by the illness. CBT can be used in the gap between perceived limitations set by the patient and the actual limitations imposed by the illness.

5. Non-standardised forms of CBT have been applied with success to various categories of older people, including people with dementia.

3.2: TWO-DIMENSIONAL FRAMEWORK FOR CATEGORISING PRESENTATIONS

Figure 3.1 provides a representation of older people's status via two intersecting continua, and is used below to provide more specific guidance regarding therapeutic requirements.

The 'physical health' dimension describes a person's status along a continuum of fitness and health. The 'intellectual' dimension describes a person's cognitive status. This line is closely linked with age, because many of the dementias and vascular problems are associated with the ageing brain. Through the dimensions described in Figure 3.1, it is possible to provide specific advice about how to work with the patients populating each quadrant. It is relevant to note that patients can move between the quadrants rapidly, as physical illness can impact on intellectual status (e.g. delirium) and vice versa. It is also worth noting that the therapeutic goals sought for the various populations will differ between quadrants. For example, for some people the goals will be to receive relief from their depression, while others may require the teaching of mnemonic strategies to help them remember to take their medication.

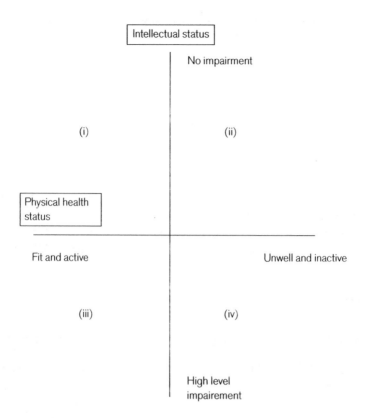

Figure 3.1: Framework for clarifying patients' overall health status

The quadrants

The next section describes features of the populations occupying each of the four (i–iv) quadrants.

QUADRANT I

The patients occupying the top left quadrant are physically fit and cognitively intact. They require few adaptations from standard treatments, although some CBT training centres advocate the use of increased numbers of sessions. For example, the Older Adult and Family Center at the Department of Veteran Affairs Medical Center, Palo Alto, advocate 16–20 sessions (Dick *et al.* 1999; Thompson *et al.* 2000). However, care needs to be taken with respect to this issue because Cuijpers' (1998) review showed that increasing sessions was associated with higher dropout rates in elderly patients treated in the community. Dick *et al.* (1999) suggest the use of longer sessions, increasing the standard format by 10–25 minutes. This recommendation is also controversial, as longer sessions may run into difficulties with sustaining patient concentration and attention (see Chapter 4). Less contentious is the view that older people benefit from the use of rehearsal and role-play to help consolidate and proceduralise new learning (Thompson *et al.* 2009).

The patients in this quadrant have generally been well researched in the psychotherapy literature (Hepple, Wilkinson and Pearce 2002; Kneebone 2006; Mackin and Arean 2005; Scogin *et al.* 2005). Evidence suggests that this population can not only benefit from psychotherapy (Hartman-Stein 2005; Pinquart, Duberstein and Lyness 2006; Pinquart and Sorensen 2001; Zalaquett and Stens 2006), but in some situations may show better outcomes than their younger counterparts (Walker and Clarke 2001). The reasons for such positive findings are complex, but it is clear that those older people experiencing non-chronic mental health conditions often demonstrate effective coping strategies, particularly those that have shown resilience in the past. With specific relevance to the treatment of depression, the systematic reviews (Mackin and Arean 2005; Scogin *et al.* 2005; Zalaquett and Stens 2006) advocate using CBT. Pinquart, Duberstein and Lyness' (2007) meta-analytic review of 57 studies concurred regarding the benefits of using CBT, but also supported the use of reminiscence therapy (Fry 1986). NICE guidelines (2009) take more of a stepped-care perspective, suggesting the use of simpler treatments prior to the use of the more intensive approaches, particularly in cases of mild to moderate depression. Thus for mild to moderate depression, self-help programmes, problem-solving/brief therapies, reminiscence and life-review therapies are suggested (Bohlmeijer, Smit and Cuipers 2003; Floyd *et al.* 2004). For the more severe presentations, CBT, interpersonal therapy (IPT, Hinrichsen and Clougherty 2006) and family and group therapies are recommended (Qualls 1999) – usually in conjunction with the appropriate pharmacological treatments. NICE advocate the use of psychodynamic therapy (Garner 2008) for the complex comorbid conditions that may present along with the depression. Despite the helpful clarity provided by the above guidelines, it is sobering to see from the recent Cochrane report (Wilson, Mottram and Vassilas 2008) that the quality of studies in the area remains poor. Further, it is interesting to note that no particular therapeutic approach appeared to be markedly better than the others with respect to the treatment of depression.

Five trials compared a form of cognitive behavioural therapy (CBT) against control conditions, and the findings showed CBT was more effective than control. Two individual trials compared CBT against psychodynamic therapy, with no significant difference in effectiveness indicated between the two approaches. (Wilson *et al.* 2008, p.2)

In relation to anxiety, a number of systematic reviews have been undertaken (Ayers *et al.* 2007; Pinquart *et al.* 2007). The evidence suggests that CBT is the best researched approach and continues to be seen as the most effective of the various forms of psychotherapy (Cully and Stanley 2008). For example, in the treatment of generalised anxiety disorder it was better than waiting list control conditions, and equivalent to other forms of active treatments (supportive therapy, discussion-groups) (Stanley *et al.* 2003; Wetherell, Gatz and Craske 2003). As yet no randomised trials have been conducted for panic disorder, obsessive compulsive disorder, or post-traumatic stress disorder, although less robust studies have demonstrated favourable results for CBT (Cook and O'Donnell 2005; Swales, Solfvin and Sheikh 1996).

The case study of Mary in Chapter 8 illustrates the treatment of someone occupying this quadrant. A standard CBT core belief formulation approach (i.e. diathesis-stress) is used in her therapy, owing to the fact that the current evidence base relates to the use of standard formats. It is relevant to note, however, that specific older adult conceptualisations have now been developed (e.g. Laidlaw, Thompson and Gallagher-Thompson 2004, Comprehensive Conceptual Framework – CCF).

QUADRANT II

The top right square is made up of diverse groups of people, many with multiple diseases and disorders (chronic pain, cancer, arthritis, stroke, Parkinson's disease, etc.). In the treatment of these presentations, the therapist is required to know about the limits posed by the diseases and physical disorders and be able to disentangle these from the limits set by the patients for themselves. The latter limits will contain biases and fears that are required to be tackled in therapy (see Table 3.1).

The CBT therapist is able to work in the gap between the actual limits and the perceived limits driven by the patient's erroneous beliefs. Thus the role of the therapist is to help the patient operate as close to the actual limits imposed by the diseases and physical disorders as possible (Figure 3.2). It is relevant to note that when working with NATs with this group of individuals, there is often a degree of 'rationality' to some of their fears (e.g. their illness *will* eventually kill them, they are *not* going to make a marked recovery, etc.). Hence, when looking for appropriate responses to people's NATs it is often useful to avoid the term 'rational re-evaluation' of the situation and adopt the term 'helpful re-evaluation'.

Table 3.1: Examples of some of the self-limiting fears and
beliefs of someone recovering from a stroke

- I'm afraid to be by myself because I may have another stroke when I'm on my own.
- I don't want to leave Newcastle because I want to be near my consultant...just in case!
- I am definitely going to have another stroke, so why bother going to physiotherapy?
- The next stroke is bound to kill me!
- It's all genetic.
- My heart has been really damaged by the stress of the stroke.
- I shouldn't raise my blood pressure – so no more exercise, or sex!
- I've got to constantly monitor myself for any signs of the onset of another stroke.
- I can't give up cigarettes. Anyway, all my brothers smoke, and they've not had a stroke.
- It's fate!

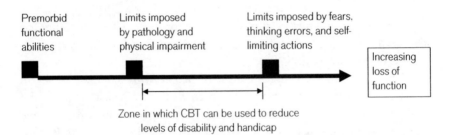

Figure 3.2: Zone of therapeutic work

The impact of an illness can be described in terms of levels of functional loss within the following five categories: pathology, impairment, disability, handicap and quality of life. While the pathology and impairments set the physical limits of functionality, CBT can work at the other levels to ensure the levels of disability and handicap are kept to a minimum. In doing so, the patient's quality of life can be maintained at its highest level. This perspective is endorsed by Rybarczyk *et al.* (1992), who emphasised the need to try to limit notions of excess disability in the treatment of chronically ill patients. They highlighted four other therapeutic requirements:

- to resolve practical barriers to participating in therapy

- to help patients to accept depression as a separate and reversible problem and not an inevitable consequence of the physical illness

- to counteract the loss of important social roles and autonomy

- to challenge perceptions of being a 'burden'.

Wilkinson (2008) suggests that in many cases therapists' interventions involve treating the anxieties stemming from the fears associated with the diseases and medical conditions. Such work typically requires one to distinguish the anxiety components from the physical symptoms and to acknowledge the roles that fears are playing (e.g. physiological arousal, anticipatory fear, safety-seeking behaviours, avoidance, etc.). Then via education, behaviour experimentation, decatastrophisation techniques and thought re-evaluation methods, the person is helped to tackle the affective component of her difficulties. Through such approaches, Stanley and colleagues were able to significantly reduce treatment duration of patients' physical complaints (Stanley et al. 2003). Further examples of positive findings have been reported in stroke (Lincoln and Flannaghan 2003), palliative care (Anderson, Watson and Davidson 2008), chronic pain (Cook 1998), and conditions such as Parkinson's disease (Cole and Vaughan 2005; Laidlaw 2008). The use of bibliotherapy for the treatment of depression for those with a disability has also been shown to be beneficial, and found to generalise two years post-intervention (Landreville 1998).

The two bottom quadrants consist of people with moderate to severe dementia. A great deal of literature has been written on how to improve the well-being of these patients but, as NICE (2009) guidelines and Cochrane reports inform us, the evidence base for many of the treatments is poor (James and Fossey 2008).

QUADRANT III

The patients populating the bottom left-hand quadrant have cognitive impairment, but remain relatively fit and active. There are a number of empirical studies demonstrating the use of psychotherapy for affective disorders with this group (Heason 2005), but many of the papers use case study formats (Spira and Edelstein 2006). Hence, the evidence base remains largely at the anecdotal level except in the area of CBT. For example, in the 1990s Linda Teri undertook a number of groundbreaking studies treating depressed people with dementia using adapted forms of CBT (Teri 1994; Teri and Gallagher-Thompson 1991; Teri and Logsdon 1991; Teri, Logsdon and Uomoto 1991). In truth, most of the interventions were behavioural in nature (e.g. use of The Pleasant Event Schedule-AD), and required the support of caregivers.

A helpful paper on adapting therapy for an older adult with cognitive impairment was published by Coon *et al.* (2007). Although it focuses mainly on the use of 'homework', it provides a wealth of description on how to adjust therapy for people with mild/moderate impairment. Another illuminating paper concerned the use of CBT for seven people with dementia and depression (Scholey and Woods 2003). These therapists identified several themes worthy of exploration when working with people with dementia. They were the need:

- to investigate patients' beliefs about the causes of their cognitive impairment, because such reasoning often leads to distress and anger (e.g. *'It was the fault of my doctor; she should have warned me about the chance of having more mini-strokes'*)

- to examine degrees of hopelessness due to feelings of loss of control

- to assess feelings of insecurity that may arise due to memory loss, disorientation, etc.

- to check out whether the impact of traumatic events has resurfaced owing to a dislocation between memory and the use of previously effective coping strategies

- to exercise flexibility, patience and tolerance with the patient, who may require the therapeutic work to be conducted slowly and repetitively

- to be aware of the systemic nature of the problem, and the usefulness of utilising a team approach in tackling the difficulties (i.e. liasing with occupational therapists, physiotherapists, social workers, etc.)

- to ask about any loss of mobility, particularly difficulties associated with transport (e.g. loss of ability to drive self independently).

Single case and group CBT have also been used by other researchers with some favourable results (Kipling, Bailey and Charlesworth 1999; Koder 1998; Teri, McKenzie and LaFazia 2005). One of the few RCT (randomised controlled trial) studies in this area was conducted by Teri and Gallagher-Thompson (1991). This study revealed a significant reduction in depression both for the patients and their carers. Despite being described as cognitive, the interventions were mainly behavioural in nature, and were aimed chiefly at family caregivers. The requirement of 'caregiver support' is common in many forms of psychotherapy with people with dementia. For example, Miller's (2009) interpersonal therapy for cognitive impairment (IPT-ci) also requires the full assistance of a caregiver; although one-to-one time with the patient is recommended. A good review of this area is provided by Logsdon, McCurry and Teri (2008).

In this quadrant, one also sees patients displaying challenging behaviours (aggression, disinhibition, vocalising, agitation, smearing, repetitive behaviours, etc.).

Over recent years a number of effective formulation-led approaches have been used with these presentations (CBT – Fossey *et al.* 2006; Wood-Mitchell *et al.* 2007; behavioural – Moniz-Cook *et al.*'s Cochrane review, 2008). In developing treatments with these patients, although one is using formulations to understand the problematic behaviours and emotions, the actual interventions employed are often simple behavioural and environmental manipulations (James and Stephenson 2007). The agents of change in this work are frequently the carers and staff, and thus much of the therapeutic work is done with them (i.e. changing carer attitudes and belief systems, using modelling and role-play techniques to reinforce effective staff–patient interactions, Beck *et al.* 1999; Moniz-Cook *et al.* 1998; Teri, McKenzie and LaFazia 2005). Behaviour management has emerged as one of the most helpful strategies in this area, although it is now more commonly known as functional analysis (Moniz-Cook *et al.* 2008). In a series of studies entitled the Seattle Protocols a clinical psychologist developed a functional-analysis programme and trained community consultants to assist family carers in developing skills to manage problematic behaviours to do with dementia (Teri, McKenzie and LaFazia 2005).

The second case study in this book, Donald in Chapter 10, illustrates an approach used to treat challenging behaviours in care home settings. The therapy is informed by group CBT principles, with the staff being a key focus of the treatment.

QUADRANT IV

At the less severe end of the fourth quadrant are those who are frail, have a moderate dementia, and are living at home. They may be maintained at home by home-care services and/or telecare services that can support them to live independently (Orpwood and Chadd 2007). With advances in computing and telecommunications, patients can be monitored, their safety maintained and medication dispensed via an internet link. Thus patients can be assisted to stay in their homes for as long as possible (James 2008a). The internet can also be used to deliver cognitive stimulation therapy (CST) packages

(Spector *et al.* 2003). CST is a therapy consisting of intellectual games designed to slow down cognitive deterioration. In the UK, those in the very bottom right-hand corner of the figure are often receiving care in elderly severely mentally ill settings, either in the NHS or increasingly within the private sector. Standard forms of psychotherapeutic work for this group are often limited (reality orientation, reminiscence, validation therapy – James and Fossey 2008; Livingston *et al.* 2005; Verkaik, van Weert and Francke 2005), and in some situations may be restricted to the use of activities (music, sensory stimulation, aromatherapy in order to provide stimulation and to relieve boredom – Ballard *et al.* 2002).

Patients in this quadrant suffering from severe dementia rarely receive CBT, but just as in quadrant iii, their families and carers are often the targets of cognitive interventions (Marriott *et al.* 2000). When working with patients from these latter groups, one is often treating carer depression, guilt, anxiety and anger. In a recent meta-analysis of psychological interventions by Brodaty, Green and Koschera (2003), a positive effect of 0.31 (CI = 0.13–0.50) was found for the treatment of carer distress. There is also evidence that family carers can be trained to reduce depression for themselves and also that trained community care staff can help family carers to reduce problematic behaviours in people with dementia (Mittelman *et al.* 2004, 2007).

3.3: CONCLUSION

This chapter has addressed the rather complex issue of therapeutic adaptation. It has attempted to reduce the complexity somewhat through the use of a simple two-dimensional grid. Further, literature associated with patients' presentations within these grids has been outlined. Currently, CBT has primarily been applied to people in quadrant i, in relation to depression and to a lesser degree anxiety (Cully and Stanley 2008). The least work has been conducted in quadrants iii and iv, and, where it has taken place, it has employed a non-standard format, often using patients' carers as the agents of change. As a general rule of thumb, working with older people requires patience and slower paced therapy and, particularly with people with higher levels of impairment, there tends to be more of a behavioural emphasis:

> Homebound frail, and/or medically ill older adults, for example, may respond more favourably to simple behavioural interventions than to more complex cognitive therapeutic techniques. As a general rule, complex psychological interventions (e.g. problem-solving, cognitive restructuring) require slower pace with older adults

> (Gallagher-Thompson and Thompson 1996), while modifications
> to the therapy process make therapy more user friendly. (Cully and
> Stanley 2008, p.251)

It is important to remember, due to the key role played by the formulation in CBT, patients in all quadrants can potentially benefit from the application of CBT at some level (e.g. a conceptualisation will help a therapist gain a better understanding of his patient's distress). Thus, at the very least the use of a CBT formulation will help identify the most appropriate approach to use (e.g. perhaps suggesting either systemic or behavioural interventions rather than CBT).

A more detailed discussion of formulations with older people occurs in Chapter 6. Yet it is worth noting that in recent years, a number of specific formulations have been developed to assist with our conceptualisation of older people (e.g. Laidlaw *et al.*'s (2004) Comprehensive Conceptualisation Framework, CCF). While these may not be regarded as adaptations, they have been developed to help our understanding of older patients' experiences.

> The CCF for CBT with older people helps therapists, particularly
> those unused to working with older people, to conceptualise older
> adults' problems within a CBT model and to formulate the patient's
> problems. (Laidlaw 2008, p.97)

Chapter 4

Cognitive Changes, Executive Functioning, Working Memory and Scripts: Their Relevance to Therapeutic Engagement

4.1: INTRODUCTION

Dementia is not a natural consequence of ageing, rather it is a common but abnormal feature, affecting one in five people over the age of 80. In contrast, cognitive decline is normal, although it is a complex process at the level of the individual. One of the few universal characteristics of ageing is a decline in executive abilities. Executive functioning is closely associated with frontal lobe activities. This area, situated in the anterior of the brain, governs many high level intellectual processes including information processing abilities, social functioning and emotional regulation (Gazzaniga, Ivry and Mangun 2002, p.499). West (1996) suggests that age-related executive dysfunction occurs as a result of accelerated cell shrinkage, decreased dopamine concentration, decreased receptor sensitivity and a reduction in receptors in the frontal cortex. It has been hypothesised that changes in this area may account for the finding that older people perform less well on novel reasoning tasks (fluid intelligence) compared to over-learned proceduralised activities (crystalline intelligence). The relevance of these problems in relation to therapy is outlined below.

This chapter acts as a link between the introductory chapters and the subsequent chapter on assessment. It begins with a discussion of the nature of mood disorders from a neuropsychological perspective. Particular emphasis is placed on the important roles that executive functioning and working memory (WM) play in patients' abilities to engage well in therapy. In this chapter WM is conceptualised as an active short-term memory store where stimuli are processed prior to passing on to long-term storage. Much of the data processing, particularly the conscious aspects, is coordinated by the executive component of WM. A simplified version of the WM framework is presented in Figure 4.1, and this shows the central role the executive plays in the processing of information. This chapter also examines WM's involvement in unconscious processing of information. It describes how people whose WMs are not functioning well tend to over-employ scripted activities that require little conscious monitoring. Unfortunately, if used excessively, this can lead to cycles of inflexible actions and thinking (e.g. NATs, processing biases, safety-seeking behaviours, etc.).

This chapter aims to illustrate:

1. The nature of age-related cognitive decline is complex.

2. Executive deficits are very common in older people.

3. Executive deficits are also found in people with psychiatric illnesses.

4. Executive functioning is related to WM.

5. WM becomes less efficient with age and during periods of low affect.

6. The information processing difficulties associated with executive dysfunction can be conceptualised via WM problems.

7. WM mainly plays a role in conscious processing, but it is also involved in unconscious processing.

8. Unconscious processes function via the use of scripts, and these inflexible scripts can be over-employed when the WM is under stress.

9. Scripts can play a role in maintaining psychiatric illnesses.

10. An awareness of the above features is helpful in understanding patients' experiences of depression and anxiety.

4.2: COGNITIVE CHANGES

4.2.i: Age-related changes

Cross-sectional studies that assess cognitive abilities indicate that competencies decline steadily between the ages of 25 and 65, and then decline more markedly in the following years. More sophisticated studies, however, suggest that the picture is more complex, with cohort differences being as large as age-related effects in many intellectual domains (Schaie 2008). Schaie's large-scale longitudinal study found great variation in individuals' scores on a set of five cognitive domains (word fluency, numbers, verbal meaning, reasoning and spatial orientation). It appeared that most people had declined in at least one domain by the age of 60, but few had declined across all of the areas. He concluded that some change was normal, but the pattern of change was different for each individual. Despite this variability, one of the few broad domains researchers agree declines with age is executive functioning (West 1996). Indeed, Salthouse (2000) boldly suggests that executive dysfunction (Edf), and the resulting reduction in people's processing speeds, accounts for much of the age differences we observe in performance.

4.2.ii: Non-age-related changes

It is important to note that Edf does not solely arise from neurological changes, because other factors can influence it. Rabbitt (2006) highlights the impact of physical health problems on people's cognitive performances (infections, diabetes, pain). He also discusses the influence of sensory loss, suggesting that poor vision and hearing place additional cognitive load on the limited capacity of the executive (Gallacher 2004; Rabbitt 2006). It is also evident that many of the drugs used to treat older people, particularly the minor and major tranquillisers, increase Edf (Ballard and Waite 2006). Poor executive performance is also a characteristic feature of many forms of mental illness, including depression, anxiety and psychoses (Watkins and Brown 2002). Evidence for such dysfunction is evident in imaging and neuropsychological studies (Elliott 1998).

Hence, older people who are suffering low affect are at a 'double disadvantage' with respect to executive functioning, owing to the influence of both their age and the clinical disorder. Due to the important role that executive functioning evidently plays in psychological illnesses of older people, the remainder of this chapter will focus on Edf and the areas associated with it.

4.3: EXECUTIVE DYSFUNCTIONING

A number of researchers have examined whether Edf impacts on performance in psychotherapy (Doubleday, King and Papageorgiou 2002). Mohman and Gorman (2005) observed a negative impact of Edf in relation to their ability to treat older people with generalised anxiety disorder (GAD). However, the relationship was not clear-cut, being complicated by the fact that some of the older people's Edfs improved markedly during the course of their CBT. Table 4.1 outlines the common problems encountered by therapists, such as Mohman and Gorman, when working with people with executive deficits (see left-hand column). In the right-hand column there is a list of potential ways a therapist could deal with such difficulties.

Table 4.1: Common executive difficulties and adaptations

Features associated with executive dysfunction	Possible adaptations in therapy
Poor concentration – leads to inability to maintain focus for prolonged periods of time. Hence, patient will find it difficult to fight against the current negative style of thinking. Note, NATs require little concentration as they have become automatic.	Reduce complexity of material, shorten session, only cover a few topics, use frequent feedback. Frequently check patients' understanding of the material covered, and pace session according to patients' needs. Use therapeutic breaks within session.
Poor attention abilities – lead to inability to direct and sustain focused attention. Additional problems with difficulties in shifting attention between different topics/ concepts.	Ensure agenda is meaningful for patient, with small number of items on agenda. Provide lots of feedback and summarise and chunk relevant information. Elicit feedback. Use simple diagrams and use written materials to reinforce concepts, but avoid being abstract. Remove any environmental distracters (e.g. therapist may need to close windows to prevent extraneous noises). Tape-record session for patient to listen to later.
Memory problems – lead to working memory deficits, and encoding and retrieval problems. Retrieval biases are in favour of negative information. Autobiographical information is often overgeneralised, preventing the patient remembering how she may have coped successfully in the past.	Prevent overloading of the patient's working memory. Provide information in a paced manner. Repeat main therapeutic concept frequently to help consolidate material and facilitate encoding. Avoid blaming the patient for inability to recall either positive events or coping strategies from the past. Educate patient about the biases. Facilitate the generation of positive memories by re-contextualising the memories, e.g. help the patient visualise the target event and reinstate contextual features (sights, sounds, smells) present at original encoding.

Interpersonal difficulties – lead to difficulties forming a therapeutic alliance, and problems in engaging in some interpersonal homework tasks.

Accept the patient's slow, inconsistent, amotivated style as a feature of the affective state rather than a feature of her personality. Plan and prepare (rehearse) the homework tasks within the session, ensuring the rationale and components have been discussed clearly.

Poor problem solving – leads to inability to define difficulties, to determine appropriate goals, and how to devise plans to meet one's goals. Memory problems mean that often people are unable to reflect on how they coped in similar situations in the past.

Reduce problem into component parts in order to simplify tasks. Use scaffolding techniques[1] to provide support in order to help the patient generate potential answers. Initially, one may need to guide the patient a great deal, until a more collaborative approach can be engaged in. Use behavioural experiments to energise problem-solving skills. The experiments need to be set up sensitively, so even if the person is unable to carry out activities, she will learn something about her depression from having attempted to engage in them. The therapist must acknowledge his potential role in any therapeutic problems (e.g. *The reason you had difficulties with this is because I didn't explain the homework task very well*).

Lack of motivation – leads to inability to fight the depression or to engage in effortful strategies to overcome behavioural inertia.

Ensure agenda and homework are meaningful for patient. Work with patient to predict obstacles. Reinforce therapeutic gains, no matter how small. Set meaningful goals that are achievable, measurable, monitored and reviewed regularly. Explain therapeutic rationale regarding treatment; such explanations will help to instil a realistic expectation regarding the course of treatment. For example, inform patient that initially engaging in tasks is unlikely to make her feel better. Indeed, getting a sense of pleasure or mastery may take some time.

Lack of awareness of own executive problems – leads to the patient being overly critical of herself, and comparing self negatively with 'old/non-depressed' self.

Assist patients to obtain an understanding of their difficulties. One can use formal neuropsychological testing; alternatively one can investigate the deficits via a discussion or checklist approach (e.g. *Are you having problems concentrating? How long before your mind starts to wander?*).

Table 4.1: Common executive difficulties and adaptations *cont.*

Features associated with executive dysfunction	Possible adaptations in therapy
Poor regulation of emotional responses– results in sudden mood shifts, including anger, tearfulness.	Conceptualise the sudden shifts in emotions and impulsive changes in emotional responses as being a feature of the affective state, and respond in an accepting manner. However, if the chief emotion is anger, take precautions about the patient's and your own safety.

1 – Scaffolding techniques are statements used by the therapist to support the patient to generate appropriate responses. For example, if you asked your patient to recall an event that happened a week ago, you may assist her recall by providing cues, e.g. What day did it happen on? Who were you with on that day? What time of the day was it? Such contextual material helps to cue the person's memory and assists her to draw on the relevant information needed.

As can be seen from Table 4.1, the impact of deficits in this area is great, and will influence the mood, level of concentration and agitation, and interpersonal abilities of an individual. Such features will clearly influence a therapist's ability to develop a good working alliance with the patient. Further, when working with people with moderate to severe executive difficulties, it may become evident that the person is no longer able to plan and/or make balanced decisions owing to an inability to judge risks appropriately. For example, inviting complete strangers into the house at times when she is lonely; gambling excessively as she is convinced she will win a major prize. In such circumstances, the therapist may need to temporarily become the patient's 'problem-solving' advocate. In some respects he may start to function as her 'executive'. If the therapist believes there is unlikely to be an improvement in his patient's executive functioning, he may then need to ask a 'trusted' caregiver to take a more active role in the patient's treatment and subsequent care. Thus the caregiver will need to be educated about Edf and how to work with the patient in her best interests. I often view this as therapist handing over the executive role from 'himself' to a 'trusted' caregiver to aid everyday functioning and decision-making abilities.

In the latter section I have examined executive functioning as an isolated phenomenon. Yet clearly it is integrated within a complex information processing system. It is most closely associated with 'working memory'. The next section discusses the role of the executive within this memory system.

4.4: WORKING MEMORY

In cognitive psychology, executive functioning is closely associated with short-term memory. Baddeley (1983) developed his working memory framework (WM) to explain experimental findings relating to short-term memory, placing executive functioning at the centre of the framework. In this model (Figure 4.1), the WM represents a store for retaining information and for performing mental operations on them. For example, in order to understand 'what someone is saying to me', my WM must remember the beginning, middle and the end of the speech, permitting its integration into a whole. The diagram shows a central processor of information, the executive (aka central executive). This is supported by a number of specialised support systems which assist with the temporary storage and coding of specific information (verbal and visual).

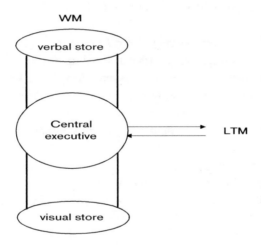

Features of working memory (WM)

- Limited capacity of information
- Serial processing
- Slow processing
- Involved mainly in conscious processing of information

Features of long-term memory (LTM)

- Unlimited capacity of information
- Multiple, parallel processing
- Speedy processing

Figure 4.1: Working memory model and its relationship to long-term memory

The executive plays a supervisory role in the information processing system. It directs conscious attention, processes incoming stimuli, retrieves relevant memories from long-term memory (LTM) and integrates the material from all support systems (see Figure 4.1). However, its supervisory role comes at a price: the executive is a relatively slow processor of information, and becomes inefficient when required to deal with a lot of information quickly.

A clinical example of overloading the executive is 'excessive rumination' as seen in GAD and social phobia, which may be defined as the repetitive focusing on oneself and one's situation. Thus, due to the repetitive 'going over of information', there is little space left to think about other things (Watkins and Brown 2002). When the WM system has become this overloaded, the therapist is likely to observe numerous information processing difficulties. For example, problems concentrating, focusing and sustaining attention, poor retrieval and storage of information in the LTM, and problems initiating and guiding intentional behaviour, as well as difficulties in shifting attention (see Table 4.1).

As mentioned above, conscious information processing tends to be slow and has only limited capacity. In order to speed up this inherent slowness in processing information, the cognitive system has evolved a trade-off strategy, whereby much of the information processing is done outside of conscious awareness – see Table 4.2. This means that the majority of the analysis of both our selves and environment is conducted rather superficially via a system of heuristics.

Thus, apart from highly prioritised material – requiring conscious analysis – much of what we process is filtered by a finite set of 'best guess' heuristics that guide our activity. The next section examines the actions of scripts and some of the errors that can occur when they are employed.

4.5: ACTIONS OF SCRIPTS

The notion of scripts comes from the work of Schank and Abelson (1977). Other people have used various terms to describe similar phenomena: Bartlett (1932) – schemas; Minsky (1975) – frames. These features are typically described as sequences of behaviour or cognitive activities that are stored as a memory sequence. Thus once the first part of the memory (or script) has been activated, the rest of the activity can occur outside of conscious awareness, e.g. once you get in the car, the remainder of the activity processes associated with driving are activated, requiring little conscious selection or monitoring. Reason (1988) believed that effective human functioning essentially involves the activation of the appropriate script, at

Table 4.2: Types of processing in working memory

Conscious processing	This is undertaken for information that requires specific problem solving and attention is processed by the executive. The system draws on information from its various support and long-term stores to deal with the information. Such processing is resource intensive and slow. The working memory system has a limited capacity for dealing with information requiring this level of analysis.
Unconscious processing	This is undertaken for information that is 'routine' and does not require either thinking through or detailed executive processing. The system makes use of existing heuristics (aka scripts) that allow familiar cognitive and behavioural processing to go on outside of conscious awareness. The working memory system acts to monitor the system at arm's length, ensuring the products are in-line with general goals. For example, when driving home from work, you do not have to think through the actions or destinations, but at certain points in the journey, and certainly at the end, one needs to be sure that one has achieved what one set out to do. It is hypothesised that the occasional monitoring and end-stage assessment takes place in the executive.

the right time. It is hypothesised that the selection of the scripts is guided by a 'best-fit' process, cued by the person's conscious intentions, script-to-script activation and/or environmental cues. In relation to the latter two features, Reason (1988) believes that the three main triggering principles of selection are *similarity*, *frequency* and *recency* (Tversky and Kahneman 1973). Thus automated selection will occur when a situation is judged as being similar to a previous one, and the script selected will tend to be the one most frequently used in these types of situations. Thus, as we go about our daily lives, these heuristics allow us to quickly pick up cues from the environment and activate familiar activities and proceduralised memories (aka scripts). Hence, when we get up in the morning our 'getting up' script is activated, involving: entering the shower, cleaning our teeth, waking up the children, preparing breakfast, etc. As one script ends, the next salient one is activated; such selection operates mostly out of conscious awareness, thereby speeding up the process and reducing cognitive load.

Such a system thus allows us to multi-task, permitting people to analyse some features in detail, while the majority of the processing proceeds out of awareness (e.g. drive to work, listen to the radio, and plan the itinerary for the day). However, like all automated systems, it is not particularly flexible and this can produce problems and errors may occur.

For example, on the first morning of the school holidays, a parent may forget to interrupt the automated sequence and mistakenly wake up the children. As outlined in Table 4.2, in this form of automated processing, the central executive still plays an important role, as a (i) script selector, and (ii) monitor. In its first role, it is operating like a film editor, splicing together action sequences (scripts) from a vast catalogue in long-term memory. In role (ii), the central executive is required to monitor the effectiveness of the system. Hence, every so often 'like a virus checker' on a computer, it undertakes a quick scan to check everything is in order and proceeding towards an agreed goal/target (e.g. periodically checking to ensure that your 'getting ready' routine is going smoothly and will permit you to get to work before 9am).

While the use of scripts is essential to allow us to multi-task and function appropriately, an over-reliance on them can result in the emergence of inflexible and rigid behaviour and thinking. Such an over-reliance is exactly what happens when the WM becomes less efficient due to increasing age and/or the presence of psychiatric problems. At such times we can start to get locked into repetitive cycles of 'thinking and doing', and if these cycles are negative, our mood will suffer – see Table 4.3.

In relation to therapy, the relevance of scripts is two-fold. First, the errors associated with the scripts help to explain some of the common phenomena we observe in our patients, both old and young, as outlined in Table 4.3. Second, the notion of scripts helps us to appreciate that many of the disorders we are treating have become personal scripts for our patients. Indeed, the characteristic patterns of thinking and behaving observed in our patients are underpinned by repetitive unconscious processes. It therefore follows that often therapy involves getting the patient to interrupt these automated patterns, by helping them to reappraise situations through conscious processing. In relation to CBT, this is achieved by getting the patient to make their experiences of their disorder more conscious. This is done by socialising the patient to the generic CBT template (Chapter 2) to help the person describe her difficulties, and then using this framework to break down the distress into meaningful, concrete and more treatable units. Hence, what was once a chaotic amorphous experience has now been slowed down, reflected upon, made less automatic, and as a consequence more manageable. Once broken down, new routines need to be scripted (i.e. constructed or reactivated, a process referred to as rescripting). Such

Table 4.3: Typical errors associated with the use of scripts

a. *Incorrect scripts can be activated*: Owing to the fact that much of the activation relies on superficial analysis, rather than conscious decision making, occasionally incorrect scripts can be activated. The mis-activation may occur if the previous script was a very frequent or familiar one, e.g. when a UK car driver is abroad, he may incorrectly move into the left-hand lane when emerging from a junction. The wrong script can also be activated at the wrong time, e.g. two weeks after retiring, an ex-employee may wake up on a Monday morning and start dressing for work. In a clinical context, these sorts of errors are also frequently seen in dementia: with people getting up at 6am, reactivating their 'job scripts', convinced they need to get to work to commence the early shift; this script is 20 years out of date. Or a woman with dementia living in care, seeing school children pass her window and subsequently thinking she needs to get home to cook her children's evening meal.

b. *Situations can be appraised incorrectly*: The appraisal of the situation may be so superficial that an incorrect script is activated. For example, a person may mistakenly get into the car of a stranger who slows down to get directions. The mistake may be caused by the walker being cued by the fact the car looked similar to the car of a neighbour. In depression, and other disorders, patients frequently base their decisions on a cursory appraisal of the available information. This can result in biases such as 'jumping to conclusions'.

c. *System inflexibility can result in biased processing*: Once scripts are activated regularly they can become established and they become more liable to reactivation due to the frequency effect (lower threshold of activation). Hence, once routine patterns of negative behaviour or thinking are established they are more easily triggered. Many 'clinical biases' can be accounted for by this feature, including the persistence of negative automatic thoughts. Indeed, as this name suggests, the thoughts tend to be triggered automatically often outside of conscious awareness.

d. *Scripts are not interrupted at the appropriate time*: When scripts are running they require little conscious monitoring. While this is helpful in terms of not taxing the cognitive system, this can be problematic on those occasions when one wants to alter established routines. For example, one might fail to interrupt a routine activity in order to conduct an additional action such as forgetting to take a newly prescribed tablet during a busy time of the day. Therapy often tries to get people who are running dysfunctional scripts to interrupt their routines (i.e. to alter their unhelpful cycles of negative thinking). Unfortunately, far too often patients find themselves trapped in these cyclical scripts, unable to alter them.

e. *Over focussing on scripts can lead to skill breakdown*: Because much of the skills are proceduralised, they work efficiently outside of conscious awareness. Hence, on those occasions where one starts to consciously analyse one's performance, the behaviour becomes less efficient. For example, if a driver over-monitors his driving, he becomes a less fluid performer. Likewise, in social phobia when people start to over-analyse their social interactions, this interferes with their social functioning.

work needs to be planned carefully and practised repeatedly through role-play and behavioural work. This is because the negative routines will prove difficult to shift as they have been the default way of viewing the world for a long period of time.

It is relevant to note that CBT intentionally only examines certain aspects of people's difficulties. The other features of the disorders (neural, hormonal, chemical, etc.) are not dealt with directly. However, these features are triggered when the script is activated, and can be targeted within a comprehensive treatment programme (see James *et al.* 2004 for a fuller discussion).

4.6: CONCLUSION

Many of the adaptations recommended for working with older people are designed to counter the information and sensory processing deficits associated with getting older (e.g. slower paced therapy, supportive literature, use of concrete language, etc.). The rate and profile of decline is highly individualised, although it is generally agreed that executive abilities are reduced as we age. It was shown that executive abilities cover a wide range of functions from problem solving to abstract reasoning, but also interpersonal skills. It was suggested that therapists should be aware of the impact of such deficits in these areas, making allowances and supporting patients – for example, being empathic towards interpersonal issues that may arise both in and outside of therapy. The model of WM, containing executive processing at its heart, was used to conceptualise the information processing deficits. It was noted that this system is easily overloaded, and at such times does not operate effectively, leading to poor concentration and attention, and delayed processing of information. Once again, this insight calls upon us to deliver therapy in structured, concrete and simple forms in order to support the functioning of the WM. Finally, the chapter examined the notion of scripts. These useful heuristics allow us to identify routine situations and carry out proceduralised tasks without putting a strain on the cognitive system. However, because they are often rigid and activated automatically, when they become dysfunctional they can perpetuate unhealthy patterns of thinking and behaving. As such, the work of the therapist may be viewed as one of rescripting of patients' actions and thoughts. Finally, it is worth noting that executive problems are a feature of psychiatric disorders, and as such the recommendations made with respect to older people are relevant to working with younger patients with mental health disorders.

PART 2

Chapter 5

Assessment

5.1: INTRODUCTION

One of the key messages of this chapter is that the assessment process is not a separate phase of therapy, but must be seen as a guide to treatment. In this sense, a therapist should not collect information that is not likely to influence the interventions. For example, if a therapist knows from the outset that he is going to solely employ behavioural interventions, he should not routinely collect elaborate personal details from the patient's past.

Assessments do not influence interventions directly, because their connections occur through the formulation: 'The aim of CBT assessment is primarily to arrive at a formulation which is agreed as satisfactory by both client and therapist' (Westbrook *et al.* 2007, p.40). From this, it is evident that the formulation plays a key role in the nature of the information that is required. As a psychodynamic therapist, the formulations would direct someone to investigate very early episodes in the patient's life. With respect to CBT, one is directed to the hot-cross bun framework. As outlined in Chapter 2, this template reduces the chaotic experience of distress into meaningful units, providing the patient and therapist with a shared conceptual model. Within this generic framework, the therapist must also work to discover his patient's idiosyncratic patterns (behavioural, cognitive, physiological), determining the links that are associated with helpful and unhelpful emotions, and devising methods to promote greater well-being. As such, the hot-cross bun framework informs the assessment process, and its features need to be reflected in the questionnaires, charts and questioning style employed. In a similar vein, if other frameworks are used (e.g. disorder specific models, or the diathesis-stress model), the assessment procedures must provide appropriate data to inform these models.

The present chapter will also provide an overview of some useful measures that can be used when working with older people.

This chapter aims to illustrate:

1. At its simplest, assessment involves detecting recurrent patterns and scripts and their links to patients' experiences.

2. Therapists uncover patterns experienced in the here and now, and attempt to identify their recurrent themes (i.e. horizontal pattern detection). Identifying similar experiential patterns from the past is termed vertical pattern detection.

3. Conducting assessments is highly complex, although it may appear simple. When undertaken badly, assessments can be overly intrusive, or at worst destructive (e.g. they may unwittingly reactivate dormant core beliefs, or generate and reinforce unhelpful ones).

The first part of this chapter provides a structural overview of the assessment process, and the latter section examines some of the common measures and questionnaires used with the older population.

5.2: ASSESSMENT PROTOCOL

The following protocol provides a step-by-step guide for conducting assessments. The detailed descriptions of the 11 steps (A–K) show the generic assessment features of standard CBT. The comprehensive list described may appear to give a sense of strict sequential order, but in reality the process is very dynamic and fluid, and some aspects may even be omitted in order to meet patients' needs (e.g. not using validated questionnaires, or a suitability assessment, etc).

A. The *referral letter* provides useful information, giving some idea of the patient's personal details, some history and presenting problems. It is particularly helpful in learning about the chronicity of the problem, as this will help determine whether one is likely to use a longitudinal approach (i.e. diathesis-stress framework), or a mini-formulation approach which does not examine the patient's early life in great detail (Charlesworth and Reichelt 2004; see Chapter 6).

B. The *first encounter* with the patient can be a rich source of information. This meeting can provide details about physical health status, mobility, posture, eye contact, confidence, facial expression, presentation of dress/attire, etc.

C. *Basic background information* needs to be *complete*. This is emphasised because one finds that some therapists gather the scantiest of information, which causes problems later on in therapy. The information will usually include:

age, marital status, children, own sibship and place in the sibship, education level, jobs held over the years, main occupation, roles since retirement, interpersonal network, including recent losses. It is also important to examine the patient's physical health status because many medical conditions are associated with depression (nutritional deficiencies, and cardiopulmonary, endocrine, neoplastic and neurological conditions). Further there is a long list of drugs that include depression as a side-effect (Kupfer 2005). Hence, it is the responsibility of the therapist to check that there are no physical illnesses and their treatments unwittingly contributing to the patient's negative affect. Consistent with this point are Thompson, Gallagher-Thompson and Dick's (1996) recommendations about gaining details from the primary care physician (GP) and family members: 'We have found that establishing a solid foundation of communication and collaboration among all interested persons can make a key difference between success and failure in the psychotherapy that follows' (p.7). Caregiver support is particularly important for those patients experiencing cognitive deficits, and it is an essential aspect of treating patients' suffering with moderate to severe impairment.

D. The *first two or three interviews* will cover:

(i) *A diagnostic assessment.* A diagnosis alone does not help to understand the complexity of an individual's problems; however, it is necessary for the formulation stage because it will direct the therapist towards specific models of disorders. Thus it gives pointers to how one is going to engage the patient (e.g. see Appendix I). If a diagnostic assessment is conducted correctly, a large amount of information is collected relating to non-symptomatic issues. For example the patient may talk about certain individuals in their lives, about specific events, about their life conditions. The therapist will then be able to help the patient elaborate on these points at a later stage of the assessment process.

(ii) *Framework-specific assessment.* When choosing to use a particular formulation framework, one must collect information relevant to that conceptualisation. For example, if employing Laidlaw *et al*.'s (2003) Comprehensive Conceptualisation Framework for Older People, one would need to collect information about core beliefs, assumptions, triggers, thoughts, feelings etc., but also details about:

- Intergenerational linkages – details about key networks in a person's life (e.g. family networks). An examination of the supports and tensions among the different generations.

- Sociocultural context – this is concerned with the relevance of one's cultural identity, politics and class in terms of one's perspectives.

- Transitions in role investment – details about recent changes in lifestyle or life-course, due to changes in roles and commitments.

- Cohort beliefs – these are beliefs commonly held by people from a specific social strata within a particular generation (e.g. those born in the 1920s, post-war, those who were hippies in 1960s, etc.).

- Health status – information about patients' physical health needs, strengths and weaknesses.

(iii) *Questionnaires.* It is useful to use valid measures of severity early on in the assessment stage to obtain a baseline against which the progress of therapy can be measured. Some of the measures are also helpful in identifying key automatic thoughts (Automatic Thoughts Questionnaire, ATQ, Hollon and Kendall 1980) or core beliefs (Dysfunctional Attitude Scale, DAS, Weissman and Beck 1978). When treating older people, many of the usual measures – Hamilton Rating Scale for Depression (HRSD, Hamilton 1960); the Beck Depression Inventory (BDI, Beck *et al.* 1961) – are confounded by physical health issues associated with this age-group. Hence, questionnaires specifically designed for older people are often preferred (Kogan, Edelstein and McKee 2000) – see section 5.4 of this chapter.

(iv) *Eliciting patterns* of thought and behaviour via *monitoring sheets*. As stated in previous chapters, a therapist needs to be a 'pattern detector'. In CBT the hot-cross bun template serves as a framework to guide the assessment. Below are three typical areas that are monitored.

Pattern 1: Examining patient activity and its relation to mood. This can be done through the use of Weekly Activity Pleasure and Mastery Schedules. These schedules monitor the patient's feelings of mastery (M) and pleasure (P) while performing everyday activities.

Times	Monday	Tuesday	Wednesday
7am – 8am	Still asleep	Got ready for visit to hospital	Still asleep
	M = 0% P = 50%	M = 10% P = 5%	M = 0% P = 0%
8am – 9am	Went for a walk	*Travelled to hospital on the bus	Still asleep
	M = 60% P = 60%	M = 80% P = 5%	M = 0% P = 0%
9am – 10am	Met friend for breakfast	Sat in the clinic waiting room	Watched TV
	M = 60% P = 60%	M = 10% P = 15%	M = 0% P = 15%

When one inspects such charts, a therapist can detect patterns occurring across the day and see how they influence mood. Also, examining the data helps the patient to recognise the role of mastery as a motivating force in tackling her disorder. For example, in the above case the patient clearly did not like travelling on the bus to hospital (*), but got a sense of achievement from doing this.

Pattern 2: Identifying pleasant events. Thompson *et al.* (2009) have developed the Californian Older People's Pleasant Event Schedule (COPPES, previously the OPPES). It is a self-report questionnaire containing 66 items (e.g. going for walks; attending a good movie; browsing in a library). Each item is rated on how frequently it occurs and how enjoyable it is. Such scales are useful as they can be employed to plot changes in activity or mood against time. This type of graphical presentation is helpful in identifying peaks and troughs, and over time can determine whether the patient is engaging in more or less pleasurable activities.

Pattern 3: Identifying links between thoughts and moods. Chapter 2, Figure 2.4 presented a typical daily monitoring sheet; alternative versions can be tailored to meet the needs of one's patients (see Coon *et al.* 2007). Below is an example of a simple version tailored to meet the requirements of a 'concrete' thinker.

Mood: Identify the following	When did it occur	Rating mood (+10 to −10)	The sorts of things going through your head
Blackest mood of the day	After waking up	−9	I can't face another day. I want to die.
Neutral mood state	Watching TV	0	Not thinking about myself, just watching the news.
Most content period of day	Grandson smiled at me	+7	He is happy to see me.

E. Generating a list of *presenting problems* (aka 'Chief complaints', Thompson *et al.* 2000). This list needs to be exhaustive, concrete and specific. Typically, it will consist of the main symptoms that may be altered by therapeutic input. For example, inactivity; loss of pleasure; avoidant behaviours; interpersonal problems; financial problems; family problems; self-related problems such as loss of self-confidence, loss of self-esteem, guilt, shame. The specific nature of the problems needs to be identified, together with concrete examples to help clarify them further.

Having defined the problems, SMART goals may be set (i.e. Specific Measurable Achievable Realistic Time-framed with a date for completion). Westbrook *et al.* (2007) suggest using the following questions to help clarify goals:

> How would you like things to be at the end of treatment?
> How would you know if treatment had been successful?
> At the end of treatment, what would you like to be different?

In answering such questions the patient is *not* allowed to answer the above with things she doesn't want (e.g. *I don't want to feel upset any more, I don't want any panicky feelings, Never to think about cancer again*). In contrast the statements should be positive and SMART. For example, a man with agoraphobia might say: 'In four weeks time, I would like to be able to walk out of the house and be able to collect the paper from the shop myself.'

F. *Raising awareness* of the features of the *hot-cross bun* cycle. During the assessment interviews, the therapist needs to raise patients' awareness about the negative scripts and cycles influencing their moods. For many people this will involve bringing their unconscious processes and actions into a higher level of awareness (see Chapters 2 and 4). Hence, through careful, slow and well-paced socialisation to the model, the patient will eventually learn how to capture and differentiate the features of the cycle. With respect to *NATs*, the therapist must help the patient to elicit her thoughts, and become aware of the common themes. One would not normally ask the patient to re-evaluate NATs in this phase as one wants to know the size and breadth of the cognitions that one is dealing with. Further, attempts to re-evaluate the NATs too early in the therapy would tend not to be successful, and may also interfere with the rapport building – as the patient may initially feel overly challenged by the re-evaluation exercises.

The patient also needs to be helped to elicit *typical emotions and learn to differentiate them*. There is a lot of co-morbidity in the mood disorders, and depression and anxiety are common bedfellows. Further, owing to the fact that anger and hostility are generally less commonly spontaneously expressed, the therapist may need to ask specific questions to elicit these.

In addition, *typical behaviours* need to be assessed to identify safety-seeking behaviours (see Box 5.1) and coping strategies used by the patient. Some strategies may have been helpful in the past, but are no longer functional and now serve to maintain the patient's problems. It is possible that over recent months the patient may have adopted a restricted range of coping strategies due to a change in circumstances (health related, financial, etc.). For example, prior to the patient's arthritic knee, the patient may have used exercise to relieve her distress.

Box 5.1: Safety-seeking behaviours

Panic
Monitoring of pulse and other physiological sensations; deep breathing, holding onto objects, inactivity, muscle tension.

Generalised anxiety disorder
Worrying, scanning for danger, mental control, distraction, thought suppression, rumination in an attempt to anticipate threat.

Social phobia
Gripping objects tightly to avoid tremor, self-monitoring, reassurance seeking, attempting not to attract attention, perceptual scanning, self-absorption, excessive self-reflection, over-rehearsing and excessive planning, post-morteming, perceptual avoidance (eye-contact, tactile).

Obsessive compulsive disorder
Neutralisations (mental and physical), control seeking, employment of rituals, checking, excessive deliberation, excessive taking of responsibility.

Health anxiety
Self-monitoring, reassurance seeking, medical consultations, hyper-vigilance, avoidance of physical exertion, selective attention to illness-related information (media, TV), bodily checking, selective attention on body.

Post-traumatic stress disorder
Thought suppression, imagery, distraction.

Box 5.1 outlines some of the common forms of safety-seeking behaviours associated with the different disorders. It is relevant to note that safety behaviours are often distinguished from avoidance and withdrawal strategies. The latter are escape strategies (e.g. avoidance of situations/objects/people), while the former are active (i.e. non-avoidant) behaviours that either (i) reduce a perceived risk, or (ii) are used by the person to cope in situations where negative feelings are being experienced.

The box provides some of the characteristic safety behaviours identified by people experiencing different mental health problems. It is important to remember that there is a large degree of co-morbidity with respect to people's mood states and thus it is common to find someone exhibiting a range of safety behaviours from each of the different categories. Thus it is essential that a thorough assessment of the patient's experience is carried out.

G. *Identifying key cognitions.* The patient may spontaneously voice beliefs regarding herself or others (e.g. carers) that will help in the formulation. An overview of the various forms of cognitions relevant to CBT is outlined below (Table 5.1). Westbrook *et al.* (2007) suggest there are three hierarchical levels of cognitions. At the lowest level ('bottom-line') there are *core beliefs*, which are 'general' cognitions that are not readily accessible nor easy to change. At the highest ('on-line') level there are the more specific and accessible *automatic thoughts*. At the middle level are *dysfunctional assumptions*, which Westbrook and colleagues perceive as acting like bridges between the levels, and whose content provides the 'rules for living' (Westbrook *et al.* 2007, p.8).

Table 5.1 provides rather comprehensive description of the various cognitions. It is noteworthy that eliciting positive cognitions is an important part of the assessment process – asking the person what they enjoy now and enjoyed previously, what skills they have possessed over different phases of their lives, etc. Working with positive beliefs and thoughts is increasingly viewed as being relevant in psychotherapy (Ranzijn 2002).

In relation to assessment, the therapist needs to know how to elicit these various types of cognitions, but also how to work with them once they have been brought into awareness or activated. In the past, I have been critical that therapists seem to be eager to elicit cognitions, particularly at the core belief level, without either sufficient care or skill to work with them (James 2001b; James and Barton 2004). This issue will be addressed further in Chapter 7.

H. *Triggers.* Information about precipitating events/triggers of both the current episode and previous episodes of low mood is essential. Such detail may reveal important patterns, thus giving insights into the individual's areas of vulnerability.

I. *Physical health issues.* If the patient has a chronic health condition, information about the impact of the condition needs to be investigated. Factual information can be obtained from various sources (literature, internet, GP, other professionals), to help to determine the limiting factors associated with the illness. As outlined in Figure 3.2 (Chapter 3), CBT tends to work in

Table 5.1: A summary of the different types of cognitions

Type of cognition	Description	Examples
Belief	These are perspectives held by people about themselves, the world, others, the future, etc. They can be positive, neutral or negative. The degree to which the person is allied to the belief will depend on various factors, including utility of the belief, length it has played a role in the person's life, values assigned to it, etc.	'Liverpool are the greatest football team'; 'My nose is too big'; 'People used to be friendlier'; 'The government has made a mess of the economy'; 'My memory is failing'.
Self-referent belief	A belief held about the self. It can be positive, neutral or negative. It may relate to the present, future or past.	'I am lucky'; 'I used to be good looking'; 'I am physically fit'; 'I've got a good sense of humour'.
Negative core belief/schema (aka unconditional beliefs)	A self-referent belief that is fundamental to the way the person views himself in the world. Such beliefs are sometimes called 'unconditional' because they are global statements that are applicable to all situations. They are often referred to as schemas, though this is not to be confused with the original notion of schema used within cognitive psychology (James *et al.* 2004)	'I am worthless'; 'I can't trust others'.
Early maladaptive schema (EMS)	Negative core beliefs that have been formed in childhood. Owing to them having been formed via immature thought processes, they often take the simple form of 'I am...' statements.	'I am inadequate'; 'I am defective'.
Late arrival maladaptive beliefs (LAMBs)	Core beliefs formed by traumatic experiences, or due to later life transitions and changes in a person's role or health status.	'I am a burden'; I am going to have another heart attack'; 'I am going to fall'; 'I am not safe any more'.

Table 5.1: A summary of the different types of cognitions *cont.*

Type of cognition	Description	Examples
Worth Enhancing Beliefs (WEBs)	Positive core beliefs that provide the person with a sense of worth. Poor affect can occur due to the lack of opportunities for these beliefs to be activated, e.g. ill health not allowing the person to either engage in exercise or socialise outside of her house. Previously the latter activities enhanced the person's well-being (see Chapter 6 for more details).	'I am good at sports'; 'I can make people laugh'; 'I get on well with people'.
Dysfunctional assumptions (aka conditional beliefs)	These bridge the gap between negative core beliefs and NATs, permitting some flexibility with regard to people's perceptions. This flexibility is achieved by providing some exceptions (or conditions) to the inflexible core belief perspective. Thus, the core belief 'I am worthless' can become the conditional belief 'I am worthless, unless I do things for others', or, put another way, 'I am OK, if I do things for others'.	'Unless I do it perfectly, it's not worth doing'; 'I'm nothing, if I don't have him'; 'I'm only happy when others like me'.
Automatic thoughts The negative cognitions are known as negative automatic thoughts (NATs)	These are thoughts that enter a person's head automatically without any conscious intent, being trigged by other cognitions and/or features in the environment. They are often so familiar to the person that there is little awareness regarding their content. CBT helps patients become more aware of people's NATs, assisting people to re-evaluate them.	'I can't do this!'; 'I'm going to have a heart attack'; 'It will end in disaster'; 'Everyone thinks I'm strange'.

the zone between the physical limits set by the condition and the perceived limits set by the anxious patient.

J. *Biography*. To help determine whether one is required to use a longitudinal approach (i.e. diathesis-stress or schema), a brief sketch of the developmental history of the patient is needed: details will include relationship with parents and siblings, key experiences at and during childhood and education, patterns of friendships and relationships, past negative events, past positive events, current social/occupational functioning.

K. *Suitability assessment.* When examining patient suitability there are a number of issues to clarify: (i) at what stage do you want to make the judgement about suitability, i.e. prior to engagement or following a trial of therapy; (ii) what features predict outcome; and (iii) whose view is relevant (i.e. therapist or patient).

Calder (2000) states that judgements of patient suitability can be made at several points in the referral-therapy process. They could be made by: the referrer; by the clinician upon receiving the letter; by the clinician after receiving pre-assessment questionnaires from the patient; after an initial assessment interview with the patient; and after a trial course of therapy by either the patient or clinician. Different types of information would be obtained at these various phases. Patient factors such as chronicity and severity can be gained without seeing the person, but the interpersonal features (teamwork, alliance, etc.) will require some form of meeting. In terms of the predictability of such factors in relation to CBT outcome, the findings are contradictory. To date, the variables associated with poorest outcome are 'severity of the symptoms prior to therapy' and presence of a 'personality disorder'. To a lesser extent both chronicity and the presence of 'non-event related' depression (i.e. endogenous) have been found to be problematic. Marriage is one of the few protective factors, while other demographic details show little association with outcome (Beutler and Crago 1991; Whisman 1993).

A further feature relating to assessment concerns 'who' makes the judgement about the person's suitability. With respect to CBT, Safran and Segal (1990) produced a ten-item, clinician-rated, post-interview suitability scale. The items are:

1. chronicity of the problem

2. compatibility with the cognitive rationale

3. alliance potential during the therapy session

4. alliance potential outside of the session (e.g. to do homework, work on the difficulties independently)

5. acceptance of personal responsibility to change

6. general optimism regarding the benefits of CBT

7. focality, and ability to attend and focus on the therapeutic material

8. absence of major obstacles to therapy (personality, circumstances – aka security operations)

9. ability to access thoughts to engage with the hot-cross bun model

10. ability to be aware of emotional change, and differentiate the different emotions from one another.

The scale has a range of 1–50, with a high score indicating greater suitability. As Laidlaw (2008) points out, many older people would not score particularly well on this scale at the *start* of therapy. Rather they would require a time of engagement in the therapy before their ability to use the CBT model could be adequately assessed. Laidlaw's view is particularly helpful, and thus while this scale is useful as a guide to highlight areas requiring specific focus (e.g. ability to differentiate emotions, optimism, etc.), it should not be used as an exclusion criterion within our clinics.

Safran and Segal's measure was strongly influenced by Bordin's model (1994) of working alliance, and as one can see it places a lot of emphasis on alliance issues. The importance of this teamwork perspective is widely recognised and has led to a number of studies examining patients' views of therapy (Krupnik *et al.* 1996). For example, Marmar *et al.* (1989) examined patient-rated alliance and its relationship to outcome in various therapies (dynamic, behavioural, CBT) conducted with older people. They found that only one of the five subscales of their alliance measures correlated with outcome, and this association was only found in the CBT condition.

5.3: CAUTIONS REGARDING THE ASSESSMENT PROCESS

This section suggests that caution needs to be taken when undertaking assessment work. Three main concerns are evident: (i) problems working at the level of core beliefs, (ii) getting trapped in an assessment-conceptualisation loop, and (iii) working at levels at which one has insufficient skills.

i. Problems working at the level of core beliefs

People's beliefs should generally be elicited via a sensitive stepped-care approach (Davison 2000; James 2001b), one that is compatible with the needs of the patient, the patient's presentation, and the skills of the therapist.

Hence, core belief work should generally be avoided with someone experiencing a first-episode disorder, or with patients with only mild depression. With regard to the therapist, this type of work should be avoided by an inexperienced therapist (James and Barton 2004). In situations where core work is deemed necessary, it is important that the methods used are truly therapeutic, and this requires planning and preparation. For example, there are potential dangers of inappropriately applying methods such as downward arrowing, as we will see below.

Downward arrowing is designed to 'bottom-out' fearful thoughts in order to determine either a person's underlying belief or her greatest fear. For example, Patient: *I am worried that I'll forget my grandchild's birthday.* (Therapist: If you did, what would this say about you?) Pt: *She'd think I didn't care.* (Th: If she thought you didn't care, what would that say about you?) Pt: *I didn't love her.* (Th: If true, what would it say about you?) Pt: *I'm selfish*, etc... This simple, yet powerful, technique takes patients from a specific situation – usually one where they have low mood – and explores the implications for them as individuals. While useful information is often elicited using this technique, accessing beliefs about being a selfish person can often serve to deepen someone's depressed mood further. For example, if she has always seen herself as a selfish person – suggesting a core belief, rather than a transient one – this could be an emotionally charged realisation, making it difficult for both patient and therapist to regulate affect.

The downward arrow strategy, in the hands of experienced therapists, can be very effective. However, owing to its simplicity, it tends to be one of the first techniques CBT therapists are taught – and therein lies a potential problem. For example, a patient may arrive at the therapy session feeling depressed, but following downward arrowing, one hour later she may be leaving seeing her life in terms of a few absolutist statements (e.g. 'I am selfish', 'I am worthless', 'I am inadequate'). As I shall discuss further, this can have huge ramifications for the person over the next few days and weeks. She may start to globally re-evaluate her whole life in terms of those beliefs (*I've always been selfish; I could have been more supportive to my mother, but I put her into care; I have had no real friends; My husband is going to leave me, because he's fed up with my selfishness*). Thus, in unskilled hands the methodology may allow access to core material (or activate processing biases) without adequate attention being given to the development of coping strategies for dealing with exposure of such details. In more competent hands, preparation would usually have taken place, and the patient would have been taught how to 'de-centre' from such material. I wish to emphasise the need for therapists to think through the possible emotional reactions and consequences of accessing beliefs, and suggest that core beliefs are brought gradually and sensitively into a course of therapy.

As therapists, aware of the potential impact that new insights can have on patients, it is important that a number of steps are taken. For example, if a therapist proposes core belief work, it is better to do this early on within a therapy session so as to leave sufficient time to work at this level of cognition appropriately (i.e. thorough evaluation of the beliefs, facilitation of de-centring skills and re-evaluation work). He should also be mindful of the patient's thinking style and biases. If the patient is prone to black and white thinking, one should expect to see dramatic shifts in perspective.

ii. Getting trapped in an assessment-conceptualisation loop

Evidence gained from supervising cognitive therapy trainees, which has involved watching many hours of video-taped CBT sessions, has informed me that many trainees over-employ assessment methods at the expense of change methodologies (see Appendix ii). I believe one of the reasons for this is that while negative beliefs can be elicited with relative ease, clinical change, particularly at the level of core belief, is difficult to achieve. When training therapists, I find a simple fishing-boat analogy helpful to illustrate the difference between elicitation and change (James and Barton 2004):

> Imagine a depressed person's thinking can be represented by a river full of negative thinking. The stream of thinking is endless and constantly flowing in a negative direction. Hence, during the assessment phase, eliciting negative cognitions is akin to throwing a fishing net over the side of a rowing boat which is gently floating on the stream of negativity. In truth, all one needs to do is open the mouth of the net (e.g. by asking some relevant questions) and then watch all the negative cognitions flow into it. However, at some point when the net is sufficiently full, one must attempt to deal with the material that has been caught. In therapeutic terms, this point would occur when one considers sufficient details have been captured in order to (a) develop a working conceptualisation, and (b) attempt to employ change strategies. Within the analogy, the latter step is equivalent to trying to row against the current of negativity. This is clearly a difficult thing to do, but to make matters much worse one is also struggling with a large dysfunctional catch and a lot of patient expectation attached to it.

At times, because of the level of difficulty of rowing against the stream, the temptation is to keep filling one's net with more examples of negative thoughts and beliefs. Such a situation can lead therapists to become stuck in an assessment and re-conceptualisation loop (A-R loop).

The A-R loop is most commonly seen with trainee therapists who may be observed eliciting more and more material, either hoping that insight alone will be sufficient to produce major changes with respect to their patient or for want of knowing what else to do. It is my belief that, because many therapists are neither confident nor highly skilled in using change methodologies, this results in patients spending too much time in the assessment and conceptualisation phases. This may be another reason for the propensity of therapists to over-examine the early years of their patients' lives – thus losing the CBT focus on the 'here and now'.

iii Working at levels beyond one's skills

The third cautionary issue, 'Not working beyond one's abilities', is reflected in both of the previous items. In order to ensure that one is appraising one's abilities appropriately and adequately reflecting on one's work, therapists need to seek the right level of supervision (Roth and Pilling 2007). The British Association of Behavioural and Cognitive Psychotherapists (BABCP) and other professional bodies operate guidelines on this issue, and in recent years there has been a wealth of literature on the use of supervision from a CBT perspective (Armstrong and Freeston 2006; James, Milne, Morse and Blackburn 2007; James, Milne and Morse 2008; Milne 2008).

The next section examines some of the measures that are helpful to use when conducting psychotherapy with older people.

5.4: MEASURES

There are a whole host of measures that can be used with older people, and there have been a number of good reviews from an older adult perspective (Burns, Lawlor and Craig 2004; Edelstein *et al.* 2008; Kogan, *et al.* 2000). The main thrust of this list suggests that one must be selective, choosing the test or questionnaire that best meets the patients' needs. For example, it is helpful to think of the function being fulfilled by a test. Some of the functions are outlined in Table 5.2.

Table 5.2: Function of measures

Function of the test or measure is:	Comments
To assess the overall outcome of the therapy (pre/post-assessments)	There are many tests in this pre/post-assessment category; often more than one questionnaire is used to assess different aspects of change.
To monitor progress made over the course of the therapy on a weekly basis	Similar to above, but because the tests need to be used repeatedly, shorter forms of the questionnaires tend to be better. Visual analogue scales and especially Goal Attainment Scales are useful methods (Thompson *et al.* 2009). The latter are flexible, Likert-style scales in which individualised goals are set jointly by the therapist and patient. The Likert score determines the degree to which the goal is/is not achieved.
To provide material to aid with the construction of the formulation	The answers given to some scales allow the therapist to identify clinical themes. Such themes can help direct the formulation and intervention strategies.
To assess patient risk	Questionnaires examining self-harm or suicidality are important, often playing a part in an organisation's management of clinical risk.
To assist with selection/exclusion criterion	Some measures are used routinely to select participants in empirical studies. Such tests may also be useful in assessing diagnosis, suitability for therapy, and/or psychological mindedness (see Edelstein *et al.* 2008).
To assess abilities, both intellectual and physical (e.g. mobility)	There are numerous tests assessing intellectual abilities, cognitive and physical performance that are useful when working with older people (see Burns *et al.* 2004).
To fulfil course requirements	The questionnaires used in this category will tend to be pre-determined and conforming to a protocol, providing little choice for the therapist to exercise judgement.

While one needs to be selective, I would advocate the use of multiple instruments rather than one when employing different treatment modalities (Mintz, Steuer and Jarvik 1981). From their experiences of studying the elderly, Mintz and colleagues think it is worth weighing the cost of adding two measures against the cost of failing to accurately assess the comparative effectiveness of various treatment modalities.

Table 5.3 provides an overview of tests that fulfil these various functions. This is not an exhaustive list of questionnaires and measures.

Table 5.3: A description of some of the tests used with older people during therapy

Anxiety	Key references	Description
Short Anxiety Screening Test	Sinoff et al. 1999	Interviewer-administered ten-item scale, with a range of 10–40. Cut-off score of 24 indicating significant anxiety. It is effective at diagnosing anxiety in the presence of depression in the elderly.
Worry Scale (WS)	Wisocki, Handen and Morse 1986	Self-administered 35-item scale, taking ten minutes to complete. Contains the worry domains of finance, health and social issues.
Penn State Worry Questionnaire (PSWQ)	Meyer et al. 1990	Self-administered 16-item scale, with a range of 16–80, taking ten minutes to complete. Examining worry in general rather than the content of worry. Frequently used with older people. An abbreviated version omits double negative items that can be confusing to some older people. The briefer version is more often used in clinical settings.
State-Trait Anxiety Inventory (STAI)	Speilberger et al. 1983	Self-administered measure comprised of two 20-item scales (state and trait), in which each item is answered on a four-item Likert-type scale to measure general anxiety.
Beck Anxiety Inventory (BAI)	Beck and Steer 1993	Self-administered 21-item scale, with a scoring range of 0 to 63, taking 15–20 minutes to complete. Effective for assessing somatic symptoms, but should be used with caution in medical settings because possibility of over-estimating severity of anxiety.

Table 5.3: A description of some of the tests used
with older people during therapy *cont.*

Anxiety	Key references	Description
Hamilton Anxiety Rating Scale (HARS)	Hamilton 1959	Interviewer-rated 15-item scale, with a range of 0–60, taking 15 minutes to complete. There are no norms for older people.
Geriatric Anxiety Inventory (GAI)	Pachana *et al.* 2006	Self- or clinician-administered 20-item scale, with a range of 0–20. Cut-off score of 8/9 for presence of anxiety and 10/11 for presence of GAD. The GAI is able to discriminate patients with and without anxiety, and those with and without GAD.
Clinician-administered PTSD Scale (CAPS)	Blake *et al.* 1995	Clinician-administered 30-item structured interview that corresponds to the DSM-IV criteria for PTSD. In addition to assessing 17 PTSD symptoms, its questions target the impact of symptoms on social and occupational functioning.
Anxiety Disorders Interview Schedule	Di Nardo *et al.* 1993	Clinician-rated interview designed to aid the diagnosis of anxiety disorders. It has been shown to have good agreement with DSM-III-R in studies with older adults.
Fear Questionnaire (FQ)	Marks and Mathews 1979	Self-administered 15-item test, taking ten minutes to complete, assessing the severity of avoidance behaviours related to agoraphobia, social and blood-injury fears.
Geriatric Depression Scale (GDS)	Yesavage *et al.* 1983	Self-administered 30-item scale, with scoring range of 0–30, taking 5–10 minutes to complete. Cut-offs 11 and 21 for mild and severe depression respectively.
Beck Depression Scale (BDI, BDI-II)	Beck *et al.* 1961; Beck *et al.* 1996	Self-administered 21-item test, with range of 0–63, taking 20 minutes to complete. Cut-off of 12/13 for presence of depression. A universal measure used for numerous purposes, including carer well-being.
Center for Epidemiological Studies – depression scale	Radloff 1977	Self-administered 20-item test, with range of 0–60, taking five minutes to complete. Four domains (depressed affect, positive affect, vegetative signs, interpersonal distress). Cut-offs 16 and 23 for mild and significant depression respectively. Used in research and as screening tool.

Hamilton Rating Scale For Depression (HRSD)	Hamilton 1960	Semi-structured interview format requires a trained clinician; in the 21 item version the scoring range is 0–60, taking 20–30 minutes to complete. Cut-off 11 for diagnosis of depression. Used in research and clinical settings.
Cornell Scale for Depression in Dementia	Alexopoulos *et al.* 1988	Semi-structured interview format requires a trained clinician, 19-item scale, involving observation of the patient (ten minutes) and questioning of the carer (20 minutes). Range of 0–38, with a score of 8 suggesting depression.
Montgomery and Asberg Depression Rating Scale (MADRS)	Montgomery and Asberg 1979	Semi-structured ten-item test, with a range of 0–60, taking 20 minutes to complete. Frequent administration is possible. Used in research; popular in drug trials.
Brief Assessment Schedule Depression Cards (BASDEC)	Adshead, Day Cody and Pitt 1992	Interviewer-facilitated test, with 19 cards containing statements (e.g. I'm not happy at all) to which the patient can answer true/false/don't know. Maximum score is 21, with 7 indicating depression. Designed for elderly medical inpatients.
Automatic Thought Questionnaire (ATQ)	Hollon and Kendall 1980 Ingram *et al.* 1995 (ATP-Q)	Self-administered 30-item scale, with range of 30–150, taking 10–15 minutes to complete. Cut-off score of 44 indicates depressive style of thinking. The responses can be used clinically, helping to identify the NATs. There is now a positive version of the scale called the ATP-Q.
Dysfunctional Attitude Scale (DAS) A and B versions	Weissman and Beck 1978	Self-administered 40-item test, with range of 40–280, taking 15 minutes to complete. Cut-off score of 113 characteristic of depression. The themes emerging from the responses are useful in identifying patients' core beliefs.
Hopelessness Scale (HS)	Beck *et al.* 1974	Self-administered 20-item scale, with range of 0–20, taking ten minutes to complete. Cut-off score of 3 indicates increased risk of self-harm. This scale is often used clinically as a risk assessment measure as hopelessness is associated with self-harm.

Table 5.3 has outlined some of the scales commonly used with older people in relation to anxiety and depression. However, owing to the pervasive effects of these two disorders on people's lives, other domains are frequently monitored and assessed. For example, some clinicians choose to monitor changes in sleep patterns during the course of treatment. Two useful questionnaires in this area are the Pittsburgh Sleep Quality Index (Buysse *et al.* 1989) and the Dysfunctional Beliefs and Attitudes about Sleep Scale (Morin 1994). The former is a useful screening tool, while the latter assesses sleep-related dysfunctional beliefs related to insomnia. For a helpful practical review of the range of questionnaires used with older people and their carers see Burns *et al.* (2004). Those requiring a more discursive overview may wish to consult Edelstein *et al.* (2008). They assess the psychometric properties of the various questionnaires used for older people in relation to suicidal ideation, personality, sleep disorder, anxiety and depression. They also examine the potential sensory deficits that could compromise assessment, and discuss various solutions to such difficulties.

5.5: CONCLUSION

It is important to emphasise that the assessment process should not be viewed as a discrete phase of therapy. Indeed, the assessment is much more than merely data gathering; it should involve socialising the patient to CBT and incorporate change strategies. The latter may take the form of experiential exercises and/or homework tasks. Such activities help both the therapist and patient become more knowledgeable about the nature of the disorder. This chapter has also emphasised the need to take care when using the various powerful questioning techniques available to therapists, particularly when working at the level of beliefs. I have emphasised the need for awareness, preparation and competence when working with such constructs. The final section of the chapter has examined some of the common measures and questionnaires employed when working with older people. It has been noted that prior to choosing to employ a measure, one needs to ensure that the potential data available from the measures matches the goals of the therapy.

Chapter 6

Case Formulation

6.1: INTRODUCTION

Central to CBT, and its teaching, is the case formulation. This is seen by many therapists to be a key skill and fundamental to successful therapy. Formulating is the link between theory and practice and several standardised models have been developed to guide therapists in this skill (e.g. Persons and Tompkins 1997). While work around cognitive theory supporting the CBT model is well developed, the area of case formulation remains under-researched. Consequently, there is a growing number of researchers becoming aware of the need to improve our knowledge of the nature and role of case formulation in therapy (Kuyken, Padesky and Dudley 2009). For example, Bieling and Kuyken (2003) have recommended exploratory work concerning how practising therapists formulate in the real world, what form this takes, and the perceived role and importance of formulation. Many researchers and clinicians may argue that there is not a 'right' way to formulate a case. However, there is also growing evidence that case formulation is an under-taught skill in psychotherapy training (Sperry *et al.* 1992).

This chapter aims to illustrate the following:

1. The general nature of formulation, including what therapists consider the essential features of a good formulation.

2. The common formulation frameworks used with older people.

3. Advice on how to select the most appropriate framework for one's needs.

4. Several useful tips for therapists regarding using formulations with older people.

6.2: NATURE OF FORMULATIONS

Eells, Kendjelic and Lucas (1998) found that most formulations did little more than describe information, with no inferred hypothesis or underlying mechanisms. Similarly, Henry and Williams (1997) suggested that trainees of CBT find case formulation a difficult skill to master and consequently widely differing hypotheses are produced for individual cases. Indeed, empirical evidence from Persons, Mooney and Padesky (1995) found low inter-rater reliability between therapists when asked to formulate the same case. Fothergill and Kuyken (2002), more recently, found higher reliability on some inferential aspects (e.g. agreement about nature of patients' core beliefs). However, this was not the case for all inferential aspects, despite the researchers using a highly systematised case formulation method to explore participants' formulating abilities.

While these findings do not necessarily imply poor outcome in therapy, they do imply that, at some level, certain case formulations will be more helpful than others. However, at present, there is a lack of consensus over what should be included in a good formulation (Eells *et al.* 1998). In teaching the skill of formulation, there is a need for appropriate guidelines (Henry and Williams 1997). This is becoming increasingly relevant as more work is being done on using an integrative approach to CBT formulations to account for wider influences, such as the systemic context (Tarrier and Calam 2002). Clearly such issues are highly pertinent to working with older people, where one is often needing to move between the intrapsychic and the environmental influences. For example, in Laidlaw's Comprehensive Conceptualisation Framework (CCF) for older adults (Laidlaw *et al.* 2004), there are 11 elements (early experiences, core beliefs, conditional beliefs, activating events, compensatory strategies, negative automatic thoughts, cohort effects, role investment, health function, sociocultural beliefs, intergenerational linkages). Thus, for therapists, the job of formulating a case is becoming an increasingly complex process, and the need for exploration into what elements make up a quality formulation is becoming more relevant.

Butler's (1998) work on case formulation guidelines has offered one of the most comprehensive considerations of what a good formulation might look like. She defines formulations at a situation-specific level. Butler also highlights the key purposes of a case formulation, for example clarifying hypotheses and prioritising problems. Similarly, Flitcroft, James and Freeston (2007) have examined the purposes of CBT case formulations. In their empirical study, Flitcroft and colleagues asked therapists two questions: (i) what were the relevant features of a case formulation, and (ii) which of these features were the most essential. Seven experienced CBT therapists helped to construct a list of 86 statements capturing concepts considered relevant to a CBT formulation of depression. A further 23 therapists rated these statements in terms of their importance, using a Q-sort procedure (see Table 6.1). Three factors emerged, suggesting three dominant opinions as to the *essential* purpose of a formulation: a state factor, a process factor and a trait factor. Most of the therapists highlighted the state or generic aspects of 'thoughts, emotions and behaviours' as being the essential features. These tended to be practical, 'here and now' aspects.

Table 6:1: Hierarchical list of the most important features of a formulation

	Q-items – Items scored from +5 to −5	Mean (+5 to −5)
1	It explains how problems are maintained.	2.87
2	It is acceptable to the client and others.	2.65
3	It helps to make sense of the apparently senseless.	2.52
4	It informs on possible ways to intervene (the how rather than the where).	2.52
5	It identifies typical negative automatic thoughts relating to the self.	2.09
6	It instils hope and optimism.	1.91
7	It acts to facilitate the therapeutic alliance.	1.91
8	It explains depression at an individual level.	1.91
9	It socialises the client into therapy.	1.78
10	It identifies typical negative automatic thoughts relating to the world.	1.74
11	It identifies compensatory strategies.	1.70
12	It identifies typical negative automatic thoughts relating to hopelessness.	1.65
13	It identifies assumptions.	1.61
14	It identifies safety behaviours.	1.57
15	It reflects an evolving process.	1.57
16	It is informed by cognitive theory.	1.48
17	It demonstrates a matching of thoughts, emotions, etc.	1.43
18	It identifies specific depressive emotions.	1.39

Table 6:1: Hierarchical list of the most important features of a formulation *cont.*

	Q-items – *Items scored from +5 to −5*	*Mean (+5 to −5)*
19	It specifies treatment goals.	1.35
20	It identifies reactive behaviours.	1.30
21	It identifies avoidant behaviours.	1.30
22	It identifies precipitating events.	1.22
23	It identifies negative reasoning biases.	1.17
24	It identifies rules.	1.13
25	It identifies typical negative automatic thoughts relating to future pessimism.	1.09
26	It identifies core beliefs developed in childhood.	1.09
27	It identifies core beliefs developed since childhood.	1.09
28	It shows a logical consistency.	1.00
29	It identifies early experiences.	0.96
30	It helps inform relapse prevention.	0.96
31	It fits with historical evidence.	0.96
32	It identifies interpersonal schemas.	0.83
33	It identifies any obstacles to success.	0.78
34	It identifies attachment issues.	0.74
35	It identifies recurring triggers.	0.70
36	It predicts potential reactions to interventions.	0.70
37	It shifts the individual's experience of their situation.	0.65
38	It prioritises primary/secondary goals.	0.52
39	It identifies interpersonal style.	0.48
40	It can be adapted in its presentation.	0.48
41	It clarifies the links between distal and proximal features.	0.43
42	It identifies secondary appraisals of the negative automatic thoughts.	0.39
43	It identifies physiological reactions.	0.39
44	It identifies beliefs about the client's own capacity to change.	0.22
45	It identifies beliefs about depression that the client holds.	0.22

46	It indicates where gaps might be.	0.13
47	It indicates when to intervene.	0.04
48	It identifies specific anxious emotions.	0
49	It indicates suitability of treatment.	−0.04
50	It helps explain co-morbidity.	−0.17
51	It identifies a problem list.	−0.35
52	It acts as a containing event.	−0.35
53	It identifies appraisal of autobiographical memories (recurring rumination).	−0.39
54	It offers a psychological understanding to the referrer and others.	−0.43
55	It normalises diagnosis.	−0.43
56	It identifies sources of pleasure.	−0.57
57	It indicates the construct system the patient uses.	−0.70
58	It avoids the inclusion of irrelevant information.	−0.70
59	It identifies recent relationship changes.	−0.70
60	It identifies social support.	−0.87
61	It identifies life transitions.	−1.04
62	It identifies a list of typical symptoms.	−1.09
63	It identifies appraisal of autobiographical memories (negative evaluation).	−1.13
64	It serves to enhance the therapist's supervision.	−1.17
65	It indicates ways to intervene interpersonally.	−1.17
66	It helps identify what to evaluate pre- and post-.	−1.22
67	It helps to reduce negative appraisals in family, carers and staff.	−1.22
68	It identifies the patient's interpersonal style in therapy.	−1.22
69	It identifies the patient's ability to self-reflect.	−1.26
70	It identifies the patient's learning style.	−1.35
71	It identifies physical health issues.	−1.39
72	It is clear and accessible to other therapists.	−1.48

Table 6:1: Hierarchical list of the most important features of a formulation *cont.*

	Q-items – Items scored from +5 to –5	Mean (+5 to –5)
73	It identifies living conditions.	−1.61
74	It indicates the time-scale of the patient's difficulties.	−1.74
75	It identifies beliefs about the therapist that the client holds.	−1.87
76	It identifies social roles.	−1.87
77	It indicates the ego strength of the individual.	−1.96
78	It identifies family background.	−2.09
79	It validates the therapy model.	−2.22
80	It identifies personality type.	−2.43
81	It indicates how much therapy is needed.	−2.48
82	It identifies financial factors.	−2.78
83	It clarifies diagnosis.	−2.83
84	It identifies educational and work history.	−2.91
85	It identifies experiences of past therapy.	−3.65
86	It tells us who has given the label of depression	−4.30

In contrast, others highlighted the importance of process features. This group of therapists were less concerned with the specifics of the CBT model, emphasising the non-specific features of therapy (e.g. socialising, explaining, clarifying, instilling hope, etc.). This view fits with established research (Safran and Segal 1990) that suggests it may not be the techniques alone that result in good outcome, rather it is the combination of therapy specific and non-specific factors (i.e. good therapeutic alliance). The third factor suggested a trait perspective, and the therapists in this group believed it was most essential to explore their patients' histories and personality features in detail.

The contrast between Flitcroft *et al.* first and third factor profiles is somewhat consistent with Perris' (2000) writings, and his distinction between first and second generation forms of CBT. In his review, he considered that early versions of CBT (first generation) worked with surface-level structures (state structures). However, he suggested that the field of CBT was evolving into a second generation of treatment approaches. These approaches differed 'to the extent to which knowledge about developmental issues is actually utilized in the practice of therapy' (Perris 2000, p.102). It was Perris' view that when one is dealing with more complex presentations, therapy needs to be conducted at a 'deeper historical' (i.e. core belief) level. Thus it is perhaps better to ask what type of framework is most suited to an individual's presentation rather than what are the constituents of a good formulation. This theme is explored more at the end of this chapter, but first there is a brief discussion of ideas on formulation that I routinely share with my trainees when they are initially introduced to working with older people.

6.3: FORMULATIONS WITH OLDER PEOPLE

One of the differences between working with older versus younger people is the potential complexity of elders' formulations. This is in part due to the amount of historical data available to populate the formulations. Indeed, the skill of good therapists is often knowing what *not* to include in the formulation, as well as being aware of what actually needs to be present. I use the following set of seven statements in my supervision to help my trainees determine the most appropriate formulation approach for the patient:

1. Identify people's own formulations.

2. Ensure interventions are formulation-led.

3. Compare utility with accuracy.

4. Avoid 'kitchen-sink' formulations.

5. Acknowledge the assumptions of the formulations.

6. Understand the differences between the CBT frameworks and acknowledging their biases.

7. Recognise your own skills and knowledge base.

Before discussing the items, it is important to recognise that there is confusion about the term formulation. Hence, for purposes of clarity, when describing formulations in this section, I am referring to the framework, and *not* the process of producing the framework.

(i) Identifying people's own formulations in their various forms: the formulation framework can be composed of *either* an elaborate model of beliefs, thoughts, links made across time, *or* a simple set of conceptual statements regarding the patient. At the beginning the therapist's formulation will probably be different to that of his patient and/or carer. However, early on in therapy the different versions need to be brought together in a form that is both helpful in relation to the goals of treatment and acceptable to all parties. An example of a simple conceptual formulation of a staff member caring for a sexually disinhibited older man is: 'He is a dirty old sod, who exposes himself when no-one else is around, so he knows what he is doing.' The latter constitutes a formulation because it is the staff member's conceptual understanding of the man, and it is likely to influence how he is treated. Clearly such a conceptual view needs to be worked with and altered; it cannot simply be ignored otherwise it would undermine the interventions. In other scenarios many of our patients enter therapy with a coherent conceptualisation regarding their disorder. One of the jobs of the therapist is to determine whether these formulations are potentially helpful, and as such whether they can be utilised in therapy. For example, if someone viewed himself as resourceful and a good 'coper' prior to the onset of his depression, the therapist could attempt to re-establish such views (Blackburn, James and Flitcroft 2006).

(ii) Ensuring the interventions are formulation-led: a defining feature of our work is the development of a conceptual understanding of the individual, which then provides the rationale for our interventions; this may sound self-evident! However, frequently one finds that therapists conduct elaborate formulations, but routinely intervene with an unrelated, unsophisticated behavioural intervention. And when one asks the therapists about how this intervention relates to the formulation, they struggle to make the link.

(iii) Comparing utility with accuracy: as outlined above, the main function of a formulation is to provide a framework to guide and support appropriate interventions. In this sense they can be seen as 'helpful stories', containing various levels of detail that promote change. No matter how detailed one's story is, clearly it can never be an accurate account of the person's disorder or her history. Therefore, the therapist should not spend excessive amounts of time fine-tuning the formulation in terms of perceived accuracy. It is more helpful to develop a shared parsimonious 'story', rather than an overly comprehensive account, and one that links well with change strategies.

(iv) Avoiding 'kitchen-sink' formulations: the expression 'everything but the kitchen-sink' is a term used in situations when people are over-inclusive in their use of material in order to achieve an outcome that could have been obtained with less detail. Hence, this item concerns a tendency by some therapists to obtain far too much information about their patients' pasts; information that will never be used to direct the interventions. This problem is common in therapy in general (James 2001b), but even more so when working with older adults because of their longer histories. This issue is discussed further in Chapter 9.

(v) Acknowledging the assumptions of the formulation: when working with older people there are a range of CBT formulations to choose from (see section 6.4). While they all have the same broad goal (i.e. to direct interventions), each has its own set of assumptions. Some assume that the patient can be an active agent in the change process, others assume that change occurs systemically. A number of formulations are aimed at the level of the core belief, while others are more behaviourally focused. Therefore therapists must be aware of assumptions underlying the formulation, and the relevance of the patient's suitability (Safran and Segal 1990) when making a choice of what formulation approach to use. In the two case examples presented in Chapters 8 and 10, the first case of Mary used a standard CBT format, whereas the second (Donald) employed a more systemic approach. With Donald, the CBT concepts were used with the staff rather than directly with him.

(vi) Understanding the differences between the different therapeutic frameworks and acknowledging their biases: the work of a therapist involves identifying the nature of the problem, then applying a model to understand the difficulties in order to direct interventions. Thus, when using a psychodynamic approach, one filters the information through a template that focuses on a patient's early life, and identifies characteristic patterns from that period. With interpersonal therapy, one applies an interpersonal perspective, using a social networking template. With respect to basic CBT, one filters people's distressing experiences through the 'generic' template. In essence, one reduces the chaotic experience of depression and/or anxiety into a small number of items. These items are fairly concrete, understandable and measurable, and therefore they are utilisable in the fight against the negative affect. Further, it is around this template that one asks for data to be collected and, therefore, many of the diaries, and monitoring sheets have the four generic features embedded within them (Figure 2.4). Also, because these features are directly related to the person's 'here and now' experiences, one tends to be dealing with factual data rather than hypotheses and conjectures.

However, working at this generic level is sometimes insufficient to produce lasting change. At such times one might need to look for historical patterns to explain recurrent difficulties. As outlined above, this is termed second generation CBT (Perris 2000). This type of work requires more information gathering, greater pattern detection, and higher levels of therapeutic competence. But also, by its nature, it involves a lot more conjecture and thus is more likely to be influenced and biased by the therapist's own theoretical leanings. For example, a therapist who has a preference for schema therapy is likely to produce a different formulation to a clinician with a bias towards attachment perspectives. Indeed, great care needs to be exercised when dealing with historical data because it is possible to create false memories, and inadvertently develop unhelpful beliefs (James 2003).

(vii) Recognising one's own skills and knowledge base – across the country there are courses in CBT. Some last a few days, while the 'gold-standard' ones are generally conducted over a nine-month period. Whether one is a graduate of a gold-standard course or not, it is essential to maintain one's skill-base through supervision and training (James, Milne and Morse 2008; Milne 2008). It is important to constantly reflect on one's strengths and weaknesses. Indeed, therapy can be a negative experience for those patients working with incompetent therapists (James 2001b). Therefore, when choosing a particular formulation approach with a patient, it is important to ask oneself whether one has the required skills, and also whether one has the resources and support to undertake it competently.

6.4: REVIEW OF FORMULATION APPROACHES USED WITH OLDER PEOPLE

The following section outlines some of the formulations that have been used in the treatment of older people, with and without dementia. The section does not examine the diagnostic-specific frameworks (e.g. panic, OCD, GAD, etc.), although these are outlined in the appendices (Appendix I).

i. Generic or 'hot-cross bun' (Padesky and Greenberger 1995)

This model highlights the inter-relationships between cognition, affect, behaviour and physiology. It is clearly a derivation of Beck's first generation generic model for CBT. Despite appearing simple, this model is often difficult for patients to work with initially. As such, simplified versions may be used early in treatment. The version used in the early part of my work is outlined in Figure 6.1.

This model places the emotion at the centre because, in truth, a 'feeling state' is conceptually different from the other items of the cycle as it is the combined product of the other features. The figure presented here is the version I use in early homework assignments. Its format is designed to clarify the information required and helps to socialise patients to the CBT model. Only one emotion is placed at the centre to ensure that the thoughts and behaviours are fully consistent with a specific feeling state. Hence, if the

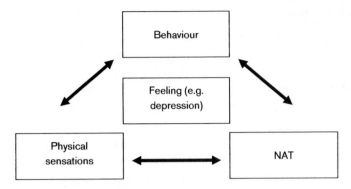

Figure 6.1: Revised version of the generic CBT cycle

thoughts recorded are more consistent with anxiety, then a second cycle is generated which centres on anxiety. The reason for doing this is to help the patient differentiate emotions and their themes and scripts associated with each of the emotions (see Table 6.2, which identifies the different themes associated with depression, anxiety, anger, guilt and shame).

Table 6.2: Cognitive themes associated with emotional distress

	Emotion	Themes
Triads[1]	Depression	A sense of self as worthless or inadequate, with a negative view of the world. One's future is perceived as unchanging and hopeless.
	Anxiety	A sense of vulnerability, a perception of the environment as chaotic, and the future as unpredictable.
	Anger	A sense of personal injustice, a perception of the environment as hostiles, a need to act to protect self from fututre harm.
Dyads	Shame	A sense of self as an object of ridicule or humiliation as judged by someone in the environment. Shame is interpersonally driven (Gilbert 1998).
	Guilt	A sense of the self as being the sourc of harm or injury, with someone in the environment suffering as a result of one's actions.

[1] Depression, anxiety and anger are represented by triadic relationships. However, other emotions such as shame and guilt are better described by dyadic relationships.

ii. Mini-formulations

According to Charlesworth and Reichelt (2004), a comprehensible formulation is more likely to be accepted by an older person than one that is comprehensive, yet incomprehensible. Thus they support the use of simple 'mini-formulations', which include: short linear chains of appraisal and emotional response, and two or three element vicious cycles.

LINEAR CHAINS (I.E. 'EVENT → APPRAISAL → EMOTIONAL RESPONSE')

Charlesworth and Reichelt (2004) suggest that basic linear chains can be useful in educating patients to the phenomenon of appraisal. Such models can be used in most circumstances as long as the term 'event' is defined broadly to encompass both external and internal experiences including life events, actions of others, and the patient's own thoughts, emotions and body sensations.

MINI-CYCLES

Charlesworth and Reichelt (2004) suggest that shared formulations with older adults can be facilitated through the use of two and three element 'mini-cycles'. The classic example of this is the 'feel low → negative thoughts and sad memories → feel worse' mood-thought cycle. Other common examples would be the 'pain → depression → pain exacerbation' cycle that can be used in conjunction with educational material such as the gate-control theory of pain (Melzack and Wall 1996). Once a patient feels comfortable with these simpler versions, they can be elaborated upon.

iii. Diathesis-stress

This formulation approach incorporates the 'hot-cross bun' model, but adds a historical perspective. The patient's early life is explored in-depth to determine whether aspects of her upbringing have led to the establishment of beliefs that over time have become dysfunctional (e.g. Don't trust anyone). Once established, the beliefs tend to be held rigidly and are hypothesised to influence the thinking and behaviour of the person in later life, during periods of low affect. This conceptualisation is sometimes referred to as a 'vulnerability' or 'Achilles heel' model (see case study 1, Mary, Chapter 8 for a worked example).

iv. Schema-focused

This framework shares many similarities with the diathesis-stress conceptualisation, but the core beliefs (aka schemas or Early Maladaptive Schemas – EMS, Young 1994) are permanently active. Hence, they are continually impacting on the person's life. Further, one cannot assume that the person has ever operated for an extended period outside the influence of the schemas. One of the major contributors to this area has been Jeff Young with his schema-focused approach; he has recently re-conceptualised his original theory and has begun to move away from traditional CBT (Young, Klosko and Weishaar 2003). However, for the purposes of the present discussion, I will examine his earlier writings on Early Maladaptive Schemas (McGinn and Young 1996; Young 1994). As the name suggests, EMS are developed in early childhood. Over time they become rigid and inflexible attributes of the personality, guiding and influencing behaviour on a day-to-day basis. In his comprehensive account, Young hypothesises 18 schemas, and for each one he outlines specific cognitive, behavioural, experiential and interpersonal strategies. Each of the strategies is grouped into five domains, and each of the domains is believed to interfere with the fulfilment of a core need in childhood (e.g. the need for security, bonding, boundaries, etc.). The domains are: disconnection and rejection, impaired autonomy and performance, impaired limits, other-directedness, overvigilance and inhibition. EMS often manifest themselves in their fullest form during periods of change. At such times, the person may perceive that the adaptations required to deal with the situation are overwhelming, threatening or unacceptable, and as such the 'core organisation of the self' becomes disturbed. Furthermore, the person engages in strategies to preserve the 'sense of self', even if this self-perception is dysfunctional. The strategies employed are schema maintenance, avoidance and compensation. Maintenance strategies are processes used by the patient to reduce the likelihood of schema activation. Thus someone who sees herself as unattractive will seek out someone she considers to be unattractive to be her partner. Avoidance strategies involve the employment of a range of avoidance activities. Hence, someone who is frightened of being rejected may avoid relationships, while someone who thinks she is stupid may avoid tests/exams/pub quizzes/'intellectuals'. Schema compensation strategies involve individuals acting in ways that appear inconsistent with the schema. In truth the actions are attempts to prevent activation of the negative beliefs. So, someone who is afraid of rejection may always reject others first – because being rejected for her would be taken as evidence 'she is unlovable'. An accessible account of the model was written by Young et al. (2003), entitled 'A clients' guide to schema focussed therapy'.

v. The Worth Enhancing Belief (WEB)

The WEB (James, Kendell and Reichelt 1999) perspective is analogous to the dysfunctional belief hypothesis, but focuses on the functional role of positive self-beliefs. It is hypothesised that the WEB framework is formed via a person's temperament, upbringing and early history, and determines the beliefs and attitudes the patient utilises to maintain a sense of worth. For example, if someone obtains feedback that she is bright and/or athletic, she is likely to develop positive beliefs regarding intellectual and sporting achievements. Once operative, the framework filters information entering the information processing system and, in a psychologically healthy individual, tends to select information consistent with the WEBs.

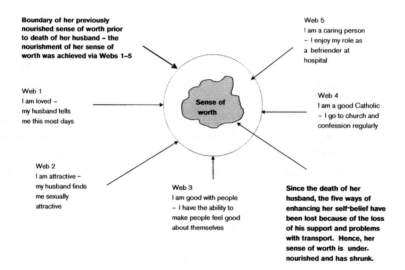

Figure 6.2: Example of the Worth Enhancing Belief model

Through the filtering process, the WEB becomes central to the way the person perceives herself. However, without continuous reinforcement (i.e. nourishing) a positive belief cannot operate effectively and therefore will not serve to enhance the individual's sense of worth. In Figure 6.2, prior to her husband's death, the patient felt loved and cared for. This belief was reinforced through a number of areas during this time. However, the positive reinforcements were reduced considerably following her husband's death. She not only lost his love, but because she cannot drive a car, she has lost the ability to maintain many of the other activities that gave her a sense of worth. For example, she cannot meet friends easily, nor get to the hospital or church. A summary outlining the nature of the WEBs is provided in Table 6.3.

Table 6.3: The nature of WEBs

- WEBs are functional structures within the information processing system through which relevant information about the self is processed. WEBs process positive information that reinforce and maintain the belief and enhance the person's sense of worth.

- A WEB must be continually fed to survive (i.e. nourishment of the belief). In an undernourished state a WEB can no longer function to enhance the person's sense of worth. In such circumstances the person becomes vulnerable to developing depression.

- The more WEBs a person has in different spheres of her life, the greater opportunities the person has of maintaining a sense of worth.

- Life events that directly threaten a key WEB represent the most serious threat to a person's self worth (e.g. an athlete experiencing a carer-threatening injury; an attractive woman growing older and 'losing' her looks).

The implications of this formulation framework are significant in terms of assessment and intervention procedures. For example, when taking someone's history the therapist should, in addition to assessing the negative beliefs, assess the patient's premorbid functional beliefs to determine how she had previously maintained her sense of worth. This will involve identifying both the positive cognitions and coping strategies she employed to maintain them.

vi. Comprehensive Conceptualisation Framework (CCF) for Older People

Laidlaw *et al.* (2003) CCF has the diathesis-stress framework at its heart, but also includes five other features regarding the patient. By obtaining this additional information (social, cultural, interpersonal, etc.), a better understanding of the patient's distress is gained. A version of the CCF is provided in Figure 6.3; in this representation the features are described within four domains to highlight the thematic nature of the additional information. Alongside the diathesis-stress feature, we have: *cohort beliefs*, which are sets of beliefs to do with 'being old' that are held by individuals who have either a shared history or grown up in the same period of time (pre-war generation, evacuees, baby boomers, etc.). The *sociological context* is concerned with the way ageing is perceived within the society and culture in which one is living; role models are often influential in people's self-perception. *Intergenerational linkages* are concerned with the relevant interpersonal networks that influence the patient's well-being. *Role investment* relates to role changes associated with life events, e.g. retirement, divorce, stroke, becoming a carer, etc. Satisfaction with the investment is dependent on the value the person attaches to what was lost or gained by the change in role. *Health status* relates to the person's physical status, both perceived and actual. As Laidlaw *et al.* (2003) state in their informative account, 'within the CCF, Beck's model is helpfully "supplemented by information and understandings from gerontology"' (p.32).

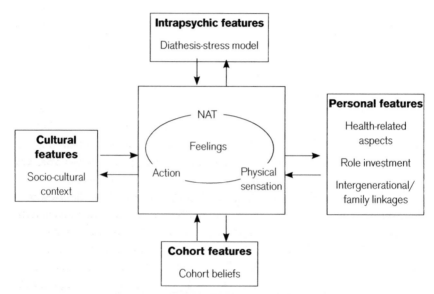

Figure 6.3: The main features of Laidlaw *et al.*'s Comprehensive Conceptualisation Framework

According to the authors, the CCF is viewed as a lifespan model, applicable for people across all the age ranges. They suggest that from time to time major life transitions disturb our homeostasis significantly (deaths, divorces, loss of job, etc.), which may lead people to seek psychotherapy. Laidlaw believes that the CCF's extra domains provide a useful aide-mémoire that assists with both the assessment and treatment processes, particularly in relation to older people. It is relevant to note that this well-crafted model is one of the few to be specifically designed for older people. It combines features of CBT and interpersonal therapy (IPT) in a helpful and well-balanced manner.

vii. Interactive Cognitive Subsystems (ICS – Teasdale and Barnard 1993)

The ICS formulation is a complex information processing perspective, which accounts for how sensory information (tactile, olfactory, taste, language-based input) is processed and how it can lead on to changes in affect. Owing to its level of complexity, it has taken some time for clinicians to employ the model in their clinical work (BABCP 2008). A simplified version of the framework was published some years ago (James 2001c). However, I acknowledge that this article failed to do justice to the detailed nature of the model, and readers should read Teasdale and Barnard's book (1993) to obtain a full account. A good account of the potential uses of the model with people with dementia is provided by Higginson (unpublished), who bases a lot of her constructs around Williams' (1994) paper.

viii. Triadic formulations

Beck's triads (i.e. models of content specificity, Beck 1976) suggest that the affective disorders (depression and anxiety – see Figure 2.1; Table 6.2) can be characterised by three themes, concerning perception of the self, the world and the future.

People suffering from depression will typically think of themselves as being unworthy, inadequate or unlovable. They will see the world as punishing or unfulfilling, and have a sense that things will not improve over time (i.e. a sense of hopelessness). A similar triad exists with respect to anxiety. For example, anxious people tend to view themselves as vulnerable, the world as threatening/chaotic, and their future as unpredictable. In addition, they do not think that they have adequate resources to cope with their surroundings, and thus are prone to the various symptoms associated with anxiety (excessive arousal and alertness, poor concentration, lack of confidence, stress). Over recent years other triadic, and dyadic, themes have been proposed to explain emotions such as anger (James 2001d), and guilt and shame (Gilbert 2003 – see Table 6.3). The triadic themes associated with anger are a 'perception of personal injustice', which is perpetrated intentionally by some external source (usually a person, organisation or deity), and there is a perceived need to react quickly either to prevent the injustice reoccurring, or in order to maintain self-esteem.

Such frameworks have proven useful in conceptualising people's experiences of distress. In practice, they help guide therapists to pay careful attention to patients' emotional states, and any inconsistencies between these states and the contents of the patients' thinking. Indeed, a therapist would almost certainly query an aggressive patient who indicates feelings of depression, and reports anxious thoughts (Charlesworth and Reichelt 2004). Although these models have their empirical basis in traditional CBT, they are also helpful when working with people who have communication or intellectual difficulties. For example, the triads have been helpful in working with people with severe dementia, who are often unable to discuss their thoughts and feelings in a structured way. Thus one of the few ways of empathising with their experiences is through monitoring of their emotional responses. Thus if one saw someone with dementia displaying signs of *anxiety*, one would ask oneself: What is happening in this situation to make her think she's vulnerable? How can we reduce the amount of chaos in her environment? What could we do to make his situation more containing and more predictable? Prompted by such questions, one may make decisions about how to: *orientate* the patient better (e.g. use of signage); provide more structure and greater predictability in her environment.

ix. Kitwood's model for dementia

Kitwood's (1997) simple linear and descriptive formulation uses five features to help therapists understand a patient's experience of dementia. The assessment requires the therapist to collect details about the patient's: premorbid personality + history + health status + intellectual impairment + environment. Although not a cognitive model, it implies that cognitions from the person's history are a common cause of anxiety and depression. For example, knowing the person had children can help us understand why she frequently asks to leave the ward at 4pm when she sees school children pass the window of her care home.

x. Conceptualisation of dementia (CoD) model (James in press)

This is essentially an ABC model (Events, Reactions, Consequences) moderated by the person with dementia's view of herself in relation to time and place. The 'perception of self' aspect is determined by the individual's premorbid personality, history and cognitive status. Indeed, the person's prior social status, personality type, previous job, life-roles, religious and sexual preferences, physical status, fears, responses to illness etc. will all influence the way she views herself during the dementing process.

In the early stages of the illness, when the level of insight remains high, the person will be aware she is having memory and processing difficulties and may take this into account in her reactions to events. For example, because she is unaware she keeps forgetting whether she's taken her tablets, she is less inclined to argue with her husband when told she's forgotten her medication. In those situations that result in negative consequences, this may lead to an undermining of confidence, a sense of shame and low mood.

As the person begins to lose insight, and her sense of reality becomes less similar to others, interactions with her environment may become more problematic. This may evoke a range of negative emotions and coping strategies. Some of these strategies (reassurance seeking, arguing one's case, avoidance, etc.) may be viewed as challenging. The environment's response (i.e. the Consequences) to the reactions can evoke further emotional and behavioural reactions, leading to 'challenging behaviours' (see Figure 6.4). For example, a resident not believing her keyworker when told that she can't leave the care home to collect the children, because the 'kids' are adults, could respond with aggression if orientated to the facts in a non-empathic manner that failed to take account of her incorrect perception of reality. Of note, her response may be more positive if spoken to in a way that accommodated her own sense of reality (e.g. via the use of validation techniques; Feil and de Klerk-Rubin 2002). The secondary consequence ($2°$) of such occurrences will have a cumulative impact on the person's self-esteem. For example, if the response of the environment is routinely punitive or hostile, the person may develop a sense of mistrust, learned helplessness or unworthiness.

While this model is helpful in understanding negative feedback loops, it is also useful as a means of promoting well-being. Indeed, it highlights the need to understand the person's level of insight and current perception of self. It also calls upon therapists to interact with people with dementia in ways that promote a positive self-perspective. This model is currently being used to conceptualise the mechanism of change, underpinning many of the treatments used to treat people with dementia (validation, reality orientation, cognitive stimulation, music therapy, doll therapy, etc.) – see James (in press).

xi. Cohen-Mansfield formulation of challenging behaviour (Cohen-Mansfield 2000b)

This 'needs-based' model highlights the fact that challenging behaviours (CBs) are usually *not* unpredictable random actions, rather they are rational activities with a high degree of predictability. Indeed, frequently CBs are manifestations of patients' attempts to cope in situations they are

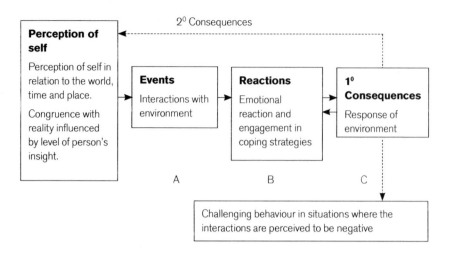

Figure 6.4: Conceptualisation of dementia (CoD) model

misperceiving or are confused by. Cohen-Mansfield's (2000a) needs-led frameworks involve obtaining two types of information: (i) background features (history, premorbid personality, physical health status) and (ii) a comprehensive description of the CB episode. The latter are the verbal and non-verbal signs displayed by the person during the challenging episode (Figure 6.5). By putting these two types of information together, one is in a stronger position to accurately identify the person's coping strategy or the need driving the coping response – e.g. to be free from pain, respond to an imagined attacker, defend oneself from perceived molestation. Within Cohen-Mansfield's (2000b) great body of work, she has also produced a 'decision-tree framework' devised to help therapists select appropriate interventions based on patients' challenging presentations (Treatment Routes for Exploring Agitation (TREA) model).

xii. Newcastle Approach for Challenging Behaviour (James 1999; James and Stephenson 2007)

This formulation incorporates features of Kitwood's and Cohen-Mansfield's work, and includes aspects of the triadic formulations. Figure 10.1 presents the framework, but this is merely one of the tools used in the approach; the figure summarises the information gained from the patient, family and staff. The methodology is designed to be used with patients across the range of cognitive impairment, from mild to severe. In the latter case, most of the

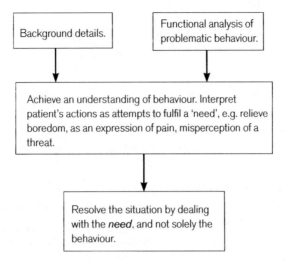

Figure 6.5: Representation of Cohen-Mansfield's model for understanding challenging behaviours

assessments and interventions are carried out with the carers and staff. It is used routinely in a number of Challenging Behaviour Services in the UK, and is embedded with a 14-week treatment protocol. It is designed to be accessible for care staff, encouraging them to be stakeholders in the treatment process and to generate behavioural interventions for their residents. The framework is explained in detail in Chapter 10, in the case of Donald.

The next section examines how therapists choose the most appropriate formulation for their patients.

6.5: CHOICE OF FORMULATION

When choosing an appropriate formulation, a number of features need to be borne in mind. The features, and their relationship to each other, are represented diagramatically in Figure 6.6. At the first level the type of formulation selected will be influenced by the *setting* in which the problem is being exhibited. For example, if someone is displaying a psychiatric illness while in an acute hospital ward, then a 30-week schema-focused approach would not be deemed appropriate.

At level two, *stakeholders*, one is called to examine who is involved in the patient's treatment and what each of these stakeholders brings with them to the therapy. In the case of therapists, they need to consider their knowledge, experience and skills with respect to the patient's presentation.

Level 1: Setting

- Family home – family carers involved
- Hospital ward – shorter stay, nurses, medical staff
- Hospice – palliative care setting
- Care home – home for life, private care, care staff (mostly unqualified)

Level 2: Stakeholders

(i) Therapist

- Training; skills; experience; confidence; risk; practice; support; supervision

(ii) Patient

- Physical issues – patient's abilities to engage in behavioural tasks and exercises
- Cognitive abilities – patient's abilities to retain information from one session to the next, and ability to give an adequate history of self
- Motivation – patient's ability to self-motivation and/or use support from others
- Concurrent treatment – medication, past approaches
- Personality

(iii) Others involved in care

- Medical staff; family; friends; advocates; social services; care home staff

Level 3: Nature of disorder

- Diagnosis; co-morbid conditions; mental and physical health of patients
- Evidence base of model with respect to the disorder

Level 4: Teamwork – therapeutic engagement

- Patient and therapist abilities to: form a working relationship, establish joint goals, take on roles, decentre, work collaboratively

Level 5: Patient manipulation of therapeutic materials (microskills)

- Patient abilities to: reflect, problem-solve, conceptualise within the session, work with abstract concepts

Figure 6.6: Levels supporting the choice of formulation

If they are working outside their zone of competence, they will need to access extra support and supervision. In relation to the patient, the choice of which formulation approach to use can be extensive if she is physically and mentally fit, motivated, has a supportive interpersonal network and has a non-chronic condition. Other stakeholders, such as family and friends, can also influence the type of formulation employed. Evidently, if the patient is interpersonally close to her carers then a more systemic approach may be deemed appropriate.

At the third level, *nature of disorder*, one sees the type of disorder and the setting. In relation to CBT, there is an evidence base regarding which formulation framework is best suited to a specific disorder. Thus, all of the diagnostic presentations (depression, chronic depression, PTSD, OCD, etc.) have their preferred conceptual model (see Appendix I).

At the next level, *therapeutic engagement*, the degree to which the patient and therapist are able to work together is examined. A good working alliance is necessary for undertaking comprehensive, long-term formulation-led approaches. Such approaches require patients to be comfortable about divulging the necessary information to construct their formulations. In some circumstances, older patients may struggle to see the relevance of the questions, and can get upset by their perceived implications (James *et al.* 1999). For example, consider a 76-year-old depressed man who did not see the relevance of discussing his early childhood. Indeed, from his perspective he believed his early physically abusive upbringing had no bearing on his current mood, which he saw as being due to a decline in his health. Furthermore, he wanted to make it very clear that he felt his brutal upbringing made him a stronger person, better able to cope with armed-service in Korea, death of his only son, etc.

At the final level, *patient manipulation of therapeutic materials*, we are concerned about the ability of the patient to manage and manipulate therapeutic materials. This requires the patient to have the ability to reflect, conceptualise, re-conceptualise, demonstrate insight, etc. If the patient is unable to carry out these tasks, a simpler and more concrete approach will be required (e.g. mini-formulations), and may need the assistance of others (e.g. carers, Teri and Gallagher-Thompson 1991).

6.6: CAUTIONS REGARDING USE OF FORMULATIONS

This chapter has discussed formulations under the general assumption that they are powerful and positive therapeutic tools. However, as discussed by a number of authors (James 2001b; Leeming, Boyle and Macdonald 2009), they can often be problematic. In Leeming *et al.*'s qualitative study, which included patients from two older adult community teams, it was noted that some patients felt pressurised by their conceptualisations. For example, if the formulation suggested that a person's disorder was associated with an abusive upbringing, then it implied blame should be attributed to a key person(s) in her life. Further, the use of the formulation resulted in some patients perceiving themselves to be inherently weak, because *why should they have become depressed when their siblings did not! – after all they had all been brought up in the same household.* Thus, attempting to provide an explanatory model for disorders is likely to have consequences, leading to reinterpretations and the development of different and not necessarily more functional autobiographical narratives. Leeming's conclusions were that there is a need to be more sophisticated about our use of formulations. In particular, we need to be clearer about their functions and consequences (Harper and Moss 2003).

6.7: CONCLUSION

This chapter has provided a brief overview of using formulations with older people. Up until relatively recently the literature on formulation in CBT was relatively sparse, but this has changed greatly in the last ten years. It is particularly pleasing to see that there are now specific models being developed for older people. It is important to remember that these models have yet to be tested in empirical studies, and, although they appear face-valid and intuitively correct, the jury is still out with respect to their value. The chapter has been wide-ranging but has attempted to provide practical advice mixed with theory and some of the recent exciting developments in the area.

Chapter 7

Change Techniques

7.1: INTRODUCTION

When discussing change techniques many texts stress the importance of patients understanding the rationale behind the interventions. This is certainly very important, but from my experience of teaching CBT, I think there is a step prior to this concerning therapists' own understanding of their therapy. For example, if one asks a group of therapists to write down the 'mechanisms of change' for CBT, many of them get lost in an incoherent mass of wordage. Their responses can become even more convoluted if one asks therapists: 'Imagine I am a patient with mild cognitive impairment, and I ask you to explain how CBT works in *really* simple terms.' In truth, like any good professional, a therapist should have a very clear notion of how their therapy works, and should be able to explain it in a relatively simple manner. This chapter will present relevant details relating to mechanisms of change. It will also provide an example of a specific change technique (i.e. the continuum), demonstrating the amount of planning and detail required to support its use.

This chapter will illustrate the following:

- Assessment and formulation processes are the servants of the change strategies. On occasions therapists can become too focused on the former, striving for the ultimate conceptual model, and paying insufficient attention to the interventions.

- Having a good understanding of the 'mechanisms of change' is crucial to delivering effective treatment.

- Modifying core beliefs is a complex process, involving improving specificity and flexibility of key cognitions.

- Devising effective interventions requires careful planning and execution – this is illustrated in a discussion of the continuum technique.

7.2: NATURE OF CHANGE

As outlined in previous chapters, achieving effective change is the goal of therapy. Thus, the assessment, formulation, interpersonal work, etc., all function to bring about this goal. It would be wonderful if change simply occurred through psycho-education or by patients gaining new insights, but such things happen infrequently. As such, therapists are called upon to identify situations that activate negative patterns of thinking and behaving, and subsequently disrupt these patterns via behavioural and cognitive techniques. As outlined in Chapter 4, some of these patterns will have become so familiar for the patients that the negative cycles of thinking and behaving will be outside of conscious awareness and may start to take the form of automatic scripts. These scripts will be characterised by the features of the CBT cycle, but will also contain neural changes, hormonal surges etc. as outlined previously (Chapter 4). A number of theoretical papers on this topic have been written by myself and colleagues at Newcastle University (James 2008b; James, Reichelt, Carlsson and McAnaney 2008). The scripts will be triggered by specific events or thoughts, and the more frequently they are triggered the lower their threshold of activation. Figure 7.1 demonstrates how the activation generalises, resulting in (i) the spiral effect, and (ii) situational generalisation.

In the spiral scenario, the first negative cycle triggers the next, and next, and so on. This phenomenon is common in both depression and anxiety, and has been discussed in the past by Thompson *et al.* (1996) and Gallagher-Thompson and Thompson (2009). In the 'situational generalisation' phenomenon, with repeated activation, a spreading effect occurs as situations that bear some resemblance to the original triggering situation activate the negative script. This effect is commonly seen in the anxiety disorders, where a fear of spiders can lead to a fear of insects, leading to a concern about sitting on grass, etc.

CBT deals with these cycles of activation patterns by making them conscious and providing a framework to describe their main features (i.e. the 'hot-cross bun'), and then attempts to disrupt the links between the features. Some techniques used to do this are outlined below.

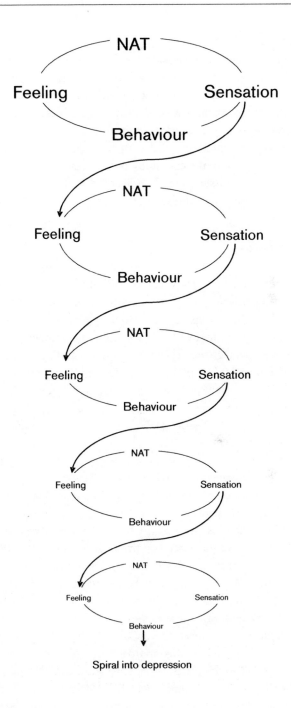

Spiral into depression

Figure 7.1: Spiral effect

7.3: CHANGE STRATEGIES

This section is presented in three parts; the first examines the use of questions, which can be considered to be the 'tools of our trade'. Despite them being one of the main forms of communication with our patients, a recent survey has shown that therapists have a poor knowledge of questioning techniques (James and Morse 2007). The second part of this section provides examples of change strategies commonly used with older people. A number of these strategies are illustrated in the case study on depression, Chapter 8. The final part examines process issues, and is concerned with how to structure and deliver the techniques to maximise their benefit.

7.3.i: Questioning skills

Within CBT, questions are used to explore an issue from different angles, create dissonance, facilitate re-evaluation of beliefs, while at the same time building more adaptive thinking styles. Skilfully phrased questions can help to highlight either links or discrepancies in the patient's thinking (Overholser 1993) and lead to new discoveries. Questioning techniques can also greatly assist patients to gain greater clarity and understanding of their thinking processes. The questioning process is a dynamic one, requiring different types and sequences of questions at various stages of therapy. Many questions may be fruitless and self-defeating. As part of developing competence in our questioning abilities, Overholser (1993) argued that an understanding of question formats is essential.

Two common questioning techniques utilised within CBT are Socratic questioning and 'downward arrowing'. *Socratic questions* may be seen as an umbrella term for a method in which questions are used to clarify meaning, elicit emotion and consequences, as well as to gradually unfold insight, or explore alternative actions (see 9.9ix, Chapter 9) (Carey and Mullan 2004; Padesky 1993). *Downward arrowing (or vertical arrow restructuring)* (Burns 1980; Wells 1997; also see section 5.3, Chapter 5) is a questioning technique used in the exploration of underlying beliefs and meanings. Here the meaning of an automatic thought is repeatedly questioned in order to determine the 'bottom line'. Characteristic questions of this process include: 'If that were to happen, what would it mean to you?' or 'If that were true, what would be so bad about that?' Thus, this approach questions the meaning of the catastrophe inherent in the patient's negative automatic thought.

A further form of questioning which is less commonly discussed in the CBT literature is the scaffolding-platforming technique. Scaffolding is defined as the process by which a therapist provides temporary support to the patient in order to help her learn something new based on the foundations of what she already knows (Graves and Braaten 1996; James, Milne and Morse 2008). There are two main aspects of the scaffolding process, namely questions and 'platforms'. One of the chief functions of questions is to drive learning forward, allowing the therapist to access new information, reflect on past experience, etc. Sometimes the questions may be simple and direct and at other times they are provided within a context. The context is often made up of scaffolding statements which function either to help focus the patient with respect to a particular issue or to facilitate ease of response. Platforms are defined as the supportive information (summaries, reminders, or statements) used to set up a question or to give it an appropriate context. Thus the platforms serve to guide the patient's responses. To illustrate, take the following two 'agenda-setting' questions, which are essentially asking the same thing. The second sequence has a platform, the former does not:

1. 'What would you like to discuss in today's therapy session?'

2. 'I want you to take a minute to think of something that would be helpful to discuss today, something that will help me to really understand what it's been like for you over the last week with respect to your depression. It's important to take a little time over this, because I don't want you leaving today's session thinking that we've missed something important. Remember, this is your hour, let's use it to deal with any difficulties or things that have gone well (minute of silence).'

Although the therapist is essentially asking the patient to do the same thing in both examples, the second question provides a rich, yet focused, context (i.e. it has been scaffolded); thus, it increases the likelihood that the patient will set an appropriate agenda. Indeed, the second example is a sophisticated sequence, reminding the patient of the function of the session, motivating her to take responsibility regarding its success, cueing her to chose concrete items from the recent past, and providing adequate space to permit reflection.

Table 7.1 summarises some of the other forms of questions that have been highlighted in the CBT literature. These follow a logical route from gathering information and clarifying to reaching thought/assumption level, moving on to creating dissonance, shifting the person's thinking and generalising from this. While it is helpful to examine question types, it is relevant to note that, as is highlighted by McGee, Del Vento and Bavelas (2005), examining single questions in isolation is overly simplistic. In truth it is the manner in which questions are combined and sequenced that determines their impact (James, Morse and Howard 2010).

Table 7.1: Examples of types of questions used in CBT

Question type		Example(s)
Information gathering/ general questions	Questions intended to open up a particular area of exploration (Wells 1997).	'When was the last time you felt anxious?' 'What was the first thing you noticed?'
Direct questions	Asking concrete and specific questions (Blackburn and Davidson 1995).	'How did you deal with that?' 'What did you find helpful/ unhelpful?'
Probe questions	These are used to follow up on answers of general questions with the aim of eliciting more detailed information and checking that the initial response was correct (Wells 1997).	'What is the worst that could have happened if you'd felt more anxious?'
Echo-probing	Reiterates part of what was said, using exact words and by repeating them with inflexion in the form of a question. Enables elaboration and active listening.	'Just so I am clear, you said "This was the *worst* moment in your life"?'
Queries	Used to clear up misunderstandings and demonstrate active listening.	'Can you tell me what you mean by...?'
Clarifications	To make something clear or easier to understand by giving more detail or a simpler explanation.	'In what way does your grandson bother you?'
Appraisals	To judge patient's qualities, successes and/or needs.	Are you satisfied with the way things have turned out?' 'What can you learn from this experience?'
Leading questions	'Contains an implied assumption, often serving as a spotlight to focus the patient's attention onto a specific area' (Overholser 1993). Phrasing of the question should not push patients towards one response over another.	'Do you think talking about this with your husband would help the two of you learn to deal with this problem, or would talking just stir up more arguments?'

Suggesting the opposite	A technique that is useful to help stimulate a client's NATs awareness is to suggest something that is the opposite of what their response or thinking might be. This stimulates an 'oh no, not like that at all...' response.	'Was it your actual intention to upset your grand-daughter and make her cry?'
Focusing and redirecting	Overtly directing the topic of conversation.	'Why don't we talk about what's happening at lunch club?' 'Could we talk a little bit about something you mentioned earlier, your reactions to this feeling?'
Question stem	Beliefs can be elicited by providing the first half of the sentence.	'If you don't complete the housework then...?' 'If you trust someone then...?'
Re-contextualising	Enables negative memories to be placed in their contexts of time and place. The contextual information provides patients with cues to aid them to recall facts about past events which can aid in the development of alternative perspectives (James and Barton 2004). This group of questions may be useful when developing responsibility (pie) charts (Westbrook *et al.* 2007).	'You feel guilty for leaving your husband after he was convicted for the assault. So did you just leave on a whim, or were there events or circumstances that caused you to leave him? Let's list some of these reasons.'

7.3.ii: Interventions used in trials with older people

Over the years a number of treatment manuals have been produced that have been empirically tested in trials (Kneebone 2006). For example, Thompson *et al.*'s (2000) manual was used in Laidlaw *et al.*'s (2008) successful application of CBT for late life depression. Also, Mohlman *et al.* (2003) used their enhanced CBT manual in a study with older people with GAD (Mohlman and Gorman 2005). A CBT group approach was manualised by Matthews and Wilkinson (unpublished) and used successfully to reduce the recurrence of depression in Wilkinson *et al.*'s study (2009). One of the most up-to-date books to read in this area is Gallagher-Thompson and Thompson's (2009) publication on empirical practice; there is also a companion text written for patients (Thompson *et al.* 2009). The latter series of books uses evidence-based material from the studies they have undertaken over the last 30 years. The following section borrows from this material, describing some of the typical interventions employed. It is relevant to note that interventions for changing core beliefs are not included here. Owing to their greater level of complexity, such interventions are addressed separately in section 7.5.

DISTRACTION METHODS

Wenzlaff and Bates (2000) inform us that distraction techniques are effective interventions, particularly if patients are encouraged to use positive stimuli that are unrelated to the unwanted thought. Thus thinking about something positive is better than trying not to think about something negative. The principle of the method is that one cannot divide one's attention easily between two competing stimuli, and thus if one is focusing on a pleasant or neutral stimulus, then the energy invested in one's distress will be less. Common distraction techniques include: physical exercise; refocusing on one's external environment rather than one's internal world; use of mental exercises, such as simple counting, mental imagery, focusing on music and other sensory modalities.

The technique of mindfulness (Segal, Williams and Teasdale 2002) shares some features with the distraction techniques. In this methodology the patient is taught to disengage from the distressing thoughts by developing self-focusing skills. Through extensive in-session and out-of-session practice, the patient learns to pay attention to the 'present moment in a non-judgemental manner' (Smith 2004) and not to process distressing thoughts even if she is aware of their presence. Hence, this method starves the NATs of cognitive and emotional energy. This technique has been used in a number of trials with older people, particularly in primary care settings (Smith, Graham and Senthinathan 2007).

IDENTIFYING COGNITIONS AND BEHAVIOURS

This group of strategies are concerned with identifying the thoughts, images, behaviours and scripts, etc. associated with the patient's distress. By making the components of the distress conscious, the patient and therapist are able to work with them to create change. The common techniques for identifying cognitions and behaviours include: diary keeping, use of clinical questionnaires, identifying cognitive biases. Key thoughts can also be identified by the therapist by asking the patient about her thinking following any sudden mood shift (e.g. becoming tearful, angry, etc.). Imagery work can also be used to elicit thoughts and behaviours, by getting the patient to imagine herself in situations that she typically finds difficult.

The imagery work can be used to explore the difficulties, and prepare the patient to tackle the obstacles and problematic thoughts and feelings in the real world.

APPRAISING THE COGNITIONS AND BEHAVIOURS

These techniques are designed to help the patient to start to assess the relative helpfulness of the CBT patterns and scripts. Many of them also assist in providing the patient with a rationale for why they have been affected by this particular type of disorder. This level of understanding helps them to normalise their distress, and gives them more information about the disorder they are trying to tackle. Techniques in this section include: devising conceptual models; understanding the origins of a cognition; weighing up the pros and cons; completing mastery and pleasure charts and examining the data from the charts; identifying distress-free places and the characteristics associated with these occasions. Gallagher-Thompson and Thompson (2009) favour using the Californian Older People's Pleasant Event Schedule (COPPES) – see Chapter 5, section 5.2. Two further methodologies, time grids and relationship charts, are described in the case example in the next chapter.

DEVELOPING NEW PERSPECTIVES

In traditional CBT one is frequently attempting to make the patient's thoughts more rational by examining the facts of a situation against biased interpretations of it. However, when working with older people there is sometimes a degree of rationality in the person's negative thinking (e.g. if a person is fearful about having a stroke, and has a heart condition, her concern is not totally unwarranted). Hence, when developing new perspectives it is often better distinguishing between helpful and unhelpful thoughts, rather than rational and irrational ones. The helpful/unhelpful distinction also assists in determining which thoughts need to be re-evaluated. For example the NATs illustrated in Table 7.2 do not appear to be helpful in any way, and clearly need attending to.

Table 7.2: Helpful and unhelpful features of NATs

	Negative automatic thought	What is helpful about this thought?	In what way is this thought unhelpful?
1.	I can't do anything correctly.	It stops me trying to do things beyond my abilities.	I feel paralysed, and my life is so boring because I don't do anything. And this makes me feel worse!
2.	No-one wants to spend time with me.	It tells me that I've only got myself to rely on.	I'm so very lonely.

When working in the older people's speciality, therapists are frequently working with carers who are experiencing very negative situations (e.g. in situations where further physical and intellectual decline of a partner is a certainty). Despite such a negative prognosis, the clinical goals still involve disentangling the facts from the unhelpful perceptions. For example, let us consider the situation of a carer called Helen. She is the wife of Joe who suffers from dementia. In this problematic scenario, Joe was insisting on doing the dishes, but did them very badly and this irritated his wife. However, he would get aggressive if she tried to stop him from doing them. Her thoughts were: *'He's always been stubborn; he can see he's making a mess. He's trying wear me down; I'm not going to let him win.'* As one can imagine, such thoughts resulted in a lot of anger and distress, and arguments! A key feature of treating Helen was first to remove the emotional tone of the situation, because the high arousal was blocking her problem-solving skills. By helping her to see this was not a battle, she was slowly able to stand back and review the situation. Also, by asking the question 'What might he be getting from washing up?' she was able to accept that his actions were probably his way of fighting the illness, and perhaps him trying to demonstrate his independence and relieve his fear of being a 'burden'. With this reframe, Helen was calmer and more accepting. Further, the new perspective permitted her to begin to problem-solve her way round the situation better. Following further reflection, she let him wash up and make a mess, but encouraged him to wash and stack only certain items of crockery. After he had finished and had sat down, she would return to complete the job to her satisfaction. At the end of treatment she made the following remarks: *'What he's doing continues to wind me up, but it is easier to think that he is getting something from doing it. And I think he's probably trying to be helpful…BUT I just wish he do something less messy!'* – for the full account of the case study see James, Powell and Reichelt (2001). This example demonstrates two things about developing new perspectives with carers: (i) in order to foster improved problem-solving skills, the therapist needs to reduce the emotional tone within the situation, and (ii) some scenarios are always going to be problematic. Helping the carer to disentangle the facts from the unhelpful perceptions is a way of reducing the degree of distress produced in the scenario (Fossey and James 2007).

EXPERIENTIAL AND EXPOSURE EXERCISES

Gallagher-Thompson and Thompson (2009) stress the importance of working multi-modally with patients. Thus, when trying to get someone to learn a new skill, the therapist needs to: 'write it down, repeat it, have the patient repeat it, role-play it, rehearse it' and ideally get the patient to carry it out as a homework assignment. Indeed, in developing new skills, a great deal of emphasis is attached to consolidating declarative learning via experimental and behavioural exercises. Common behavioural strategies include: role-play, graded task assignments, systematic desensitisation tasks, social skills training, and relaxation exercises. Another strategy proposed for older people is the 'coping card' method (Thompson *et al.* 2009). It is suggested that the therapist should provide his patients with laminated cards containing helpful expressions, which may be used when the patient is feeling distressed. The key to the success of such cards appears to be related to the valency of the message. It may take some trial and error with respect to the use of the card before the most effective statements are being used (see the case example in the next chapter).

BIBLIOTHERAPY

This strategy involves the use of self-help books that aim to guide and encourage people to make changes, resulting in improved self-management rather than merely providing information. This method fits well with CBT as the onus is on the patient taking an active part in the therapy, and undertaking written work and assignments between sessions. The approach has been widely used with older people, because it can be readily used with frail patients who are unable to attend regular clinic appointments. There have been four good controlled trials of its use with older people (Floyd *et al.* 2004; Landreville and Bissonette 1997; Scogin *et al.* 1987, 1989), making the elderly one of the best researched groups in this area. Anderson *et al.*'s (2004) systematic review of the use of bibliotherapy provides a helpful guide regarding this emerging technology. It also provides guidance on the various texts and their evidence base. The three main books used in the trials are: *Managing Anxiety and Depression* (Holsworth and Paxton 1999), *Feeling Good* (Burns 1980) and *Control your Depression* (Lewinsohn, Munoz, and Youngren 1992). Anderson and colleagues also recommend two other books, but these have not been tested empirically as yet: *A Clinicians Guide to Mind Over Mood* (Greenberger and Padesky 1995) and *Overcoming Depression: A Five Areas Approach* (Williams 2001).

In addition to using published texts, Thompson *et al.* and Dick (1996) suggest that patients should keep their own therapeutic notebooks to support them in their therapy. The books seem to be particularly helpful when the patient has memory problems, or requires additional time to reflect on key issues. Further, when the concepts or ideas are no longer needed, the pages associated with this redundant material can be torn out, keeping the contents of the notebook lean and specific.

REFORMULATING

The previous chapter discussed the use of formulations in depth, including issues about their forms and functions. Now, as one moves towards the final stages of therapy (sessions 8–12), it is hoped that new perspectives will have emerged and old ones altered. Hence, many of the details in the original formulation will have changed (e.g. negative beliefs weakened, cycles disrupted, etc.), thus requiring it to be revised and updated. It is my preference to record the revised formulation as a simple 10–20 line narrative (see next chapter for an example of this). Presented in this form, the reformulated conceptualisation of the patient can be carried around in her purse/wallet in a readable and accessible form.

7.4: PROCESS ISSUES ASSOCIATED WITH CHANGE TECHNIQUES

In Chapter 9 of this text, CBT process issues are discussed in detail in relation to therapeutic competence. A competent therapist is expected to pace the session appropriately, demonstrate interpersonal effectiveness and collaboration, provide and elicit feedback. Performing therapy with such skills prevents the CBT techniques simply becoming isolated strategies with little chance of success.

Mohlman *et al.* (2003) have recently produced an 'enhanced CBT protocol' for treating anxiety in older people. This approach involved in-session assignments of weekly reading, graphing exercises of mood ratings, cognitive restructuring, progressive muscle relaxation, strategies for tolerating negative affect, worry exposure and behavioural exercises. They emphasised the need to use a slow pace, frequent repetition and paraphrasing to ensure the patients had a clear understanding of each task and concept. Homework tasks were also carefully planned and reviewed throughout the course of the 13 weeks of therapy.

Coon *et al.*'s (2007) case study on adapting homework assignments also provided good examples of process issues, and because their work was adapted for someone with cognitive impairment, the CBT was made clear, concrete and person-centred. For me, this paper provides a good example of KISS (Keep It Simple and Slow), and therefore how therapy should be conducted in most situations. Specifically, this paper showed how patients' preferences could be incorporated into their therapy. For example, it demonstrated how the patient (Mrs W) designed her own 'Thoughts record form'; she had earlier declined to use both the traditional five and three column versions (Coon and Gallagher-Thompson 2002). Her personalised form had three columns: 'Unhelpful thoughts/More helpful thoughts/New feelings'. Mrs W was also encouraged to keep a therapy notebook throughout the CBT. It functioned as a memory aid, a socialisation tool, recorder of key concepts, a diary, etc. The case study also showed the importance of utilising social supports and cultural features (religion) within the treatment process. Coon's comments were as follows:

> Mrs W's sociocultural context – including the support of her husband, family, best friend, church, family and neighbor – played substantive roles in supporting treatment progress and completion of her home practice activities. The case described here highlights yet again the important roles that informal caregivers play in our society. Clearly, additional research is needed to investigate the role of both cognitive and behavioural interventions. (Coon *et al.* 2007 p.259)

A further process strategy adopted by many therapists in the speciality is the use of telephone calls to patients in-between therapy sessions (Floyd *et al.* 2006; Gallagher-Thompson and Thompson 2009). These are brief 'check-in' calls that serve to motivate the patient, and allow the therapist to tweak the homework assignment if required.

The next section of this chapter will examine change techniques for core beliefs. Due to the fact that many of the studies supporting CBT with older people have used the diathesis-stress (d-s) model, the change techniques outlined below are described within this framework. The d-s model suggests that dysfunctional beliefs developed early in life act as vulnerability features (i.e. an Achilles heel) that can lead to difficulties later in adulthood (see Chapter 6). According to Westbrook *et al.* (2007), when working with core beliefs, a CBT therapist is operating at the most complex level of change.

7.5: MODIFYING CORE BELIEFS

This section describes some of the assumptions one is making both implicitly and explicitly when using the d-s model, followed by the theory of change underpinning the model.

7.5.i: Assumptions of working with d-s frameworks

When developing treatment programmes based on the diathesis-stress framework, a number of assumptions are made regarding the nature of the patient's cognitive difficulties. One of the key features is the notion that the person's dysfunctional core beliefs are the engine room of the negative thoughts and affect.

In relation to the core beliefs, it is assumed that they are inaccurate characterisations of the patient. It is also believed that when the person is not experiencing the affective disorder, she is capable of keeping 'in-check' the negative thoughts relating to the theme of the core belief. Furthermore, it is assumed that in the past, when not experiencing the affective disorder, the patient will also have behaved in ways that were inconsistent with the core beliefs (e.g. someone with a core belief 'I am inadequate' would have previously compared themselves favourably with others in some situations). An awareness of such inconsistencies is important, as these examples can be used as dis-confirmatory evidence later in treatment. It is also assumed that the patient's normal coping strategies have only temporarily become overwhelmed since the activation of the core belief, and that equilibrium can be restored once she feels more contained. To this end, it is important to help the patient understand why she has been affected so greatly by recent events; this is done by giving the patient a rationale via the formulation. In addition, we assume that once she is feeling more contained within the therapeutic relationship, she will be able to re-engage her coping strategies. It is relevant to note that the above assumptions cannot be made in the case of Axis II (personality disorder) presentations, as it may be case that the core beliefs of this group of patients have been continually active throughout their lives (James 2008c).

Working with core beliefs is often problematic because, when active, they are accompanied by a debilitating level of emotion, preventing the patient rationally disputing the dysfunctional thinking. Hence, it is the task of the therapist to first slow down the activation process for the patient in order to introduce rational evaluation of the situation. As described in Chapter 2, the provision of a diagnosis, framework, etc. are all key steps in reducing the pace of the thoughts and give structure to the experience. Once the thoughts have been brought into conscious awareness, they can be worked upon via a number of techniques as described above.

As outlined above, it is important to provide the patient with a rationale regarding the development and maintenance strategies underpinning her core belief. This is to enable the therapist to employ the 'straw man' technique later on (see Table 7.3). This technique involves the building of a conceptual story regarding the formation of the core belief, including the reasons for its recent activation, followed by the systematic investigation of its evidence base (e.g. establishing the patient has a belief 'I am stupid', then systematically examining the evidence to support this). Obviously this technique exploits the assumption that the core belief is an inaccurate characterisation of the individual, and contrary evidence is available to dispute the veracity of the core beliefs.

Table 7.3: Straw man technique
_____

A method for demonstrating the lack of sustainability of the patient's negative self-perspective

1. *Assessment phase*: Gaining information about the patient's view of herself. The view is likely to be negative, full of inconsistencies and contain negative biases. The above perspective is developed into a conceptual story and starts to be constructed within a formulation.

   At this stage, much of the negative information is not challenged, as the therapist is attempting to get an in-depth assessment of how the patient sees herself.

2. *Formulation*: The patient's conceptual story is summarised and consolidated within a formulation. Embedded in the formulation is the 'battle-plan', containing the many inconsistencies and biases that the therapist has been noting during the assessment phase. These issues can be viewed as weaknesses in the patient's case supporting her negative self-view. This weakness will be exploited in the intervention phase.

3. *Intervention phase*: In the intervention phase, the therapist exploits the weaknesses in the patient's self-perceptions, using questioning techniques and behavioural experiments to do so. For example, 'From our discussions you say that you have *always* thought of yourself as inferior. Yet, you have also told me about many successes throughout your life – for example, you passed your 11+ examination, won an apprenticeship, got top marks in your typing exam, etc...and last year appeared in the local paper as "neighbour of the year". Now the *moment* you heard the news of *each* of these successes, did you think of yourself as *inferior*?'

4. *Reformulation*: The last phase of this process is to re-conceptualise the patient's story into a new formulation; one containing less biases and which accounts for her situation in a more balanced manner.
_____

The exact nature of the treatment strategies employed will depend on the therapist's view of how change occurs (i.e. the therapist's change mechanism), which is discussed in the following section.

7.5.ii: CBT change mechanisms

The three most common perspectives, which are not mutually exclusive, are core belief eradication, core belief modification, and coping strategy enhancement (Barber and DeRubeis 1989; Williams 1992). The core belief eradication perspective suggests that core beliefs can be changed completely, such that the patient will no longer hold the dysfunctional core belief. The modification view considers that core beliefs can never be eradicated, but may only be weakened. Thus, it is believed that the individual will continue to be sensitive to issues relating to the core beliefs. Yet, following successful treatment, the core beliefs will not be triggered as frequently, and the NATs associated with them will be re-evaluated in a more helpful manner. The third approach does not tackle the core beliefs, but attempts to improve the patient's ability to cope with their products (i.e. the NATs and the emotions) (see section 2.3, Chapter 2).

It is my view that for older people, and many adults, it is very difficult to eradicate core beliefs that have been formed in childhood as they have been in place for a long time, and thus core belief modification and coping enhancement approaches are preferred. In many of my cases, the aim of the therapy has been to weaken the effects of patients' core beliefs, initially by refining them (i.e. *core belief refinement*) and then by attempting to make them less rigid (i.e. *increasing flexibility*). Reducing rigidity can be achieved by looking for past evidence of episodes when patients have contradicted their beliefs about being 'stupid', worthless, evil etc. (see Table 7.3). As stated in this table, these techniques are normally employed once the initial formulation has been constructed.

BELIEF REFINEMENT

Core belief refinement is often one of the first cognitive interventions undertaken. It involves obtaining greater specification with respect to the problematic beliefs. Many unconditional core beliefs are expressed in rather woolly, global and under-specified ways (e.g. I am useless, worthless, stupid, etc.). In some respects, this 'non-specific globality' is why the beliefs are able to elicit huge affect and also why they are often difficult to challenge. Indeed, because of their lack of specificity, many of the problems patients encounter on a daily basis tend be attributed to themselves, which serves to reinforce the beliefs (see fragile egg, Figure 2.2, Chapter 2). Hence, disputes with spouses or children, mistakes made at the grocery store, forgetting to file one's tax return on time, losing the dog while on a walk, etc., may all be used by the patient to confirm her inadequacies.

In chronic conditions, the patient will have developed the art of generating many examples of occurrences and episodes that support her belief. Hence, it is important to assist the patient to clarify the nature of any belief and its parameters. Some of this boundary-setting with respect to the belief can be achieved via questioning and procedures like the continuum technique (see section 7.6).

A further aspect of 'belief refinement' involves assessing the extent of the beliefs' influences, and uncovering how globally the cognitions affect the patient's life. If, for example, core beliefs can be triggered by a wide range of cues and are active in many different areas of a person's life (home, family life, work, leisure), then clearly they are global phenomena. However, if they are triggered in only certain domains, their influence will be more circumspect, and they can be defined with a higher degree of specification. For example, if someone who perceives herself to be totally incompetent discovers, via the use of diaries, that her self-belief is only triggered in the presence of her daughter, then a more accurate core belief would be: 'My daughter can make me believe I'm stupid.' As one can see, this is a less dysfunctional perspective than the belief 'I am totally stupid'.

INCREASING FLEXIBILITY

As outlined above, many of the dysfunctional beliefs are held rigidly. This is a product of when and how they were developed (i.e. formed in childhood, thus are a feature of simple immature problem-solving skills). Unfortunately, maturation in thinking style does not always allow for the development of a more balanced set of self-appraisals. This may be due to the three features previously described in 'schema-focused therapy', section 6.4, Chapter 6: belief avoidance, maintenance, compensation (Young 1994). Thus by constantly avoiding facing up to issues, overcompensating, and maintaining the status quo, the patient becomes stuck in self-fulfilling cycles from childhood in adulthood.

A key aim of treatment is to increase the flexibility of the person's cognitions, making the beliefs permeable to factual/helpful information. Thus, following successful treatment, a patient's interpretation is no longer based on biased thinking, but a balanced assessment of the situation, such as: *My son did not ask me to baby-sit because he knows I'm quite tired at the moment. It is not because he doesn't trust me.*

With respect to core belief work, greater flexibility could begin by making her unconditional beliefs become conditional.

For example:

'I'm untrustworthy' becoming *'I'm untrustworthy, when I'm ill and feeling depressed.'*

'I am evil' becoming *'I feel evil, when I have that thought about harming my husband.'*

Once the beliefs are in conditional form, one can work on these cognitions to make them even less rigid and more flexible. A method of increasing flexibility (and specificity) is the continuum technique, which will be discussed in detail below (see also James and Barton 2004). The technique is described in detail to demonstrate the level of knowledge and preparation required of a therapist prior to undertaking such strategies.

7.6: COGNITIVE CHANGE WITH THE CONTINUUM TECHNIQUE

The following guidelines are the main steps involved in setting up and using a continuum; 11 steps are described. A practical example of the technique is provided in the next chapter. As the name suggests, the technique involves applying *continuous properties* to beliefs that are held in a *discontinuous fashion* (e.g. 'I am a total burden'). This reflects thinking biases such as absolutism and black-and-white thinking, and dysfunctional core beliefs are typically held in this way. In practice, a continuum is set up diagrammatically by labelling one end of a 10cm line with the core belief (e.g. 'total burden'), then eliciting the opposite of the belief, and using it to label the other end (e.g. 'very useful'). This continuum can then be used by the patient to make a number of self-ratings or judgements, often involving contrasts with other people. Creating a continuous space for these judgements opens the possibility of less extreme or dichotomous thinking, and in relation to core beliefs can begin to sow the seeds of doubt about inflexibly held views. There are a number of variants on this, which I will illustrate below through the development of a set of guidelines for using this method effectively. For a fuller account of these guidelines see James and Barton (2004) (also see Padesky 1994; Wells 1997).

i. Assess suitability during the session using probe questions

The therapist should check out that the patient will be able to engage in the method appropriately. Any doubts about the patient's focus and ability to move between concrete and abstract thinking can be assessed at this stage. Prior to discussing the method with the patient, the therapist should also attempt to develop a conceptualisation, predicting the impact of the use of the continuum in this situation.

ii. Explain the rationale to the patient

It is beneficial to explain the procedure prior to engaging the patient in the strategy. Not only is this good teamwork, but the structure provided reinforces effective learning. During this socialisation phase, the patient should be informed that the methodology is likely to be used routinely throughout her period of treatment.

iii. Discuss the potential benefits and forewarn the patient about the potential reactions and hindrances she might experience or engage in (e.g. emotional avoidance)

In order to increase motivation, therapist and patient should jointly explore the potential benefits that are expected to occur through the successful implementation of the continuum technique. It is also important to make explicit the sort of dysfunctional processes that are likely to produce problems for the patient: belief maintenance, avoidance and compensation strategies (McGinn and Young 1996; see section 6.4, Young's schema-focused therapy). Indeed, by describing and explicitly acknowledging the experiences commonly reported by people when working on core issues, the patient can feel more contained.

iv. Collaboratively agree on a core belief to target

The next step is to agree on the content or material to be used with respect to the continuum. One would normally select an unconditional statement (i.e. I am worthless; I am evil). One must work collaboratively with the patient when determining the most appropriate belief to change.

v. Set a goal relating to the change processes being employed

It is important for the therapist to determine the process of change that he is endeavouring to use to achieve the agreed goal. This decision will have an impact on the style of continua employed and the labels ascribed to the end points (Padesky 1994). It will also determine whether adaptive or maladaptive descriptors are used at the poles (Table 7.4). For example, if the therapist believes that the continuum method can result in core belief change, then he needs to socialise the patient to this expectation. The aim of treatment should be to get the patient to re-examine the evidence relating to her beliefs, and in so doing reduce the credibility of the dysfunctional cognitions. Simultaneously, the therapist should be working to develop and support a more adaptive perspective. In contrast, if the therapist thinks that the core belief can never be eradicated and will frequently be triggered in a given situation, he should socialise the patient to a different and less ambitious expectation. In this case, the goal of the continuum may be to refine the belief so that it is less global and more flexible (e.g. becoming a conditional form of the belief rather than an unconditional – *from* 'I am a burden' *to* 'I often feel a burden, when I ask others to do things for me'). In both of the above change scenarios, the therapist is also likely to help the patient to develop better coping strategies to assist her to deal with the dysfunctional core belief when active.

vi. Select the most appropriate form of continua
The therapist needs to think through the theory of change underpinning the methodology. This will help to construct the most appropriate form of the continuum to meet the patient's needs. Table 7.4 presents three different forms of continua, and their different functions.

vii. Engage the patient in an integrated CBT change process
Despite the continua process being viewed as a cognitive change strategy, it is essential that the other elements of the CBT cycle are addressed. Thus, questions should be asked about the links between belief and emotions, physiology and behaviours.

viii. Employ CBT processes competently
In order for the strategy to work well, the therapist must employ all the conventional skills required of good CBT. The therapist should elicit and provide feedback; use good interpersonal skills; pace the work effectively; work collaboratively; use an effective questioning style, and a guided discovery approach (see earlier section 7.3.1, on questioning skills). It is important that the continuum method is not dominated by the structural aspects of the technique, rather it should be directed through the use of competent therapeutic skills.

ix. Ask the patient to summarise the learning achieved, and whether the goals were met
After completing the continuum, the patient should be asked to summarise what she thinks has been achieved. For maximum effect, the summary is best done in written form on the page on which the continuum was drawn. The patient can also be asked to give a written statement concerning the degree of progress made towards the overall treatment goal.

x. Discuss the pros and cons of strategy
As in all change methodologies, after completing the strategy the patient should provide specific feedback concerning her experience of undertaking

Table 7.4: The different forms and functions of continua

Nature of continua	Example	Function
Use of positive poles (e.g. case example of a woman who views herself as being worthless) (see Padesky 1994).	Instead of: 0% _____ 100% worthless worthless Use of: 0% _____ 100% OK OK	Use of positive poles ensures that (i) the person can identify a positive or preferred belief that she wants to move towards (e.g. being OK), (ii) any successful re-evaluations are directly related to her goals, (iii) any positive movements can also be reinforced, and the means of achieving them operationalised in concrete terms. For example, one can ask the patient what she has actually done to move 5% further along the positive scale (i.e. seeing herself as being more OK).
Use of multiple continua lines to help break down global concepts into concrete formats to enable the patient to make more helpful/rational judgements (see Chapter 8 for an example).	By examining a single concept along a number of dimensions, one increases the specificity of the original concept (e.g. 'worthlessness' could be examined in terms of five dimensions, and the patient may not view themselves negatively on all of these.	To break global, over-generalised beliefs into smaller conceptual features. As such, the absolutist nature of the perception begins to be challenged.
Use of non-linear representations (e.g. case example of a man who perceives himself to be inadequate: he would continually compare himself to highly successful people as reported in the media).	The horseshoe presentation (Elliot and Kirby-Lassen 1998): 0% totally adequate adequate	By getting the patient to rate herself on this type of scale, she appreciates that the most functional area is to be in the mid-section. This area represents flexibility.

the task. This feedback can help with the debriefing process, and also assists in future adaptations should another continuum be employed in subsequent sessions.

xi. If any change occurs, assess how it will impact on subsequent functioning

In order to reinforce the impact of in-session change, and to help it generalise to outside the session, time should be spent discussing the implications of the change. It is advisable to get the patient to reflect on how her changes in thinking could be operationalised outside of the therapeutic arena (i.e. in their interactions with her friends; when dealing with her doctor). Such reflections could be elaborated and developed through the use of experiential exercises and further consolidated via the setting of a relevant homework assignment. A different, yet associated, feature relating to subsequent functioning concerns patient containment. Working at the level of core belief can sometimes produce great emotional and cognitive shifts for the patient. The therapist may not always be able to 'ground' such a shift appropriately prior to the end of the session. In such circumstances, the patient's destabilised state may lead her to make dramatic life-changing decisions prematurely (i.e. to separate from her partner; to stop taking important medication; to confront an abuser). In order to prevent this from happening, the therapist should carefully assess the impact the continuum-work has had on the patient prior to the end of the session.

The above guidelines have highlighted that a lot of preparatory work and therapeutic skill are required to employ this methodology, and many of the other change techniques, competently.

7.7: CONCLUSION

This chapter has examined the nature of interventions. It has stressed the importance of therapists having a clear notion of the nature of change. It is only when one has a good grasp of what one is intending to do that one can recognise when things are going awry and adaptations are needed. A description of some of the common change techniques has been given. It is noted that such a list of strategies is helpful, but only when accompanied by effective change processes, such as effective use of feedback, interpersonal skills, etc. Finally, the various themes of the chapter were brought together in a discussion of the continuum, a typical technique used to alter core beliefs. The level of detail discussed in this example demonstrates the complexity and preparation required when working with CBT change methodologies.

PART 3

Chapter 8

A Case Study in Depression: Mary

8.1: INTRODUCTION

In this case a diathesis-stress model was used to formulate and treat the patient's difficulties. The case is introduced with a summary of the referral letter received from the psychiatrist. The conceptual model is then presented and the treatment strategy briefly outlined. Following this brief overview, the structural and process features associated with the case are unpacked and discussed in more detail to provide greater learning opportunities.

This chapter will illustrate the following:

- how the various phases of the therapy work together to produce an effective episode of care

- the typical obstacles that one encounters when treating people with depression

- the use of the continuum technique with case material.

8.2: OVERVIEW OF THE CASE

Referral letter: The letter from the consultant psychiatrist read as follows:

Dear Cognitive Therapy Team,

I saw Mrs Mary Jones, aged 67, in my clinic today. At interview, Mary was well presented and articulate. However, both her eye contact and concentration were poor, and she reported having lost 10lb in weight. This is the first time she has been referred to psychiatric services, but has been prescribed anti-depressant medication on two previous occasions by her GP. She states that she has experienced low times throughout her life. On this occasion she has requested a trial of a 'talking therapy' prior to the use of medication in the hope of obtaining a more permanent resolution to her difficulties.

She met criteria for depression, with a five months history of low mood. This was triggered by an argument with her husband during the Christmas period. Despite receiving a lot of support from her husband, Mary continues to experience 'black spells'. In April she expressed some suicidal thoughts, which precipitated her referral to psychiatric services.

She previously worked as a company secretary and is the wife of a retired vicar. She is a middle child of three and stated that she missed a lot of schooling due to the combination of having chronic asthma and an overprotective mother. She left school without qualifications, feeling she had not achieved in any area. She married Michael 46 years ago; they do not have any children. Owing to his job as a vicar, they previously had a hectic social life, which she found difficult. I would welcome your assessment of this case, with a view of taking her on for therapy.

Yours sincerely, Consultant Psychiatrist

Assessment and formulation: The psychiatrist's letter presents a picture consistent with a diathesis-stress model of depression with additional elements of social unease. This model suggests that owing to difficulties in her past, Mary developed a vulnerability to depression. She had not suffered from a severe depressive episode previously, with her minor episodes being successfully treated by her GP. The severity of the depression was assessed using the Geriatric Depression Scale (GDS score of 22 – severe range), and this scale was used weekly over the course of the therapy to provide her with feedback regarding her progress (see Figure 8.2). On the Hopelessness Scale (HS), a measure of suicidal risk, she scored 16 (severe range – high suicidal risk). Her score on the Dysfunctional Attitude Scale (DAS) was 124 (major depression); for a review of these measures see Chapter 5.

Questioning revealed that the trigger for the present episode was her husband letting out his frustration at Mary's performance during a game of bridge. He said 'Now that was a bl**dy stupid thing to do… You're so stupid!'. She took this badly, particularly as a number of the other people present ribbed her about the incident. Mary was unable to settle for the rest of the evening, and so made an excuse to leave early. Subsequently, she refused to attend all the other social functions arranged over Christmas. When asked about this incident in therapy via a Socratic questioning technique, Mary stated that this incident had publicly exposed her own thoughts about herself. She said it had opened the Pandora's box containing all her beliefs about being stupid.

When these issues were explored historically and across different settings in the present, it was evident that there was a self-referent belief around the issue of being 'stupid' that was fuelling her distress. Mary had been aware of this issue for most of her life, and had consequently avoided testing herself in many domains because of a fear that the 'truth' of her self-belief would be exposed. Due to similar fears she had not gone for job promotions, nor driving tests, or even to pub quizzes. She said that she found socialising with her husband's friends particularly difficult because they all had university degrees. However, she also said that she had learned to deal with these graduates by rarely ever expressing an opinion, and by perfecting the role of the 'interested' listener. In addition to these strategies, she always prepared herself carefully prior to social evenings. For example, she would read the *Daily Telegraph* and listen to Radio 4 for a few days prior to a social event. She noted that these compensation strategies, although giving her only a 'veneer of intelligence', had proven most effective up until this point. Yet, such strategies led her to believe that no-one knew the 'real her' – and if they did, they would reject her. Hence, in her blackest moments she also considered herself to be a *'deceitful fraud'*. Mary's initial formulation is presented in Figure 8.1.

Treatment plan: In attempting to help Mary, four broad strategies were used early on. Initially, a risk assessment was undertaken regarding her intentions concerning the suicidal ideations (Duberestein and Heisel 2008). Major concerns were: (i) a high score on the Hopelessness Scale, and (ii) her rejection of her support systems, particularly contact with her husband, elderly mother and best friend. Second behavioural reactivation was also an early goal, and this was facilitated through the use of mastery and pleasure charts (section 5.2, Chapter 5). Third, she was gently socialised to the CBT model. This needed to be done slowly and concretely owing to the reduced information processing capacity and executive deficits resulting from the depression. Fourth, in session five, the therapy focused on developing Mary's formulation collaboratively. This became the road map for targeting subsequent interventions. It was evident that the engine room for much of her distress was the core belief *'I am stupid'*, and thus either it needed to be modified or its impact coped with better. In discussions with Mary, she

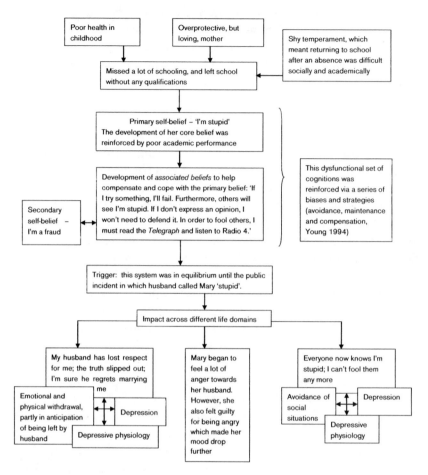

Figure 8.1: Mary's initial formulation

thought that the belief was too much a part of her to be changed, and so she chose to make it more flexible (i.e. less of an unconditional belief and becoming more conditional). Over a period of nine further sessions, she was able to move towards self-referent statements such as: *'I do stupid things sometimes, but this doesn't make me stupid'; 'My stupidity is relative to whom I'm with'.* Other useful statements were: *'My husband often upsets people by saying stupid things'; 'I can't change the past'.* In order to develop and give credence to these alternative cognitions, Mary needed a lot of support. The support helped her develop an ability to reframe scenarios, using more balanced and helpful thinking about the situations. This work involved using many behavioural (demonstration, role-play) and cognitive (continua, imagery) methodologies.

The coping card method (see below) as discussed in Chapter 7 were also particularly helpful, and the self-referent statements outlined above were used as the material for the cards. Some of these interventions are discussed in more detail below.

At the end of the 14 sessions of therapy, she was discharged with clinically significant improvements evident on three of the original assessment scales (Table 8.1).

```
-------------------------------------
|          Mary's Cue Card          |
|                                   |
| * I don't have qualifications, but I do |
| have LOADS of common sense        |
| * People who know me often seek   |
| me out for advice. They trust my  |
| judgement                         |
-------------------------------------
```

Table 8.1: Psychometrics pre- and post-treatment

Measure	Baseline score	Discharge score
GDS (Yesavage et al. 1983)	22	6
HS (Beck et al. 1974)	16	6
DAS (Weissman and Beck 1978)	124	60

The changes in the GDS scores are presented in Figure 8.2. Each week at the start of the session she was asked to complete this depression measure in order to monitor her own progress. A discussion of this progress was a standing item on her agenda.

8.3: REVIEW OF THE WORK UNDERTAKEN WITH MARY
The following section unpacks in greater detail some of the clinical work undertaken with Mary in order to promote reflection and better learning.

8.3.i: Assessment
In relation to Mary's depression, a diagnosis was given and tools were used to detect her characteristic patterns of thinking and behaving. Throughout all phases of the treatment, recordings of the sessions were undertaken both

GDS scores

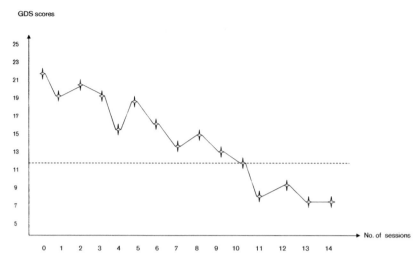

Figure 8.2: Progress chart showing changes on weekly GDS scores

as a record of progress and a memory aid. She was also encouraged to keep a therapy diary, using this as a treatment workbook and a prospective aid to be used post-treatment.

Diagnosis: She described the typical biological symptoms of depression (lethargy, poor sleep, early morning wakening, etc.), and hence was formally given this diagnosis.

Charts and diaries: 'Here and now' CBT data collection methodologies were employed to generate information about what she was experiencing on a day-to-day basis. In keeping with the adapted hot-cross bun framework outlined in Figure 6.1, details were collected about feeling states and the behaviours, thoughts and sensations associated with them (Figure 8.3). This information enabled us to obtain an idea of her changing mood and the patterns associated with them. I was particularly interested in things that triggered her low mood, and her responses to them.

Establishing links between the above episode and previous episodes (i.e. vertical links) was also important in understanding her disorder and the beliefs underpinning it. Historical data logs proved helpful, as well as the use of time charts (Figure 8.4). Typically, the time charts assist patients to recall events in sequence, often helping to cue key memories. It is also interesting to see what people include and do not include in their time line. Further, one can be surprised by the mood ratings attributed to the various events, with major dips in affect sometimes triggered by events that one might perceive as being relatively minor occurrences. Table 8.2 shows a summary of Mary's personal details and problem list.

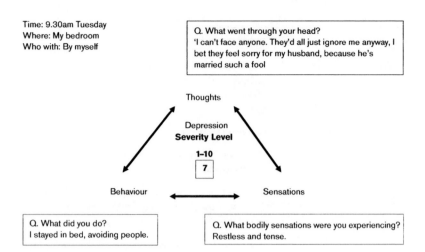

Figure 8.3: Triadic CBT cycle

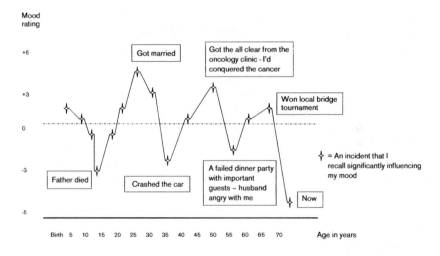

Figure 8.4: Some of the features on Mary's time line

Table 8.2: Summary of Mary's personal details and problem list

Key areas	Details
Family of origin	Middle child of three, and only daughter. Father was a labourer, died when Mary was 13. Mother history of anxiety, worked in grocer's shop after death of father. Mother still alive.
Marital status/family	Married to Michael for 46 years. He is a vicar. No children.
Education	Missed lots of schooling. Unable to make good relationships with classmates due to absenteeism.
Social network	Socialised with husband's colleagues and parishioners. She views these people as her husband's friends rather than hers; this is not necessarily an accurate perspective.
Career	Worked as a secretary, although role of vicar's wife often involved administrative duties.
Relevant medical details	Chronic asthmatic; arthritis in the left leg and hip. Previous episodes of depression.
Interests/hobbies	Reading non-fiction, won prizes for playing bridge.
Baseline questionnaries:	GDS = 22; HS = 16; DAS = 124.
Medication	Previously prescribed imipramine, then citalopram. Currently not on any psychotropic medication.
Problem list	1. Views herself as stupid 2. Thinks her husband will decide to leave her 3. Avoids people 4. Avoids speaking to her husband about her problem 5. Angry feelings and thoughts towards her husband 6. Neglect of self (dress and make-up) 7. Lethargy

8.3.ii: Formulation

Formulations have been discussed in detail in Chapter 6. In relation to Mary's difficulties, a diathesis-stress methodology was employed. Figure 8.1 summarises Mary's formulation, which suggests her core belief was forged in childhood. Thus the core belief regarding 'stupidity' is hypothesised to have been central to the way she has seen herself, particularly during periods of low mood. In order for her to be able to navigate life's trials and tribulations with such a negative sense of self, she developed a number of conditional beliefs, life rules and behavioural strategies to help her cope (e.g. *'Don't test yourself in public'; 'If you are with clever people, never express an opinion'*). These strategies served to maintain the belief. Her negatively biased cognitions (i.e. minimisation of the positive, personalisation of negative outcomes) and her use of compensatory strategies (e.g. reading the *Telegraph*, listening to Radio 4) meant that any evidence contrary to her belief was dismissed – see the fragile egg (Figure 2.2). In many ways, in the past, she had attempted to shield her vulnerable side away from the rest of the world. Unfortunately, her husband's recent comments, spoken in a moment of pique in public, triggered her worst fear. Now, perceiving herself as being publicly exposed, she withdrew. In her eyes, her negative sense of worth has been confirmed, and thus she is now helpless in an unkind world and with few prospects for a brighter future (i.e. negative triad, Figure 2.1). Furthermore, owing to the maelstrom of emotions she is experiencing, she is unable to think rationally. She is extremely confused, sometimes cycling between extreme levels of depression, anger and guilt in the space of a few minutes. The anger is mainly directed towards herself, but occasionally at her husband. The guilt is associated with her belief that she was deceiving others (i.e. I am a fraud).

It is noteworthy that Figure 8.1 also highlights another key belief, regarding a 'fear of rejection'. Indeed, it could be argued that Mary's underlying fear is that people, particularly her husband, will recognise she has been hiding her 'true inadequate' self, and as a consequence will reject her. Despite Mary acknowledging the potential logic of such hypotheses, she was very firm in the view that her core dysfunctional belief was around the notion of 'stupidity'. Hence, as this made sense to her, and provided a focus for treatment, this cognition formed the centre-piece of the formulation framework employed.

This case also illustrates a number of important points about core beliefs with respect to their development and maintenance. First, core beliefs tend to develop initially as 'functional' heuristics that help the person make sense of her world. They can develop any time in a person's life (James *et al.* 2004), but are often associated with childhood perspectives. In the case of Mary, viewing herself as 'less clever' than her peers was adaptive because it gave her a compass by which to navigate the complexities of growing up. It informed her that she had less academic knowledge than her peers (which she interpreted as stupidity), and that she could avoid ridicule by not competing with others. Second, the contents of her beliefs (the 'I am...' statements) illustrate that core beliefs are often over-simplified and unconditional in nature. This is probably due to the fact that her cognition developed in childhood, when her thinking style was immature. Thus, Mary simply summed herself up as: *'I'm stupid'*. In core belief therapy, these simple, rigidly held, absolute statements are termed unconditional core beliefs – as outlined previously in Chapters 5 and 7.

It is relevant to note that Mary had taken active steps, both behaviourally and cognitively, to prevent activation of her unconditional beliefs. She had avoided testing herself too much, settling for an administrative job that did not over-tax her. She had also developed a set of conditional beliefs and rules. For example, *'I must never go to a party without my husband'; 'If I am with clever people, then I shouldn't say anything controversial'; 'Unless I have read a recent article about a topic, then I must not offer an opinion'.*

8.3.iii: Treatment

An overview of her whole treatment has been outlined above (section 8.2). In contrast, this section goes into detail about one of the main intervention strategies used (i.e. the continuum). The theoretical features underpinning this strategy are provided in the previous chapter (Chapter 7, section 7.6). And in line with the key principles, its purpose was to make Mary's dysfunctional core beliefs more flexible and less absolutist.

In the case of Mary's continua, an arrangement of lines was constructed – see Figure 8.5. As part of the experiential exercise, she was asked to construct a continuum line, and rate herself in relation to the two ends of the pole. As expected, she initially rated herself high on the stupidity end, saying she would 'give anything to be intelligent'. In order to help her achieve greater flexibility regarding these constructs, she was asked about what features she associated with intelligence. These features were then also constructed into continua. Then for each of these features she was asked to rate herself on the line. As can be seen from the diagram, and the comments she made about the constructs, she was able to recognise that she had numerous abilities and skills that she had previously not taken sufficient account of. Thus the continua exercises helped to (i) sharpen up the definition of what features underpinned her sense of stupidity, and (ii) facilitate the 'self re-assessment' process that became the focus of future sessions.

However, having reflected on the matter over the following week, and being disturbed at having rated herself positively, she came to the next session feeling angry. She stated firmly that she had changed her mind about the ratings, and actually all the ratings should be negative. She said that on reflection, and based on the work we had done together, it was apparent that she was a fraud. *'I have been pretending to be intelligent all these years, when really I've been fooling people. I was being a parrot, revising before parties, etc. in order to*

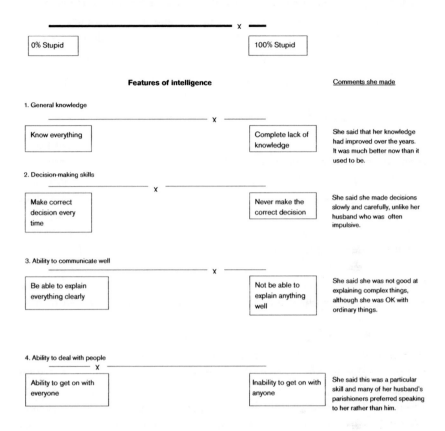

Figure 8.5: Mary's continua

hide my own insecurities!' This notion of being a fraud is a common comment made by people when undertaking core belief work. If it is present, it needs to be challenged as it can become a major obstacle to core belief change if left in situ. In the current case, Mary was given the opportunity to re-examine previous situations and motives for engaging in some of her 'fraudulent' strategies. For this task we first examined her notion of being a fraud. From these talks it became evident that she was afraid that if people knew the 'true' Mary, they would neither like nor want her. So next she was given the following instructions:

> From the work we've done, it seems that certain beliefs from your childhood may have influenced how you have behaved and portrayed yourself to others. The main concern is the notion that

you have fooled everyone into thinking you're bright. Your fear is that perhaps you were acting fraudulently, and if your husband and friends had been fully aware of your stupidity, they would not have liked/wanted to be with you.

Well, here's the chance to check this out. I want you to examine some of your relationships. What do key people in your life obtain and value from sharing a relationship with you?

The change methodology used to facilitate this exercise was a 'relationship chart and table'; this grid is frequently used in interpersonal psychotherapy (Miller 2009). First a relationship web is constructed as shown in Figure 8.6, and then the people outlined in the web are used to populate the top row of the accompanying grid. Along the vertical axis of the grid are features that the patient considers to be important to her. She is then asked to rate the extent to which a given relationship provides satisfaction in relation to this feature on a scale of 1–10, where 10 represents high levels of satisfaction. Thus Mary's grid summarised the characteristics of each of her relationships, and explored the quality and the nature of her current contact with these important people.

From this grid it is apparent that she has only a small group of friends whom she trusts and with whom she can relax. Further, since the start of her depression she has tended to avoid these people and spend more time with people she feels less comfortable with. This observation was developed into a homework assignment running over a period of weeks. The goal arising from this work was to get her to spend more time with people she felt comfortable with, and whom she felt stimulated by.

Through the information discussed during the construction of the relationship chart and the various exercises developing from it, a number of relevant pieces of information arose concerning 'facts' she has uncovered about herself from the therapy. She was asked to summarise these points as part of another homework assignment.

FACTUAL POINTS ARISING IN DISCUSSIONS

From data derived from the homework assignment and following further discussions, she drew up a list of features regarding her notion of being a fraud.

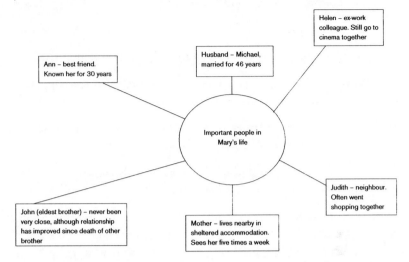

——— = The distance of this line from the centre indicates how important this person is *currently* in Mary's life. Mary remarked that prior to depression, Ann and Judith would have been much closer to the centre, but since her illness she'd avoided them.

Helen – ex-work colleague. Still go to cinema together

Husband – Michael, married for 46 years

Ann – best friend. Known her for 30 years

Important people in Mary's life

Judith – neighbour. Often went shopping together

John (eldest brother) – never been very close, although relationship has improved since death of other brother

Mother – lives nearby in sheltered accommodation. Sees her five times a week

Feature – To what extent (scale 1–10):	Husband	Mother	Ann	Judith	Helen	John
Do you enjoy his/her company	7	6	8	7	7	4
Do you trust the person	8	6	9	8	6	5
Are you able to open-up to him/her	6	5	9	7	5	3
Does he/she like you	7	7	9	8	7	5
Are you keen to spend more time with him/her	6	6	7	6	6	4
Would you turn to him/her in a time of crisis	8	3	8	7	5	3
Would you like to go to a party with him/her	5	4	9	8	8	4
Does he/she provide you with stimulating conversation	8	5	8	7	5	7
Are you able to be relaxed with him/her	7	5	9	7	7	3
Are you being a fraud with this person	2	3	2	2	2	4

Figure 8.6: Mary's relationship chart and table

- My husband knows all about my past, lack of schooling etc. and so I've not been hiding things from him.

- My husband always consults me when making important decisions.

- Some people know me well and they value my common sense.

- Many of the female parishioners often preferred speaking to me rather than him (her husband) about difficulties.

- My favourite newspaper is the *Telegraph*, and I enjoy reading it. Hence, I don't simply use it as a prop.

- I enjoy listening to Radio 4 on a daily basis, and so I listen even when there isn't a social event in the diary.

These statements were particularly powerful in helping her to achieve a more balanced view of her actions and self-perceptions. One might think that the work engaged in regarding her being a fraud was somewhat risky, because there was the chance that no positive evidence would be found to counter her views. However, it is relevant to note that because a comprehensive formulation had been undertaken, I had a good idea of how she would react to such a task and what data was available to construct the list. And as predicted, after being given the opportunity to re-evaluate decisions in her life, she stated that she was *'good at making difficult decisions'*. As such, she acknowledged that people had generally received good advice from her, thus countering her earlier view she was acting fraudulently. Further, she acknowledged that when making judgements about people, she was better than her husband – who tended to be rather impulsive. Also, she recognised that her rather slow and deliberate style of thinking was not actually a sign of stupidity, but of a determination to get things right first time.

This re-evaluation procedure had a number of important effects. First, it made her feel positive about herself, and reduced the belief of being a fraud. Second, it reactivated many positive memories from her past, memories that had been difficult to access because of the impact of the depression on her memory (mnemonic interlock, Williams 1992). Third, it emphasised that these 'I am…; If…then…' statements were too simplistic, and actually they had not ruled her life in the manner initially suggested in Figure 8.1. Indeed, she informed me that on many occasions in the past she had been put in difficult scenarios in which she had been required to act intelligently. Thus, this realisation demonstrated that she had actually been pretty flexible in the past with respect to her thinking and behaviour. And thus she had more control of her core belief than she had initially given herself credit for.

8.3.iv: Reformulation of the case in a narrative form

Having undertaken the continuum and engaged in the life re-evaluation, we set about revising the formulation in a narrative form. The narrative incorporated the new information, and provided the rationale for further interventions.

Mary's reformulation: a narrative account

As a child, I missed a lot of schooling, resulting in a poor education and grades. This made me feel bad about myself, and I convinced myself I was stupid.

This view of myself has influenced me in many situations in my life. Even when I have been successful, I have attributed the success to hard work rather than intelligence. Indeed, I have been in a 'no win' situation. If things went wrong, I'd say 'it's because I'm stupid', and if anything went right, I'd say it was 'due to luck or hard work'.

Over the last few weeks I have learned that I have been too hard on myself. I now recognise that there are many different types of intelligence, and I possess aspects of some of them. So while I don't think I am good academically, I believe that I am a good, careful thinker and have lots of 'emotional intelligence' – which other people recognise and value.

As one can see with this narrative, the 'straw man' technique (see Chapter 7) has been brought to its conclusion, with the patient now able to see the flaws in the original formulation. Further, she has now gained an awareness of why she was affected so greatly by the triggering event.

Over three further sessions (sessions 12–14) Mary was able to build some adaptive coping cognitions. For example, we collaboratively developed a number of helpful self-referent statements such as: *'I am sensitive about being seen as stupid'; 'I do stupid things sometimes, but that doesn't make me stupid', 'Having a degree doesn't bestow you with common sense'.* As one can see these are generic level statements that relate directly to the core beliefs. However, with time we also moved to statements which related to the specifics of the situation causing the activation of the core beliefs. Regarding this scenario, we came to following statement: *'On that evening my husband was being impulsive and overly competitive'.*

In order to develop and give credence to these alternative cognitions, Mary needed a lot of support. Some of the statements were committed to cue cards, and used by Mary during her times of self-doubt. Her husband attended some of the later sessions, and the resulting work was helpful in reinforcing a lot of the earlier material. By the end of therapy, Mary had developed the ability to reframe scenarios, using the facts of the situation rather than her biases. In the final sessions, relapse management was undertaken (section 2.3iii, Chapter 2). Thus, she was warned that she was still likely to be troubled by NATs from time to time. It was explained that such occurrences should not be seen as evidence that the therapy had failed, rather that these negative cognitions had not been eradicated completely and she would need to take care not to let them grow and reinforce themselves again.

8.4: CONCLUSION

Mary's treatment was reviewed briefly, before conducting an in-depth analysis of certain key features. The description given outlines a rather standard case, with someone in quadrant one of the categorisation chart (Figure 3.1), indicating little adaptation was required. This case has been presented in this format because the evidence base to date supports the use of the diathesis-stress framework, with the value of the newer models waiting to be established. Despite indicating the case as 'standard', a number of features mark it out as an 'older adult case'. For example, it has a strong interpersonal component, both borrowing from interpersonal psychotherapy (IPT) and engaging the help of her husband in her treatment. The use of recording equipment in supporting the work can also be regarded as a typical feature of older people's therapy. The use of cue cards, and the constant generation of key sentences and prompts are again typical methods used in this speciality.

It is also worth noting that numerous aspects of Mary's life have not been discussed in the chapter, and neither did they play a major role in the therapy. For example, I did not spend much time discussing her close relationship with her mother, nor her physical difficulties. There were three reasons why these issues were not explored further: (i) they did not arise as key issues during the assessment phase, (ii) there is only so much detail one can discuss from an older person's history without becoming overwhelmed, and (iii) the more information brought into the therapeutic arena, the greater likelihood of confusion. Indeed, it is my opinion that when one is working with older people – 'Good therapy is often about being comfortable *not* knowing everything, but knowing *sufficient* to promote lasting change.'

Chapter 9

Assessing and Developing
Clinical Competence

9.1: INTRODUCTION

This chapter examines the skills required to work competently as a CBT therapist, treating patients in quadrant one of Figure 3.1, Chapter 3 (i.e. those with little/no cognitive impairment, such as Mary in the previous chapter). It presents details from the Cognitive Therapy Scale-Revised (CTS-R), which is a scale for measuring therapist competence in CBT and is based on the original Cognitive Therapy Scale (CTS, Young and Beck 1980, 1988). The CTS-R was developed jointly by researchers at the Newcastle Cognitive and Behavioural Therapies Centre and Newcastle University, UK (Blackburn *et al.* 2001; James, Blackburn, Milne and Reichelt 2001) The content of this chapter is taken mainly from the scale's manual, which describes the items of the CTS-R (James *et al.* 2000).

It is relevant to note that the appendices (Appendix II) include a second manual developed alongside the CTS-R, which I use in my teaching programmes (James, unpublished). This 'Training Manual' provides tips on how to enhance practice, and improve one's score on the CTS-R!

This chapter will illustrate the following:

- the key features of the Cognitive Therapy Scale-Revised, which assesses therapeutic competence

- how structural and process features combine to deliver competent therapy.

9.2: THE COGNITIVE THERAPY SCALE-REVISED

The CTS-R contains 12 items (Figure 9.1), in contrast to earlier versions of the CTS which contained 13 (Young and Beck 1980) and 11 (Young and Beck 1988) items respectively. One of the frameworks that underpins the revised scale is the cognitive cycle. This cycle represented in Figure 9.1 demonstrates how the CTS-R items address specific aspects of the 'hot-cross bun' framework. At the heart of the scale is the conceptualisation. In order to move the patient from a dysfunctional cycle, dominated by a dysfunctional conceptualisation, the therapist must address the four features highlighted in the outer ring of the circle: cognitions, emotions, physiology/arousal and behaviour, using the cognitive-specific items (items 6–12). To facilitate the smooth movement around the cycle, the therapist must also demonstrate competence in areas assessed by the remaining items 1–5 (agenda and adherence, feedback, collaboration, pacing, interpersonal effectiveness).

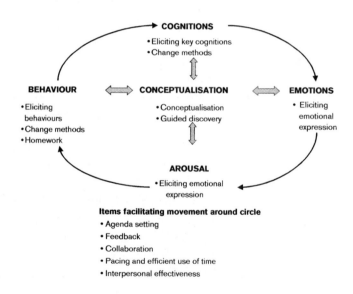

COGNITIONS
• Eliciting key cognitions
• Change methods

BEHAVIOUR
• Eliciting behaviours
• Change methods
• Homework

CONCEPTUALISATION
• Conceptualisation
• Guided discovery

EMOTIONS
• Eliciting emotional expression

AROUSAL
• Eliciting emotional expression

Items facilitating movement around circle
• Agenda setting
• Feedback
• Collaboration
• Pacing and efficient use of time
• Interpersonal effectiveness

General items	Cognitive therapy specific items
Item 1: Agenda Setting and Adherence*	Item 1: Agenda Setting and Adherence*
Item 2: Feedback	Item 6: Eliciting Appropriate Emotional Expression
Item 3: Collaboration	Item 7: Eliciting Key Cognitions
Item 4: Pacing and Efficient Use of Time	Item 8: Eliciting Behaviours
Item 5: Interpersonal Effectiveness	Item 9: Guided Discovery
	Item 10: Conceptual Integration
	Item 11: Application of Change Methods
	Item 12: Homework Setting

*Item 1 can be regarded as both a general and CT item.

Figure 9.1: The relationship between the CTS-R items and the cognitive cycle

It is generally accepted that it is not appropriate to use the CTS-R to assess performance in either the initial or final sessions of the therapy. This is because of the differing functions of the assessment and termination phases of the therapy. Dick *et al.* (1999) identified three distinct therapeutic phases of therapy for older people (early sessions 1–3; middle 4–16; end 17–20). In the early sessions the main aims are to: establish a baseline and goals, socialise patients to CBT, and form a working alliance. The middle stages involve working towards the attainment of the goals, while the end sessions involve reviewing, relapse management work and dealing with the dynamics of treatment termination. The following section describes CTS-R items for sessions conducted in the middle sessions of therapy, outlining their 'key features' and associated details.

9.2.i: Item 1 – Agenda setting and adherence

The agenda helps ensure that the most important issues are addressed in an efficient manner. The key features of the 'agenda' are outlined in the CTS-R as follows.

Key features: To address adequately topics that have been agreed and set in an appropriate way. This involves the setting of discrete and realistic targets collaboratively.

Three features need to be considered when scoring this item:

(i) presence/absence of an agenda which is explicit, agreed and prioritised, and feasible in the time available

(ii) appropriateness of the contents of the agenda (to stage of therapy, current concerns, etc.), a standing item being a review of the homework set previously

(iii) appropriate adherence to the agenda.

Short-term cognitive therapy requires that the important issues are discussed sensitively but managed in a business-like way. In order to cover a lot of material adequately in a relatively short space of time, specific and realistic targets need to be set in a collaborative manner, and adhered to appropriately. Indeed, it is of limited use to set a good agenda and then not be guided by it.

On setting the agenda, the therapist must ensure the items are appropriate. They should be suitable for the stage of therapy, amenable to a CBT rationale, consistent with the formulation, and conceived to take the therapy forward. In addition, the items should be clear and discrete. If the items are too vague, this may lead to confusion and also result in divergent and tangential material being discussed. It is important to note, however, that the therapist must be aware not to let the patient go into too much detail about any one item at this stage, as this will disrupt the agenda-setting process. The list of items should include material from both the patient and therapist. A discussion of the homework that was set previously should be a 'standing' item.

Part of socialising the patient to CBT is to establish an expectation that she will need to come to each session having thought through the key topics for that day's therapeutic work.

Following the setting of the agenda, the patient should be asked to prioritise her list of items. The prioritisation permits the therapist to plan the session and allot appropriate time for the material. Efficient prioritising facilitates the pacing of the therapy.

Helpful advice about agenda setting with older people is provided by Laidlaw and Thompson (2008, p.107). They stress its relevance, but acknowledge that numerous therapists perceive it as being overly structured and thus some therapists are uncomfortable using it. In order to socialise patients to this feature, Thompson *et al.* (1996) recommend that patients are socialised to the item from the outset: 'It is very important to begin to do this quite early on in treatment so that bad habits of rambling, or unstructured use of time do not get established; they are harder to break once established than to prevent from occurring!' (p.10).

9.2.ii: Item 2 – Feedback

The therapist should both provide and elicit feedback throughout each session. The key features of 'feedback' are outlined in the CTS-R as shown in the box.

This item stresses the importance of two-way feedback. By 'summarising' and 'chunking' information at regular intervals, the therapist can emphasise the major features, synthesise new material and highlight issues that require further clarification. By eliciting the patient's feedback (thoughts and feelings) regarding the therapy, the therapist can check the patient's attitude, knowledge base and understanding.

Chunking information and eliciting feedback should occur frequently. On occasions, when either particularly important or confusing material is being discussed, the feedback should occur after each major point; this can

Key features: The patient's and therapist's understanding of key issues should be helped through the use of *two-way feedback*. The two major forms of feeding back information are through general summary and chunking of important units of information. The use of appropriate feedback helps both the therapist to understand the patient's situation, and the patient to synthesise material enabling her to gain major insight and make therapeutic shifts. It also helps to keep the patient focused.

Three features need to be considered when scoring this item:

(i) presence and frequency, or absence, of feedback; feedback should be given/elicited throughout the therapy – with major summaries both at the beginning (review of week) and end (session summary), while topic reviews (i.e. chunking) should occur throughout the session

(ii) appropriateness of the contents of the feedback

(iii) manner of its delivery and elicitation (NB: can be written).

also help 'contain' distressing issues. During normal short-term CBT, the two-way feedback should occur at least every ten minutes.

Major summaries should occur at the beginning and end of each session, to help reinforce and consolidate therapeutic material. In Mohlman and Gorman's (2005) study, using enhanced CBT for older people, during the last five minutes of each session, the therapist led an 'expanding review' of all concepts and techniques learned to date.

It is important that the feedback be appropriate. For example, when providing feedback the therapist must choose the salient material presented to her, and then summarise these features in a way that both clarifies and highlights key issues. This form of summarising and feeding back is the foundation for many forms of cognitive techniques (e.g. Socratic questioning). There is a similar feedback technique called 'platforming', a process by which key information fed to the patient enables them to access information they already possess in order that they may achieve a better conceptual understanding of an issue (see section 7.3.1, Chapter 7).

Thompson *et al.* (1996) suggest that it is important to provide feedback concerning process issues relating to the session. For example, providing praise concerning contributions, and raising issues about problems arising within the therapy (e.g. *I have been really impressed today by the way you have made connections between the formulations and the difficulties raised in the homework task. Do you think the questions I'm asking are making you too anxious?*).

9.2.iii: Item 3 – Collaboration

Good therapeutic teamwork is a fundamental feature of CBT. Thompson *et al.* (1996) describe it as the 'heart and soul of cognitive therapy'. Collaboration should be consistent throughout the session, although at times didactic approaches may be necessary (e.g. educating the patient about the physical effects of anxiety). The key features of 'collaboration' are outlined in the CTS-R as follows.

> Key features: The patient should be encouraged to be active in the session. There must be clear evidence of productive teamwork, with the therapist skilfully encouraging the patient to participate fully (e.g. through questioning techniques, shared problem solving and decision making) and take responsibility. However, the therapist must not allow the patient to ramble in an unstructured way.
>
> Three features need to be considered; the therapist's style should encourage effective teamwork through her use of:
>
> (i)   verbal skills (e.g. non-hectoring)
>
> (ii) non-verbal skills (e.g. attention and use of joint activities)
>
> (iii) sharing of written summaries.

The therapist should adopt a style that promotes an egalitarian relationship, whereby he and the patient work actively towards shared goals. This is achieved by the development of a 'teamwork' approach. Hence the therapist should avoid being overly directive, too intellectual, controlling or passive.

The therapist needs to strike a balance between being structured on the one hand and on the other allowing the patient to make choices and take responsibility. In order to achieve a good therapeutic alliance, the therapist must assess the patient's needs, and particularly her preferred modes of learning. For example, Beck *et al.* (1983) suggest that individuals who display sociotropic traits respond better to a warm supportive therapeutic relationship, while those with autonomous traits prefer to take a high level of responsibility within the therapy and respond better to a more task-oriented approach. Good collaboration will also involve striking a balance between the verbal and non-verbal features: for example, deciding when to talk and when to listen; when to confront and when to back-off; when to offer suggestions, etc. According to Laidlaw and Knight (2008) good collaboration is essential when working with older people as it demonstrates respect for the experience of the person. Thompson *et al.* (1996) suggest that the process can be facilitated through the use of a notebook and whiteboard. Indeed, material presented in the written form can make abstract comments more concrete.

9.2.iv: Item 4 – Pacing and Efficient Use of Time

The therapist should make optimal use of the time in accordance with items set in the agenda. He must maintain sufficient control, limit discussion of peripheral issues, interrupt unproductive discussion, and pace the session appropriately. The key features of 'Pacing and Efficient Use of Time' are outlined in the CTS-R as follows.

Key features: The session should be well 'time managed' in relation to the agenda, with the session flowing smoothly through discrete start, middle, and concluding phases. The work must be paced well in relation to the patient's needs, and while important issues need to be followed, unproductive digressions should be dealt with smoothly. The session should not go over time, without good reason.

Three features need to be considered:

(i)   the degree to which the session flows smoothly through the discrete phases

(ii) the appropriateness of the pacing *throughout* the session

(iii) the degree of fit to the learning speed of the patient.

The session should be well time managed, such that it is neither too slow nor too quick. For example, the therapist may unwittingly belabour a point after the patient has already grasped the message, or may gather much more data than is necessary before formulating a strategy for change. In these cases, the sessions can seem painfully slow and inefficient. On the other hand, the therapist may switch from topic to topic too rapidly, thus not allowing the patient to integrate the new material sufficiently. The therapist may also intervene before having gathered enough data to conceptualise the problem.

The pacing of the material should always be accommodated to the patient's needs, memory and speed of learning. For example, when there is evidence of difficulties (e.g. emotional or cognitive difficulties), more time and attention may need to be given. In such circumstances the agenda items may be shuffled or adapted accordingly. In some extreme circumstances (e.g. disclosure of suicidal thoughts), the structure and pacing of the session will need to change drastically in accordance with the needs of the situation. It is important that the therapist maintains an overview of the session to allow correct pacing throughout. This may involve the therapist politely interrupting peripheral discussion and directing the patient back to the agenda.

A well-paced session should not need to exceed the time allocated for the period and should cover the items set in the agreed agenda. It will also allow sufficient time for the homework task to be set appropriately, and not be unduly rushed.

9.2.v: Item 5 – Interpersonal Effectiveness

The ability of the therapist to form a good relationship with the patient is deemed crucial to the therapy (Lazarus and Sadavoy 1996). Indeed, in order for the patient to be able to disclose difficult material, there must be both trust and confidence in the therapist (Safran and Segal 1990). The key features of 'Interpersonal Effectiveness' are outlined in the CTS-R as follows.

Key features: The patient is put at ease by the therapist's verbal and non-verbal (e.g. listening skills) behaviour. The patient should feel that the core conditions (i.e. warmth, genuineness, empathy and understanding) are present. However, it is important to keep professional boundaries. In situations where the therapist is extremely interpersonally effective, he is creative, insightful and inspirational.

Three features need to be considered:

(i) empathy – the therapist is able to understand the patient's experiences and uses this understanding to promote change

(ii) genuineness – the therapist has established a trusting working relationship

(iii) warmth – the patient seems to feel liked and accepted by the therapist.

In order that the appropriate levels of the three features are conveyed, careful judgement is required from the therapist. Personal and contextual needs must be taken into account. For example, towards the end of therapy lower levels of warmth may be used, as compared to the beginning, in order to promote patient disengagement (Miller 2009).

Empathy concerns the therapist's ability to make the patient aware that their difficulties are recognised and understood on both an emotional and cognitive level. For example, the promotion of a shared-value system between therapist and patient will help to enhance this aspect of the relationship. The therapist should avoid appearing distant, aloof, patronising or overly critical. A good therapist should adopt a genuine and straightforward therapeutic style.

It is also important for the therapist to convey warmth and concern through both his verbal and non-verbal behaviour. The therapist should avoid being critical, disapproving, impatient or frustrated by the content or slow progress/pace of the session. He should convey an attitude of acceptance of the person, but not of course with respect to the style of thinking. It is also important to highlight that appropriate use of humour can often help to establish and maintain a good therapeutic relationship.

9.2.vi: Item 6 – Eliciting Appropriate Emotional Expression

The ability of the therapist to deal effectively with the emotional content of the therapy session is a crucial feature of therapy. The therapist should then be able to use the patient's emotions to promote therapeutic change. The current item reflects the degree to which the therapist is able to create the circumstances through which emotional change and expression can be elicited and then used effectively. The key features of 'Eliciting Appropriate Emotional Expression' are outlined in the CTS-R as shown in the following box (see below).

Cognitive therapy requires both cognitive and emotional shift. In order to produce emotional change the therapist must first facilitate the patient to express herself on an emotional level. The therapist should ensure that emotions associated with a particular situation or cognition are elicited and assessed for intensity. The therapist must also be able to assess the emotional shift within a session and work with it accordingly, increasing and decreasing the level of emotionality as appropriate.

There is an optimal level of emotional affect required to motivate a person to change constructively. Too little emotional energy (i.e. apathy, lack of motivation, avoidance) will be insufficient to create change. In these cases

---

Key features: The therapist facilitates the processing of appropriate levels of emotion by the patient. Emotional levels that are too high or too low are likely to interfere with therapy. The therapist must also be able to deal effectively with emotional issues which interfere with effective change (e.g. hostility, anxiety, excessive anger). Effective facilitation will enable the patient to access and express her emotions in a way that facilitates change.

Three features have to be considered:

(i)   facilitation of access to a range of emotions

(ii) appropriate use and containment of emotional expression

(iii) facilitation of emotional expression, encouraging appropriate access and differentiation of emotions.

---

the therapist must first be able to stimulate the patient (through verbal and non-verbal behaviour) to become an active participant in the therapeutic process. On the other hand too much emotion (i.e. anger, despair, fear, etc.) will interfere with therapy. The therapist should be able to contain the energy, or use or dissipate it, in order that it no longer serves as an obstacle to effective change.

A skilled therapist will also recognise inconsistency between the emotional and cognitive content, and explore such discrepancies accordingly. For example, if a patient expresses no distressing emotion when talking about some unpleasant event, careful questioning will help the patient access her associated emotions.

A number of tools can be employed to facilitate the differentiation and monitoring of moods. For example, the Daily Mood Rating Form has been used in many of the Thompson and Gallagher-Thompson studies (Thompson *et al.* 2009). The form has four columns: Trigger and time; Mood state (depression, anxious, angry); Mood score (1–9); Comments on 'Why I think I felt this way'. The data from such forms are helpful in demonstrating that mood states vary during the course of the day, and that the scores relate to events, thinking states and actions.

9.2.vii: Item 7 – Eliciting Key Cognitions

This feature addresses the ability of the therapist to elicit important cognitions in an effective manner. The key features of 'Eliciting Key Cognitions' are outlined in the CTS-R as follows.

Key features: To help the patient gain access to her cognitions (thoughts, assumptions and beliefs) and to understand the relationship between these and their distressing emotions. This can be done through the use of questioning, diaries and monitoring procedures.

Three features need to be considered:

(i)   eliciting cognitions that are associated with distressing emotions (i.e. selecting key cognitions)

(ii) the skilfulness and breadth of the methods used (i.e. Socratic questioning, appropriate monitoring, downward arrowing, imagery, role-plays, etc.)

(iii) choosing the appropriate level of work for the stage of therapy (i.e. automatic thoughts, assumptions, or core beliefs).

A therapist should be able to identify and elicit those thoughts, images and beliefs that are fundamental to the patient's distress (i.e. the key cognitions). These key cognitions often take the form of negative automatic self-statements or beliefs relating to the self and the world that either drive or maintain negative emotions.

In the case of depression, such negative automatic thoughts (NATs) might be:

– *No one could ever love me; I'll always be rejected.*

– *My future is bleak, and it will always be this way.*

} DEPRESSION

In panic with agoraphobia:

– *I'm having a heart attack.*

– *Unless I'm very careful, I'll collapse.*

} FEAR AND ANXIETY

In post-traumatic stress disorder:

– *The world is a hostile place; I'm never quite sure when the next thing will go wrong.*

} ANXIETY

– *I can't cope with things like I used to.*

Other types of key cognitions are dysfunctional core beliefs (see Table 5.1, Chapter 5 for a summary of types of cognitions). These are rigid, inflexible and dysfunctional self-beliefs which are not open to the 'normal' corrective processes of logical thinking. These can be expressed through basic assumptions and rules (If…then; I should…; people should…).

The negative automatic thoughts, basic assumptions, rules and core beliefs often exist in the face of overwhelming contradictory evidence (e.g. *The eminent ex-professor who thinks she is a fraud*). As part of the assessment, it is also important for the therapist to identify the different forms of cognitive biases being used to support the patient's thinking (see Chapter 2, Table 2.1). For example, the patient may be engaging in 'minimising the positive': reducing the frequency or impact of good events, perhaps even focusing on the negative side of such events (e.g. *'Now that I've got a new job, I'll have no time to see the grandchildren'*) or 'catastrophising': exaggerating the potential negative impact of an occurrence out of all reasonable proportions (e.g. *'Mark didn't call last night; I don't think he likes me any more'*).

On certain occasions the patient may display a great deal of emotion (cry, shake, etc.) while discussing issues. At such times, the patient's thinking needs to be checked out as she may be experiencing dysfunctional thoughts (such thoughts are termed 'hot cognitions'). During such an episode, the therapist will need to exercise a great deal of empathy and skill when eliciting these cognitions.

9.2.viii: Item 8 – Eliciting Behaviours

Behavioural problems are observed frequently in psychiatric disorders. They take numerous forms, including withdrawal, avoidance, compulsions and various types of *safety-seeking behaviours* (see Box 5.1, Chapter 5). As such, it is important that the therapist elicits the roles these behavioural features play in the maintenance of the patient's problems. The key features of 'Eliciting Behaviours' are outlined in the CTS-R as follows.

Key features: To help the patient gain insight into the effect of her behaviours with respect to the problems. This can be done through the use of questioning, diaries and monitoring procedures.

Two features need to be considered:

(i) eliciting behaviours that are associated with distressing emotions (including use of safety-seeking behaviours)

(ii) the skilfulness and breadth of the methods used (i.e. Socratic questioning, appropriate monitoring, imagery, role-plays, etc.).

It is important to examine the role that behaviours have in triggering and maintaining the patient's disorder. Behaviours often reinforce both negative thoughts and feelings. For example, the typical avoidance observed in social phobia prevents the person overcoming her fear, and obtaining the skills necessary to engage in social interactions.

Some activities can be termed 'safety-seeking behaviours' as patients employ them as a means of reducing their levels of distress (e.g. self-monitoring procedures, holding tightly onto objects). However, safety behaviours can often serve to unwittingly maintain a person's problems, ensuring that the dysfunctional cycles are preserved (see Box 5.1, Chapter 5). On occasions the patient might react to difficulties by over-compensating in some manner (e.g. becoming aggressive when feeling vulnerable); such behavioural patterns clearly ought to be elicited and examined in relation to the relevant emotions associated with them.

Gallagher and Thompson (1981) have developed a scale for assessing baseline behaviours and activities engaged in by older people. The measure, Californian Older Person's Pleasant Event Schedule (COPPES), assesses the frequency of categories of pleasant events and the magnitude of pleasure experienced from them. An example of how the COPPES is used is provided by Coon *et al.* (2007); also see Chapter 5, section 5.2(iv)d).

9.2.ix: Item 9 – Guided Discovery

Guided discovery is a form of communicating (e.g. questioning) that assists the patient to gain new perspectives for herself without the use of debate or lecturing. It is used throughout the sessions in order to promote patient understanding. It is based on the principles of Socratic dialogue, whereby a questioning style is used to promote discovery, to explore concepts, synthesise ideas and develop hypotheses regarding the patient's problems and experiences.

The key features of 'Guided Discovery' are outlined in the CTS-R as shown in the next box.

It has been observed that patients are more likely to adopt new perspectives if they perceive they have been able to come to such views and conclusions for themselves (Vygosky 1978). Hence, rather than adopting a debating stance, the therapist should use a communication style to engage the patient in a problem-solving process.

For example, skilfully phrased questions, which are presented in a clear manner, can help to highlight either links or discrepancies in the patient's thinking. In order to accommodate the new information or learning,

---

Key features: The patient should be helped to develop hypotheses regarding her current situation and to generate potential solutions for herself. The patient is helped to develop a range of perspectives regarding her experience. Effective guided discovery will create doubt where previously there was certainty, thus providing the opportunity for re-evaluation and new learning to occur.

Two elements need to be considered:

(i)   the style of the therapist – this should be open and inquisitive

(ii) the effective use of verbal and non-verbal techniques (e.g. Socratic questions) should encourage the patient to discover useful information that can be used to help her to gain a better level of understanding.

---

new insight is often achieved. Padesky (1993) emphasises that the aim of questioning is not to 'change minds' through logic, but to engage the patient in a Socratic dialogue. Within this dialogue the patient can arrive at new perspectives and solutions for themselves. The questions posed should not be way beyond the patient's current level of understanding, as this is unlikely to promote effective change. Rather they should be phrased within, or just outside, the patient's current understanding in order that she can make realistic attempts to answer them. The product of attempting to deal with such intelligently phrased questions is likely to be new discoveries (see Chapter 7, Table 7.1).

Other methods of 'guiding discovery' include the use of metaphor, analogies, stories and appropriate self-disclosure. Used together, the above communication techniques permit the patient to make connections to assist in the development of the formulation.

9.2.x: Item 10 – Conceptual Integration

Conceptual integration encompasses both the generic CBT cycle and the individualised formulation. Through these conceptual models, the patient will gain an understanding of her disorder, its underlying and maintaining features, and relevant triggers. The key features of 'Conceptual Integration' are outlined in the CTS-R as shown in the box.

Conceptualising is one of the key processes of therapy through which change takes place. It provides the theoretical overview of the work. Its absence can lead to disjointed therapy, which might prevent major insight

Key features: The patient should be helped to gain an appreciation of the history, triggers and maintaining features of her problem in order to bring about change in the present and future. The therapist should help the patient to gain an understanding of how her perceptions and interpretations, beliefs, attitudes and rules relate to her problem. A good conceptualisation will examine previous cognitions and coping strategies as well as current ones. This theory-based understanding should be well integrated and used to guide the therapy forward.

Two features need to be considered:

(i)   the presence/absence of an appropriate conceptualisation which is in line with goals of therapy

(ii) the manner in which the conceptualisation is used (e.g. used as the platform for interventions, homework etc.).

being gained by the patient. When it is not appropriately integrated within therapy, the work may lose its focus and only consist of a set of unrelated techniques.

In order for effective therapy to occur, the conceptualisation must be appropriate. To arrive at an appropriate cognitive rationale a thorough assessment needs to take place, in which both therapist and patient collect information to increase their understanding of the problem. Through this data-gathering process the patient learns to monitor the important features of her disorder (NATs, feelings, behaviours, safety behaviours, cognitive biases, etc.), and thereby gain further insight. To instigate this process effectively, the therapist must have a good theoretical understanding of generic cognitive therapy and the specifics of the patient's disorder (i.e. the cognitive models of depression, panic, OCD, PTSD, etc. – see Appendix I).

During this period, patients learn to break down situations using the rationale. In essence, they begin to become their own therapist. This process is often facilitated greatly through the use of suitable written material. Typically the therapist will illustrate relationships via diagrams or through the use of examples, stories and/or metaphors. If not performed adequately, the patient can feel misunderstood and alienated. She may become less active both in and out of sessions.

It is important to note that the patient's self-conceptualisation will not be entirely negative and dysfunctional. Therefore it is vital, when helping to define herself, that the therapist highlights the patient's strengths too. This more balanced conceptualisation may also help clarify areas that could be used effectively in promoting change. See Chapter 6 for a review of the main types of formulation used in the treatment of older people.

9.2.xi: Item 11 – Application of Change Methods

Change methodologies are cognitive and behavioural strategies employed by the therapist that are consistent with the conceptualisations and designed to promote therapeutic change (see Chapter 7). In relation to older people, Coon *et al.*'s (2007) case study describes various cognitive and behavioural strategies to be used at the initial, middle and last phase of treatment, and outlines the patient's responses over these periods. The key features of 'Application of Change Methods' are outlined in the CTS-R as follows.

> Key features: Therapist skilfully uses, and helps the patient to use, appropriate cognitive and behavioural techniques in line with the formulation. The therapist helps the patient devise appropriate cognitive methods to evaluate the key cognitions associated with distressing emotions, leading to major new perspectives and shifts in emotions. The therapist also helps the patient to apply behavioural techniques in line with the formulation. The therapist helps the patient to identify potential difficulties and think through the cognitive rationales for performing the tasks. The methods provide useful ways for the patient to test out cognitions practically and gain experience in dealing with high levels of emotion. The methods also allow the therapist to obtain feedback regarding the patient's level of understanding of prospective practical assignments (i.e. by the patient performing the task in-session).
> Three features need to be considered:
>
> (i) the appropriateness and range of both cognitive methods (e.g. cognitive change diaries, continua, distancing, responsibility charts, evaluating alternatives, examining pros and cons, determining meanings, imagery restructuring, etc.) and behavioural methods (e.g. behavioural diaries, behavioural tests, role-play, graded task assignments, response prevention, reinforcement of patient's work, modelling, applied relaxation, controlled breathing, etc.)
>
> (ii) the skills in the application of the methods
>
> (iii) the suitability of the methods for the needs of the patient (i.e. neither too difficult nor complex).

In deciding the appropriateness of a method it is important to determine whether the technique is a coherent strategy for change, following logically from the patient's formulation.

It is important to remember that the same technique can have a different function depending on the stage of therapy. For example, a diary can act as an assessment tool early on in therapy, but later may serve as an effective way of promoting the re-evaluation of thought processes. The timing of the intervention is vital and must be suited to the needs of the patient. For example, if a therapist challenges basic assumptions or core beliefs too early in therapy, before she has a clear understanding of the patient's view of the world, the patient could feel misunderstood and alienated. Only after sufficient socialisation should the therapist get the patient to start to reassess that level of cognition. The evaluation of automatic thoughts starts earlier, first as part of the socialisation into the cognitive model and then as a change method to improve mood and to improve on coping behaviour (see Chapter 2).

As with the application of cognitive techniques, the therapist must display skill in applying behavioural methodologies. The rationale for employing the tasks should be carefully explored, and clear learning goals established. It is important to remember that behavioural tasks play a key role with respect to the reinforcement of new learning. For example, by engaging a patient in a role-play, one can assess whether the theoretical information has been truly learned and integrated into her behavioural repertoire. The role-play will also allow the person to practise new skills. Behavioural tasks are also useful methodologies to employ prior to asking the patient to use the activity in a homework task. For example, it is useful to get the patient to complete monitoring sheets within the session in order to ensure the task is understood correctly. In this way the behavioural methodologies are important feedback and reinforcement activities.

In addition, the therapist needs to elicit and develop practical plans with the patient in order that effective change takes place (e.g. the where, what, when and how of a desensitisation programme). Indeed, part of the process of producing effective behavioural change is the development of plans that help to test out hypotheses and break unhelpful patterns of behaviour. For example, when setting a behavioural task, the therapist should get the patient to:

- think through the relevance of the assignment

- be confident in her ability to perform it, and be sufficiently motivated

- check through anticipated level of arousal

- plan what needs to be done carefully, and be cognisant of potential obstacles

- practise the behaviour, or aspects of it, in session

- be able to relate either success or failure to a change in perspective.

Gallagher-Thompson *et al.*'s CBT manual stresses the importance of using behavioural interventions with older people (Gallagher-Thompson and Thompson 2009). They think it is particularly important for patients to re-engage in pleasurable activities dropped as a result of their disorder. These clinicians also advocate training in relaxation to reduce potential anxieties associated with such re-engagement. Further, they recommend teaching in communication and assertion skills to help patients get their needs met (see also Dick *et al.* 1999).

9.2.xii: Item 12 – Homework Setting

Coon and Thompson (2003) note that patients who undertake homework tasks achieve better therapeutic outcomes. An excellent case study, providing a detailed description of how to adapt homework for an older adult with cognitive impairment, was published by Coon *et al.* (2007). This work explains how to overcome the numerous barriers one finds when trying to set assignments. The key features of 'Homework Setting' are outlined in the CTS-R as shown in the box.

Homework provides a structure for helping patients gather data and test hypotheses. It also encourages autonomy rather than reliance on the therapist, and therefore plays an important role in relapse management. To help empower the patient, and encourage compliance, the assignments should be negotiated. It also is important to explore possible difficulties, and how these might be overcome. To mitigate against potential problems, it is often useful for the therapist to suggest that the patient visualise carrying out the assignment to identify future problems.

In addition, it is desirable to get patients' feedback regarding a specific assignment (*'In what ways would it be useful to carry out such a task?'; 'Sometimes I explain things too quickly, so are there any aspects I could explain more clearly?' 'What will be learned from the accomplishment/non-accomplishment of the task?'*). These questions will help to determine whether the patient is both clear about the task, and understands the cognitive rationale underpinning it. It is vital that the patient is aware of the cognitive aspects of the assignment and how

Key features: This aspect concerns the setting of an appropriate homework task, one with clear and precise goals. The aims should be to negotiate an appropriate task for the stage of therapy in line with the conceptualisation; to ensure the patient understands the rationale for undertaking the task; to test out ideas, try new experiences, predict and deal with potential obstacles, and experiment with new ways of responding. This item ensures that the content of the therapy session is both relevant to, and integrated with, the patient's environment.

There are three aspects to this item:

(i) presence/absence of a homework task in which clear and precise goals have been set

(ii) the task should be derived from material discussed in the session, such that there is a clear understanding of what will be learned from performing the task

(iii) the homework task should be set jointly, and sufficient time should be allowed for it to be explained clearly (i.e. explain, discuss relevance, predict obstacles, etc.).

the results will impact on her interpretations. Indeed, one of the important features of homework tasks is that they bring about cognitive shift, and so they must be seen as more than just isolated behavioural assignments.

Homework assignments can be set at any time during the therapy session; however, because they tend to occur towards the end of the session, there is sometimes a tendency to rush the process. This tendency should be avoided, as it can lead to ill-prepared and unclear tasks being set. Hence it is good practice to leave sufficient time to set the homework appropriately.

Helpful descriptions of 'homework assignments' are outlined in Mohlman and Gorman's (2005) study with older GAD sufferers. In their sessions typical assignments included daily mood records, worry records, anxiety work sheets, relaxation and breathing logs, perspective taking, worry exposure, sleep hygiene, daily activity scheduling and behavioural practice. An example of each homework assignment was completed before leaving the session so that the therapist could ensure that the participant understood the assignment. Additionally, mid-week homework reminder/troubleshooting telephone calls were made by the therapists for the first four assignments. All homework tasks were photocopied and returned with ample feedback.

A helpful overview of the topic is also provided by Tompkins (2004), and useful guidelines in relation to older people have been outlined by Laidlaw and Thompson (2008) and Kazantzis et al. (2005). Kazantzis et al. (2005)

developed the Homework Rating Scale, a 12-item self-report questionnaire, assessing quality and quantity of compliance with homework assignments.

9.3: CONCLUSION

This chapter has examined issues to do with working competently with older people using the CTS-R. The whole area of therapeutic competence has received increased attention of late due to the extensive circulation of the Department of Health's publication of *The Competences Required to Deliver Effective Cognitive and Behavioural Therapy for People with Depression and with Anxiety Disorders* (Roth and Pilling 2007). In this document, Roth and Pilling describe a framework consisting of five domains (generic, basic CBT, specific CBT techniques, disorder-specific skills, metacompetences). A helpful summary of the framework in the form of an assessment tool is provided by Holland (2009).

Part of the renewed focus on competence is due to the introduction of the Improving Access to Psychological Therapies (IAPT 2006) programme. This initiative, which is discussed at length in Chapter 11, involves training a large number of therapists in a short space of time to deliver effective forms of psychotherapy; mainly CBT. In addition to clarifying what is meant by 'competent', the developers of the programme are stressing the importance of employing effective training and supervision methods. In relation to the above chapter, the CTS-R has been used both as a training and supervision tool (James, Milne and Morse 2008; Milne 2008) and, in an adapted form, as a method for assessing competent supervision skills (James *et al.* 2005).

Chapter 10

Use of Psychotherapy in the Treatment of Challenging Behaviours in Care Facilities: A Staff-Centred, Person-Focused Approach

10.1: INTRODUCTION

This chapter outlines therapeutic work undertaken with patients in the lower quadrants of the adaptation grid presented in Chapter 3 (Figure 3.1). It describes the treatment of a person exhibiting challenging behaviours in a care home setting. Challenging behaviours, also known as Behavioural and Psychological Symptoms of Dementia, are actions or activities that cause difficulties for either the person or others within the settings they are performed. Table 10.1 outlines some of the typical behaviours classified as challenging.

When attempting to understand CBs, Emerson (1998) claims that there are three important aspects to take account of:

CB is a social construct – CBs usually transgress some social rule within a particular context. The significance of the transgression will depend on the nature of the behaviour, the setting and how carers interpret it. Hence their treatment is context specific, and thus it makes sense to try to deal with the behaviour within the setting it is being performed in rather than simply moving the person elsewhere. It is also illogical not to 'treat' the setting (i.e. alter the environment, work with the staff), because if the person engaging in the CBs is removed temporarily (e.g. an inpatient admittance) as soon as she returns the behaviour is likely to re-emerge.

Table 10.1: List of common challenging behaviours

Aggressive forms of CBs	Non-aggressive forms of CBs
Hitting	Repetitive noise
Kicking	Repetitive questions
Grabbing	Making strange noises
Pushing	Constant requests for help
Nipping	Eating/drinking excessively
Scratching	Over-activity
Biting	Pacing
Spitting	General agitation
Choking	Following others/trailing
Hair pulling	Inappropriate exposure of parts of body
Tripping	Masturbating in public areas
Throwing objects	Urinating in inappropriate places
Stick prodding	Smearing
Stabbing	Handling things inappropriately
Swearing	Dismantling objects
Shouting	Hoarding things
Physical sexual assault	Hiding items
Verbal sexual advances	Falling intentionally
Acts of self harm	Eating inappropriate substances
	Non-compliance

CBs have wide-ranging personal and social consequences – the behaviours tend to affect not only the quality of life of the resident, but also that of the carers and others in close proximity (e.g. fellow residents). How these 'other' individuals respond to the perpetrator is likely to have a major impact on her behaviour. Some responses may include abuse, exclusion and deprivation, which clearly will result in detrimental consequences for the resident's well-being. Thus when devising appropriate interventions, a therapist must both reduce the impact of the behaviour (frequency, duration), and attend to any negative reactions and consequences associated with the CB.

CBs are defined by their presentation and impact – CBs vary greatly in their manifestation and aetiology (see Table 10.1). Thus no one management approach alone will be appropriate for dealing with all forms of CB.

As the above definition highlights, an important issue concerning CBs is how they are interpreted. For example, aggression is usually seen as being more challenging if perceived as intentional. Indeed, the degree to which the perpetrator is perceived to have intended her disruptive behaviour is crucial in determining the carer's reaction to that behaviour.

Adler (1927) has provided a useful framework for analysing the mechanisms behind a person's actions at a more concrete level. He suggests that therapists should look for evidence for each of the elements listed in Table 10.2.

Table 10.2: Adler's explanation for behaviour

Does the person's behaviour help:	
a.	to initiate an emotional state?
b.	to stop an emotional state?
c.	to avoid an emotional state?
d.	to reduce the intensity of an emotional state?
e.	to intensify an emotional state?
f.	to maintain an emotional state?
g.	to elicit a response from the physical environment?
h.	to elicit a response from the interpersonal environment?
i.	to act in a way that is consistent with personal values, standards and goals?

The above section has highlighted that CBs come in many forms and have a wide-ranging impact on people and the environment. For this reason the treatment needs to be systemic in nature. It suggests that people's responses to the individual displaying the CB are likely to significantly affect the patients and the manifestation of the behaviour; in some cases the responses may exacerbate the disruptive behaviour. A crucial feature in determining carers' abilities to manage the CB is their interpretation of its causal roots.

The present case study illustrates a form of psychotherapy that has been used over the last ten years in Newcastle-upon-Tyne, UK, for this patient group (James 1999; James, Mackenzie, Stephenson and Roe 2006). The approach employed by the Newcastle Challenging Behaviour Service (NCBS) is a formulation-led, case-specific method that shares features with the successful non-pharmacological interventions undertaken by Cohen-Mansfield, Libin and Marx (2007) and Bird, Llewellyn-Jones and Korten (2009).

The approach is called a 'staff-centred, person-focused' method due to the fact it is systemic, viewing the staff's input as crucial to the treatment.

The chapter will illustrate the following:

1. a formulation-led, systemic approach, incorporating cognitive behaviour therapy principles, for treating challenging behaviours

2. the key structural and process features of the 'Newcastle' framework

3. the range of psychotherapeutic skills required to work competently with residents and staff in 24-hour care facilities.

10.2: DESCRIPTION OF THE NCBS AND ITS TREATMENT PHILOSOPHY

The NCBS was developed because of a gap in the existing clinical services in the area, which meant that some of the most complex people in our communities were not receiving adequate psychological care. Traditionally, the private sector care homes had proven difficult places to work into, because they had not previously received sustained attention from health service psychotherapists. Thus they were rather wary of input when it was offered, preferring medication to therapy, owing to the clinical commitments the latter entailed. This, in turn, had made NHS therapists reluctant to engage with these settings due to the poor reception they received (James, Powell and Kendell 2003a, 2003b). In order to break this negative cycle, the NCBS was established, with the following aims:

- to treat challenging behaviour in a competent and person-centred manner

- to treat challenging behaviour in the setting in which it was being exhibited

- to work collaboratively with care facilities to improve the well-being of people in care

- to prevent unnecessary admissions to hospital

- to facilitate easier discharge from hospital to appropriate care settings

- to facilitate transfers of patients to appropriate care settings (from hospital to care facilities and between care facilities)

- to develop links with statutory and regulatory organisations.

Currently the NCBS is made up of two senior nurses and four mid-grade nurses. It is managed by a psychologist and receives sessional input from a psychiatrist. Over the last decade, 1000+ people have received interventions using this approach; currently the NCBS sees approximately 200 residents per year. Empirical evaluation of the work has demonstrated its efficacy (Wood-Mitchell *et al.* 2007). I believe the reasons for its success are to do with its values and desire to empower all people involved in dealing with the 'problematic' behaviours (i.e. the resident, staff, family, care home manager). This systemic stance helps to ensure that the formulation-led care plans are initiated and adhered to appropriately.

The formulation framework used by the NCBS draws heavily from Cohen-Mansfield's (2000a) model for challenging behaviour. This 'needs-based' model highlights the fact that challenging behaviours are usually *not* unpredictable random actions, rather they are rational activities with a high degree of predictability. Indeed, frequently the behaviours are manifestations of patients' attempts to cope in situations they are misperceiving or are confused by. Cohen-Mansfield's framework involves obtaining two types of information: (i) background features (history, premorbid personality, physical health status) and (ii) a comprehensive description of the challenging episodes. The latter are the verbal and non-verbal signs displayed by the person. By putting these two types of information together, one is in a stronger position to accurately identify the person's coping strategy or the need driving the coping response – e.g. to be free from pain, respond to an imagined attacker, defend oneself from perceived molestation during a personal care activity (see Chapter 6).

The case outlined here is typical of the patients seen by a member of the team from the NCBS, and has been discussed previously by members of the team (Kennedy and Mackenzie 2007). First, an overview of the case is presented, in terms of the referral letter, assessment, formulation and treatment. Following this, the structural and process features associated with the case are unpacked and discussed in order to provide greater learning opportunities.

10.3: OVERVIEW OF THE CASE
10.3.i: Referral from the medical practitioner

Dear Challenging Behaviour Team,

I would be grateful if you would see Mr Donald MacKay, aged 90, residing at Rosey Meadows care home. Staff report they are finding it difficult to manage his increasingly aggressive behaviours and inappropriate urination. Donald was admitted to the home six months previously as an emergency admission due to mobility problems and dehydration. Donald has significant visual and hearing impairments that make communication with him difficult; this also means that a Mini-Mental State (Folstein, Folstein and McHugh 1975) cognitive assessment could not be completed.

The home manager informs me that Donald has recently become 'demanding', wanting things to be done immediately, and he can become physically aggressive when things are not forthcoming. He is also urinating in communal areas in the home and in the presence of other residents.

I have undertaken a physical examination and all tests have been negative and thus there is no obvious physical reason for his deterioration. I would be grateful for your support in this matter. I have resisted the pressure to prescribe any anti-psychotics thus far due the increased risk of falls, with the promise of a speedy intervention from your team.

Yours sincerely, Consultant Psychiatrist

10.3.ii: Assessment

The referral was discussed at a team meeting and allocated to a member of the service; the therapist subsequently visited the care home. On the first visit it was evident that some carers, although not all, were distressed by Donald's physical aggression. One carer was afraid to work with him because she had been nipped badly. Increasingly, Donald was responding to personal care interventions by spitting, hitting, slapping, kicking, grabbing and scratching.

When waiting for his meals, Donald would sometimes become verbally and physically aggressive, throwing objects such as cups if he could not get what he wanted immediately. Staff found him very difficult to please, particularly with regard to meals – he would frequently refuse the choices he had made earlier, but when offered alternatives would refuse these too. Donald was also urinating inappropriately in his room, the dining room and lounge.

Not all the information provided from the staff was negative. Indeed, he was recognised as being someone who liked to 'have a chat' and who made efforts to talk with staff and fellow residents. Staff would engage him in conversation when possible, though on occasions it was difficult to understand what he was saying.

In order to obtain factual information about his various behaviours, a series of monitoring charts were explained and given to the staff. The therapist left some examples of completed charts at the home to provide templates to assist with their completion.

Information about Donald was also obtained from both case notes held in the care home and medical notes held at the hospital. He, and his advocate, gave permission for the therapist to consult with his medical practitioner.

Further information was obtained from a sister although she was unable to give many details because she had lost contact with her brother in recent years.

At this stage the therapist's role was mainly to engage in a fact-finding process in relation to both his past (biography, health status, etc.) and his present behaviours. The next stage involved putting the information together into a presentation format to assist the staff to understand and empathise with Donald's current experiences of living in care. A specific session was organised to do this; this was called the Information Sharing Session (ISS, see below). It is suggested that armed with this greater level of awareness gained during the ISS, staff would be able to re-conceptualise his behaviours.

10.3.iii: Information Sharing Session (ISS) and formulation

All cases seen by NCBS receive an Information Sharing Session (ISS), which is a 60-minute meeting coordinated by the therapist and conducted at the care home. At this meeting all the background information collected is presented, and put together with the data from the behavioural charts. During the session, the therapist helps the staff to make links and reflect on the behaviours in relation to the resident's needs. Thus, by the end of the session they will have developed ideas about what might be underpinning his behaviours, and from these ideas start to develop appropriate interventions. The therapist always asks that as many of the staff as possible attend the ISS. Details of the information that was presented to the staff regarding Donald are outlined below:

Background details:

- Donald has always been very physically active. He worked all his life in physically demanding jobs, and played competitive football, and used to love to walk for miles.

- Donald has been self-reliant all his life. He is used to making his own choices – he may be uncomfortable about being dependent on others.

- While living alone after his wife's death, Donald was burgled. After this he felt very vulnerable – he set up traps around the house to slow down any potential intruders. Some of these fears and the anger may have stayed with him.

- Donald has very poor eyesight – he has cataracts. His perceptual difficulties mean that he sometimes misidentifies objects. He has also been diagnosed with Charles Bonnet Syndrome, a condition that causes visual hallucinations. These visual hallucinations can be very vivid and (for some people) unpleasant, frightening and disorientating. Donald is reported to have experienced visual hallucinations. However, they do not appear to cause him distress.

- Donald is not always orientated in time or place. Also, the speed at which he thinks has slowed considerably. When people are approaching him or moving around him he may not fully, or immediately, understand what is happening. He may also forget that certain things have happened, e.g. that he has already had his tablets.

During the ISS, the staff also provided further information from their own observations of Donald:

- He experiences great difficulties in hearing and understanding what others are saying to him. While his speech can be clear, and at times he can communicate well, there are also times when he mutters and his speech is difficult to follow. These communication problems appear to be a source of frustration to him.

- Donald enjoys the company of others, but his communication difficulties make socialising with staff and other residents hard for him. He has a sense of humour and can be playful, and he likes to be entertained (e.g. he enjoys armchair exercise, and 'sing-alongs' and carers have found that he is using a hearing device (inappropriately) for 'karaoke' i.e. he will sing into the microphone amusing himself and his carers).

Towards the end of the ISS, armed with the above formulation, the therapist helped the staff to think about Donald's experiences of his current situation. This process involved getting the staff to empathise with his situation, and hypothesise about his needs. The following views emerged regarding Donald and his behaviour:

- He is confused when he senses movement around him because he cannot hear properly or see what is going on – e.g. he has knocked his tablets over accidentally when reaching for them, and he has sometimes hit out at staff when they have been standing beside him.

- At times, he probably feels that his space is being invaded. That is why he says 'Get out of here'; 'Go away'.

- It is likely that he feels he needs to defend himself.

- He would like more choice and control over what is happening to him. He often says: 'It's my room – I can do what I want.'

- He probably feels isolated and bored.

Typically at the end of the session, the therapist assists the staff to devise some appropriate interventions. These interventions form the basis of a care plan (see next section). A written summary of the discussions from the ISS was given to the staff on the therapist's next visit. This summary is termed the 'formulation', and it provides a concise description of the resident's behaviour in relation to background information (Figure 10.1).

10.3.iv: Intervention and care plan

Based on ideas discussed in the ISS, the following five interventions were agreed, summarised and attached to the formulation sheet. These care plans are a user-friendly synopsis of the interventions suggested by the staff during the ISS.

CARE PLAN

1. Communicate more effectively: Approach Donald slowly and calmly from the front. Speak loudly and clearly before you get too close so that he can recognise who you are. It helps to communicate face-to-face at eye level, using simple language – use key words spoken very clearly, e.g. 'Cup of tea, Donald?' (showing him a cup) or 'Your tablets, Donald?' (showing him the tablets). Let Donald know what you are about to do, and engage him in conversation (e.g. about activities that are going to happen).

Staff know that he is sociable and likes to chat. Thus talking with him will make him feel valued and cared for. It will also add interest to his day.

2. Increase his sense of control and choice: Give Donald as much choice as possible – ask him 'Can I come in? Is it all right if I…? Would you like to…?' When possible, prepare in advance for Donald's needs so that he doesn't have to wait or ask for things (e.g. always have the sugar near at hand). This will give Donald a better sense of control over situations and will help him feel independent and respected.

3. Increase independence to reduce frustration: When Donald becomes aggressive, give him space, leaving him time to calm down. Then re-engage

Life story

90 years of age.
Father died in 1914 during World War 1. Mother owned her own business – she had a physical disability and Donald would help her.
During his teens Donald had rheumatic fever. In his youth he played competitive football.
Worked on buildings and retired at age 65. Married to Jane, who had dementia. Jane also had a physical disability in later life and Donald cared for her. She died ten years ago. Sister Margaret alive, but little contact with each other.

Personality

Likes to be called by his full name. A private person, pleasant and friendly but not very outgoing (spending much of his time alone or with his late wife) – but does like to talk with other people and enjoys sitting in the dining room and sitting room watching the activity around him. Liked walking and used to walk for miles.
Worked hard all of his life. Known to sing when in a good mood and likes to join in with group singing.
Recently has become quite demanding, wanting his needs to be met immediately. Changes his mind frequently about what he wants to eat. Insists on having soft food – asks for porridge, cake and custard. Prefers sweet foods – likes four sugars in his tea, pears and custard and custard creams. Also used to like pork crackling. Has a sense of humour (possibly likes to tease). Has enjoyed visiting entertainers, a day trip, parties, church services and fortnightly armchair exercise sessions held in the home.

Neurological impairment

1995 Charles Bonnet Syndrome, dementia and visual hallucinations MMSE 8/30 difficulties. Disorientated in time and place.

Medication

Only for physical ailments.

Physical health

Various age-related physical problems
Emergency admission – dehydrated and 'off his legs': has not regained ability to walk.
Sleeps well – sitting up.
No teeth – tried wearing dentures but prefers not to use them.
Prone to chest infections.

Conversations and vocalisations

Donald states that staff are liars and too rough with him. When refusing things he says 'Get out of here, go home' 'Go away' 'Liar' 'It's my room'.

Triggers

When Donald has communication difficulties he often gets frustrated and angry. Halluoinations may act as triggers.

Behaviours

Verbal aggression (swearing, muttering, threatening to get someone to 'chop off' staff's heads or kill them).
Physical aggression (spitting, hitting, slapping, kicking, grabbing, scratching and nipping; throwing objects).
Inappropriate urination (despite provision of a bottle).

Needs and possible thoughts

To communicate better with staff.
To feel more independent – that he has choice and is in control.
Reassurance.
Engagement in activity.

Social environment

Lived alone after wife died and managed fairly well. Neighbour visited him at home on a daily basis.
While living alone was burgled – following this set up traps around the house to impede any intruders. Kept walking sticks by him at all times as a form of protection.
Has been in residential care for six months.

Mental health

As a result of communication difficulties Donald becomes distressed and agitated. Mood can alter rapidly.

Appearance

Can rapidly become agitated/angry, particularly when he thinks his rights are being infringed.

him and explain what you are trying to do, or ask him what is upsetting him. Give lots of reassurance by telling Donald that you want to help him. Ask him if there is anything you can do for him, and give him positive feedback when he is interacting in a positive way with you. If there are things that he is able to do for you when you are caring for him, ask him for his help. This will help him to feel useful and cared for and will boost his self-esteem.

4. Encourage him to urinate in urine bottles: Continue with existing programme aimed at helping him to use the toilet, but also place more urine bottles in his room. His current preference to wee in large containers (e.g. waste bins) may be due to his poor sight and perceptual difficulties. Thus give him better access to the large-sized urine bottles (or experiment with the use of washable plastic bins or containers). Use absorbent pads in those areas where he is likely to urinate to reduce the likelihood of him slipping on a wet floor.

5. Increase his levels of stimulation and activity: Donald enjoys sing-alongs, armchair exercise sessions, visiting entertainers, parties and church services. Though he cannot see or hear the TV clearly, he may still enjoy 'watching' TV with other residents – sitting facing the TV in a group may increase his sense of belonging. Donald may also enjoy listening to songs, music or football commentaries on the radio. His receptive abilities might be improved by experimenting with the bass and treble controls on the music system. The care home, or his sister may want to purchase an audio amplifier which may assist with his hearing.

10.3.v: Outcome
After a period of three weeks, during which the member of the NCBS visited to check on the implementation of the interventions, staff reported a marked improvement in Donald's mood. Donald appeared more relaxed, less demanding and generally more playful. He also showed more signs of affection with some carers. For example, when waiting for staff to attend him, rather than appearing frustrated and making angry demands, Donald would sing his request to staff in an easy and relaxed manner. His aggressive behaviours during care episodes reduced in frequency, with Donald becoming much more likely to respond cheerfully and affectionately towards staff during interactions. The care plan directed at the 'inappropriate' urination had a limited impact on his behaviour. However the practical measures, coupled with the staff's greater understanding of the behaviour, meant that they found this situation more manageable.

The latter section gave an overview of the case; the following sections provide a guide and theoretical perspective on using the Newcastle framework. The clinical work undertaken with Donald is thus unpacked to illustrate the change mechanisms underpinning the therapist's approach. It is my view that this approach is consistent with a label of a 'psychotherapy'. This is a term seldomly used in this area, although Bird *et al.* (2009) have also started to describe their interventions in this manner.

10.4: PROTOCOL OF THE NEWCASTLE APPROACH

This section examines the methodology used in more detail, reviewing the mechanism of change employed with Donald.

There are a number of stages to consider when using the NCBS's 14-week approach and these are outlined in Table 10.3. As one can see, it is a 'front-loaded' method of working, with most of the intensive work taking place in the first few weeks of the case. In the later stages the therapist tends to be monitoring and tweaking both the formulation and interventions as a consequence of staff feedback.

In the following sections we will examine the process and structural features of the approach from assessment through to outcome.

10.5: PROCESS AND STRUCTURAL FEATURES OF THE ASSESSMENT PHASE

The function of the assessment is twofold, first to collect relevant data to help inform the intervention, and second to collect the information in a manner that increases the likelihood that the staff will carry out the interventions. The latter requires therapeutic engagement with the staff: empathising; collaborating; asking Socratic questions (see Table 10.4, adapted from Fossey and James 2007). Indeed, it is by using such processes that the NCBS therapist can encourage staff to become inquisitive to learn more about the patient and the causes of the 'target' behaviour.

Thus this method can be seen as a repersonalisation process (Kitwood 1997). This is the reverse of Kitwood's earlier notion of depersonalisation, whereby residents in care often lose their sense of identities due to staff not knowing, or not having regard, for them and their personal histories. Using the Newcastle approach, repersonalisation begins during the information collection phase. The repersonalisation process was clearly evident in the case of Donald, as it became clear that the staff knew little about him. Thus, as one can see, the approach is a 'systemic' methodology, with every endeavour being made to make the staff true stakeholders in the treatment strategy.

Table 10.3: Stages engaged in by NCBS therapist

Guiding ethos: When using the approach in care settings, it is always important for staff to feel they are involved in the various stages of the work; from the assessment to the delivery of the intervention.

Week 1: Having received the referral, and been allocated the case, the therapist commences the 'fact-finding' process. An important step is to make sure that all the physical checks have been completed by the medical practitioner to ensure that the problematic behaviour has not arisen from either an acute infection or transient difficulty (e.g. pain resulting from a fall, constipation).

Wk 2: By the second week, the therapist will have made contact with the home on a number of occasions and spoken to the relevant people, including the patient. In the conversations with staff, it is made clear what the service's expectations are. To reinforce the latter issue, an information sheet is left with the home describing the service and each other's responsibilities in delivering the package of care. During this week further information is collected from the various sources, and a detailed analysis of the behaviour is undertaken via monitoring charts. A pre-treatment measure is undertaken with the patient's key worker (i.e. Neuropsychiatric Inventory, Cummings *et al.* 1994).

Wk 3: The information collected thus far starts to undergo analysis, and greater clarification and specification of the problems are made. If not done previously, the feedback from the family is added to the growing data set.

Wk 4/5: The main event taking place in this phase is the delivery of the Information Sharing Session (ISS). This is a specific session, attended by staff in the care setting (ideally with all levels of staff represented), lasting approximately an hour. In these sessions, the information about the person's problematic behaviour is presented in the context of her background. The idea of the session is to develop an understanding of the behaviour in relation to the wider context, allowing staff to speculate on the patient's 'needs' i.e. what is driving the behaviour. This process helps to inform the interventions, which are developed by staff during the ISS. One of the goals of the Newcastle therapist is to ensure that the interventions devised meet the Specific Measurable Achievable Relevant and Timely (SMART) criteria.

The therapist facilitates the meeting using effective questioning techniques, feedback, summarising, education, challenging strategies and guided reflection techniques. These methods are designed to get the staff to 'step back' from the situation, and look afresh at the behaviour within its historical and situational context. Collaboration with staff is particularly important when trying to identify the patient's needs and possible interpretation of the situation.

Thus the goal of the ISS is to assist staff to become more knowledgeable, empowered and motivated to improve the resident's well-being, through the setting of appropriate interventions. Within the process, an effective ISS will have used information from many sources to give staff an understanding of what factors are contributing towards the patient's actions Within this approach, it is vital that the interventions are developed by the staff, so that they have ownership of the treatment process.

Table 10.3: Stages engaged in by NCBS therapist *cont.*

Wk 6: Following the ISS, it is the therapist's responsibility to take away the details discussed at the meeting, and recorded on the flip chart, to produce an A4 summary sheet (aka formulation, Figure 10.1). Attached to the formulation sheet will be a detailed description of the interventions (i.e. a care plan). A vital feature underpinning the success of the interventions is that they are carried out consistently and uniformly by all staff. To gauge how well the information is disseminated, the home is provided with a sheet on which all staff must sign to indicate that they have read and understood the invention sheet.

Wk 7–11: The remaining sessions involve follow-up work, visiting the home to ensure the interventions are being carried out consistently. In some cases, the formulation may require changing or the interventions tweaking.

Wk 12–14: Unless there are exceptional reasons for continuing input, this milestone results in discharge. At this meeting a discharge interview takes place, where the key worker is asked to complete a post-treatment NPI.

It is evident from Table 10.4 that it requires good interpersonal skills to work into care settings. Further it is my belief that the skills of a competent clinician in this area would match the abilities of therapists working in any other area of mental health.

The structural framework in which the information is presented is called the formulation. This framework is outlined in detail below and presented diagrammatically in Figure 10.2 (also see Figure 10.1).

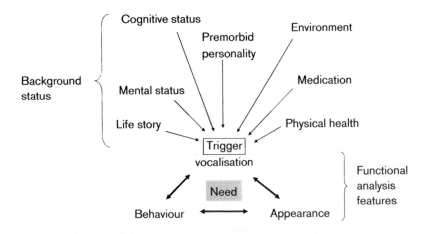

Figure 10.2: Formulation template (James 1999)

Table 10.4: Some of the skills required to work with staff in care facilities

Technique	Definition	Examples: statements you might hear NCBS member say with a respect to theme
Setting goals of the ISS	Negotiating with the staff about the contents and preferred methods of discussion during ISS.	Today we're going to be discussing Donald's behaviour and some of the reasons for him communicating this way. In your view what are the three things it's essential that we talk through before finishing the session?
Collaborating	Ensuring the staff feel part of the teaching process, encouraging them to be active participants.	You've had lots of experience of this, so before I discuss this issue further, who can tell us what's the best thing to say to him when he calls you a 'bitch'.
Gathering information	Fact finding and obtaining information from the staff about the situation, feelings, thoughts and/or behaviours.	What time does he tend to wake up? What expression did he have on his face after he hit you?
Feedback	Providing specific feedback that aids learning, and asking for feedback to help guide the teaching.	The current care plan is too vague. The ideas we have discussed today are much clearer and specific, well done!
Summarising/ clarifying	Chunking information to help clarify links and highlight key features.	Great, now let's see if I understand what you did there. You saw him searching for the toilet, and knew he'd be too embarrassed to ask you, so you asked if he'd like to wash his hands and then guided him to the sink in the toilet.
Supporting and understanding	Providing verbal and non-verbal signs that provide reassurance and encouragement to the staff.	That was difficult, but you seemed to have handled it really, really well.
Informing/ educating	Providing factual information aimed at increasing staff's knowledge.	Multi-infarct dementia is a type of vascular dementia. It is often very difficult to distinguish multi-infarct from Alzheimer's disease.
Aiding reflection	Working with the staff to get them to think through issues in order to come to an increased understanding of key issues.	Let's stop a second and think through the implications of this. If, indeed, pain is a common cause of challenging behaviour, what should we do?

Table 10.4: Some of the skills required to work with staff in care facilities *cont.*

Technique	Definition	Examples: statements you might her NCBS member say with a respect to theme
Formulating	Working with the staff to develop a framework that helps to explain residents' behaviours and needs.	OK, we seem to have gathered quite a lot of information about Donald now. Let's put it all together and see how it helps explain why he's so depressed.
Self-disclosing	Informing staff about personal experiences that help to illustrate issues or concepts.	I must admit, I wasn't aware that diabetes was a side-effect of neuroleptic use. One of the nurses told me during our training session two weeks ago.
Challenging	Getting the staff to rethink their views, often by pointing out inconsistencies in their thinking.	Well, both of you can't be right. One of you is saying he is like this with everyone, while the other thinks he is cooperative when with certain individuals.
Disagreeing	Taking a different viewpoint to the staff, in order to highlight an alternative perspective.	I am going to have to disagree with that. He is not just being awkward. Remember he has a dementia and thus can struggle at times to make sense of what is happening to him during personal care tasks.
Behavioural tasks	Using activity-based tasks (role-play, modelling) to help demonstrate skills.	Now that we have discussed the problems and possible strategies for communicating with Donald, let's try to demonstrate it via a role-play.

1. Background assessment

Background details concerning the person's life and health status etc. are collected from staff and family (see section 10.7).

2. Assessment of the triggers

Information is obtained to determine the events or people who are likely to elicit the behaviours. Diaries and assessment charts are helpful to identify the triggers.

| Behavioural chart for .... |
| Target behaviour ....
 Please record any episodes of the above behaviour (day/night).
 Aim – to record frequency and circumstances of incidents. |

Date and time	What was the person doing just before the incident? (A – antecedent)
Where the incident occurred	What did you see happen? (B – actual behaviour)
Which staff were involved (initials)	

What did the person say at the time of the incident?

How did the person appear at the time of the incident? (maybe more than one tick)

Angry	☐	Frustrated	☐
Anxious	☐	Happy	☐
Bored	☐	Irritable	☐
Content	☐	Physically unwell	☐
Depressed	☐	Restless	☐
Despairing	☐	Sad	☐
Frightened	☐	Worried	☐

How was the situation resolved? (C – consequences)

A – Antecedents are the features happening just prior to the emergence of the behaviour that may have served to trigger or reinforce it.
B – Behaviours are simply the factual acts witnessed by the staff. The staff are taught not to interpret the behaviour, rather provide factual details.
C* – Consequences are the responses of others to the behavioural disturbance. An analysis of this aspect helps to determine what the person might be achieving by acting this way. Also by examining the consequences, one can check the behaviour is not being inadvertently reinforced.

* Answers in this column give therapists ideas for interventions, and provide clues about which staff are dealing with the situation well (or not so well).

Figure 10.3: Example of a behavioural chart incorporating an ABC analysis together with elements of the Newcastle approach

3. Assessment of the challenging behaviour

It is very important to obtain a rich description of the challenging behaviour. This, again, can be done through personal observations of staff, the use of diaries and assessment charts. An example of one of the assessment charts used by the service is presented in Figure 10.3.

4. Formal assessment measure

The NCBS routinely use the Neuropsychiatric Inventory (Cummings *et al.* 1994) as a pre-/post-assessment measure; the version used includes the caregiver distress scale (i.e. the NPI-D). This informant-rated scale measures both the frequency and severity of problematic behaviours and the emotional/psychological distress of caregivers in relation to 12 neuropsychiatric symptoms. For each of the 12 symptoms, a behaviour score is obtained by multiplying the frequency (1–4) by the perceived severity of the behaviour (1–3). A total behaviour score is achieved by adding the individual behaviour scores of each symptom (maximum score = 144). The distress caused to caregivers for each symptom is also scored (0–5), and then totalled (maximum score = 60).

In the case of Donald, prior to treatment the carers rated the frequency and severity of Donald's behaviours as 19 and staff distress as 12. At the end of treatment these scores were reduced to 10 and 4 respectively.

10.6: INFORMATION SHARING SESSION (ISS) AND GOAL-SETTING PROCESS

In the ISS, all the background information collected is presented and put together with the data from the behavioural charts. Patterns are explored and detected, potential triggers elucidated, staff are encouraged to relate their experiences of the behaviour and then lessons are unpicked from these accounts. In many respects it is the therapeutic work done in the ISS that most resembles a traditional session of psychotherapy for the therapist. As with any therapy, the goal of the ISS is to arrive at a shared conceptual understanding of the problem and develop a plan to deal with it. In terms of the Newcastle model, the problematic behaviour is perceived as an expression of an unmet need on the part of the resident (Cohen-Mansfield 2000a). By the end of the ISS a set of interventions and approaches will have been developed in collaboration with the staff. It is relevant to note that the therapist plays a major role in ensuring that the goals are realistic and feasible. Indeed, for each intervention that therapist is routinely instructed to employ the SMART criteria with respect to the goal setting (Fossey and James 2007). Further discussion about the goals is presented in the section on interventions (section 10.8).

10.7: FORMULATION

Following the Information Sharing Session (ISS), a formulation is produced (see Figure 10.1). Much of the information in Figure 10.1 will already have been presented to the staff in the ISS via a flip chart. This flip chart information will have helped generate discussion and assisted the staff to achieve a greater level of understanding regarding Donald's behaviour. However, with respect to the formulation the information is condensed and written-up in the form of a single A4 sheet of paper. The experience of the Newcastle team suggests that supplying staff with an overly comprehensive formulation presented on multiple sheets is both offputting and less likely to be read. In contrast, it has been found that a single formulation sheet with a brief care plan attached provides the most effective treatment strategy The following section discusses the components presented in Figures 10.1 and 10.2, both the background features and the features associated with the analyses of the problematic behaviours.

10.7.i: Background status
PHYSICAL HEALTH

Many older people experience declining physical health (for example, visual and auditory problems) and age-related illness (arthritis, backache, cancer, toothache, constipation and chiropody ailments). It is important to note that many challenging behaviours are related to pain and physical discomfort, which is often worsened during staff/resident interactions (such as toileting, transfers and washing).

PREMORBID PERSONALITY

It is important to recognise that a person's personality endures through the course of dementia; their individuality will be apparent in various ways and at various stages of the illness. People with severe dementia may still wish to express lifestyle preferences (relating, for example, to accommodation, religious practices, food and sexual orientation). While some personality changes are related to changes in brain pathology, others are associated with psychological factors – for example, someone with dementia may feel they are vulnerable, become more emotional and seek out more physical attention. Finding out how the person coped with difficulties in the past can be revealing. Current problems may be explained by someone being unable to use familiar methods of coping, such as managing stress by going out for a walk.

MENTAL STATUS

Mental health problems are common and it is important to acknowledge their potential influence. Past difficulties may interact with current problems; for example, a person with long-standing social phobic tendencies who develops dementia and moves into residential care may feel very anxious in a busy communal room (James and Sabin 2002). Changes in brain pathology may result in psychotic symptoms such as visual hallucinations, paranoid ideations or delusions of theft.

LIFE STORY

Gathering information about the person's life, relationships, roles and losses is critically important in order to put their behaviour in context. In many types of dementia, the person's long-term and procedural memory (memory for performing familiar roles, actions, music and dance, etc.) often remains relatively preserved. Such information can be used to engage the person in meaningful activities: for example, providing an ex-cleaner with cleaning materials and an area of the home to brush and polish. Knowledge of the person's life story is therefore crucial both in understanding her behaviour and what they are communicating and in establishing a good therapeutic relationship. Important parts of the person's life story (losses, traumas) may also re-emerge during the development of the dementia.

ENVIRONMENT

Environmental factors are important influences on the well-being of older people owing to their levels of dependency. This is particularly the case for people with dementia who have particular difficulties with memory, problem-solving and orientation. We need to recognise the link between people's level of well-being and the opportunities they have to engage in fulfilling personal relationships. It is also worth checking whether a person's 'challenging behaviour' might be triggered by her being too hot, too cold, hungry or being exposed to excessive stimulation such as a loud television or radio.

COGNITIVE STATUS

The way in which a person experiences an event will be affected by their ability to process information. All cognitive impairments must be taken into account. Deficits in memory or problem-solving ability may lead to distress, particularly when a person has insight into their difficulties. Mental health problems such as anxiety and depression may add to cognitive difficulties, decreasing concentration and having a negative effect on memory and problem-solving skills. Different forms of dementia affect different abilities and they also progress at different rates.

MEDICATION

The framework also considers the effect of medication. By considering medication and physical health as important, the framework acknowledges biological factors as well as social and psychological factors. The team often tries to minimise the use of neuroleptic drugs, but frequently encourages the use of pain relief and anti-depressant medications. However, where medication is required, it is tailored to the needs of the individual and is always in keeping with the information obtained from the formulation as per current guidelines (Howard *et al.* 2001; Sink, Holden and Yaffe 2005).

Information on all the background factors listed above is normally obtained by examining case files, speaking to carers and relatives, and the person with dementia where possible. Specific forms have been devised by the NCBS to aid data collection, such as the personal profile questionnaires. These are questionnaires given to family that ask about the person's past, likes, dislikes, coping style, favourite pastimes, foods, music preferences, etc.

10.7.ii: Observing and understanding the behaviour

Figures 10.1 and 10.2 show a triangle comprised of three themes: vocalisation, appearance and behaviour. The framework uses this triad to understand the person's experience of the episode of challenging behaviour. One way of finding out what a person is experiencing is to talk to her; however, the person with dementia may not always be able to tell you what is driving her behaviour. Valuable information can be gained simply by observing the person. There are three key features to pay attention to:

- the person's behaviour

- what they say and/or vocalise (whether coherent or not)

- how they appear to be feeling (i.e. the person's appearance).

These observations can give us important clues to what patients are thinking and towards a better understanding of their needs. It is relevant to note that if there is more than one challenging behaviour present, there will be more than one trigger and triad.

TRIGGERS

The box labelled 'triggers' is situated between the background details and the triad. This box simply highlights the circumstances in which the problematic behaviours are observed.

BEHAVIOUR

Part of the assessment involves gathering details of what exactly happens during an episode of challenging behaviour (i.e. a functional analysis). General labels such as 'aggression' or 'wandering' tell us little about what a person is actually doing, and less about why they are doing it. Thus a careful analysis of the behaviour is essential.

Such an analysis will need to consider antecedents and consequences, and where and with whom the behaviour does and does not occur (see Figure 10.3).

CONVERSATIONS OR VOCALISATIONS

It is helpful to gather information about the patients' difficulties by asking them directly. Most of this information will come from conversations and listening to the person. The verbal communications of people with severe dementia are not always coherent. However, it is important to take into account the type of vocalisation (shouting, type of screaming – pain related, calling for help), when it occurs and its content (the words used).

APPEARANCE

It is important to observe the patient's appearance. Do they look anxious, depressed or angry? Observing how the people appear is key to understanding their experiences. The three most common forms of emotional distress are anxiety, anger and depression. Empirical research informs us that each of these has a characteristic theme associated with it (Beck 1976; James 2001d). These themes are outlined in Table 10.5 (also see Figure 2.1, Chapter 2), which shows that when someone is feeling anxious, they often see themselves as vulnerable and unable to cope with the demands of the situation. When someone appears depressed, they often see themselves as inadequate, worthless and the situation as being hopeless. Finally, when someone is angry, they tend to see themselves as having been badly treated

Table 10.5: Cognitive themes and their relationships to emotional appearance

Appearance of resident	Cognitive themes
Depressed (e.g. a resident sitting by herself not taking any interest in her surroundings).	The person has a self-perception of being worthless or inadequate, perceiving the world as hostile or uncaring, and viewing the future as being hopeless and unchanging.
Anxious (a resident looking frightened and confused).	The person has a self-perception of being vulnerable, perceiving his environment to be chaotic, and the future as unpredictable.
Angry (a resident hitting out when told he couldn't leave the building).	The person perceives that someone is acting unjustly towards him, and his rights are being infringed. Also there is a perception of the environment as being hostile, and a need to act immediately to protect his self-esteem from future harm.

or misused in some way. Understanding these signs helps to inform us what people's needs might be. The anxious person may be fearful for his safety, needing to be helped to feel less vulnerable. The depressed person will need to be given a greater sense of worth. While the angry resident will need to feel her rights are not being infringed.

NEED AND POSSIBLE THOUGHTS

The behaviour, vocalisation and appearance observed during an episode of challenging behaviour, when combined with the background information, can be used to try to understand what is causing the problem. Part of our role is to try to get staff to empathise with the person's situation, to think what she might be thinking in that situation and to try to understand the reasons behind the challenging behaviour. In other words, the aim is for staff to develop a 'theory of mind' perspective with respect to the person with dementia. The following table (Table 10.6) summarises how the information obtained above can be used in devising appropriate interventions.

10.8: TREATMENT AND OUTCOME

As stated above, the interventions are based on staff suggestions and are developed and refined at the end of the ISS with the therapist's help. After the group meeting, it is the therapist's role to take away the suggestions and put them together into a coherent treatment programme. As a result a new

Table 10.6: Illustration of how the emotional presentation of the person can help identify need and develop the intervention

Emotional appearance	Themes	Behaviours associated with theme	Need	Possible actions to deal with theme
Angry when carer removes his dinner plate without asking whether he had finished	He thinks he is not being shown enough respect	Swearing, nipping, throwing cup	To be respected	Prior to touching his plate, make good eye-contact. Then ask Donald whether he enjoyed the meal and then whether he's finished, using non-verbal gestures to assist with the communication.
Depressed and lonely because unable to communicate with others	Thinks no-one wants him	Frequently asking for things he does not need or want (e.g. cup of tea, glass of water)	To feel valued by others	Organise a film afternoon at the home, encouraging the residents to attend as a community. Show 1920s silent movies/comedies that do not require good receptive skills.
Shame followed by *anger* when member of staff points out to Donald that he has been incontinent	Initial theme is to do with a sense of embarrassment, but due to his reduced range of coping strategies to deal with the situation, he goes on the offensive	Threw cup on floor and struck out at staff member. Swore again when staff tried to change him	To have his dignity maintained, but a competing need to assist him in personal care owing to reasons to do with hygiene/ skin integrity	Use of a therapeutic lie informing him that he must've spilled some water over himself. Hence ask him would he like assistance to get changed

care plan is produced based around the problematic behaviour. The care plans are honed down to the bare essentials because once again it is found that overly complex treatment goals are not adhered to and often not read. It is relevant to note that psychological approaches are usually the first-line intervention used by the Newcastle Team.

10.9: REFLECTIONS

On reflection, the important factors in this case were that care staff became more positive, interested and consistent in their approaches. Although Donald continued to demonstrate some of the problematic behaviours, staff stated that through the ISS and formulation work they had gained a better understanding of Donald's needs. As a result, they felt better able to understand his behaviours and more equipped to manage them. Not only that, they stated they now enjoyed his company, which was a complete turn-around. The information about Charles Bonnet Syndrome was considered particularly valuable, giving insight into the role visual hallucinations played in Donald's behaviour.

This chapter has demonstrated the NCBS approach, which like CBT is an intensive formulation-led intervention. As outlined in Table 10.4, many of the skills required by the therapists using the approach are similar to those used in CBT. More specifically the ISS's process features share much in common with group CBT processes. In addition, the formulation itself contains elements that have been taken directly from CBT theory, especially the triadic element that records behaviour, verbalisations and appearance (the latter a proxy for emotion).

The NCBS approach is clearly not the only psychological framework that can be used with this group of people. For example, Cohen-Mansfield (2000b) has produced a helpful 'structured decision tree' protocol to guide individualised interventions (the TREA – treatment routes for exploring agitation). A further approach has been described by Bird et al. (2007), which includes psychotherapeutic methods for working closely with the staff and family members. A Cochrane review of functional analytical (ABC) approaches is currently underway (Moniz-Cook et al. 2008), and will highlight some of the other key papers in the area.

The development and modus operandi of the NCBS is consistent with the guidelines of the National Dementia Strategy (2009), National Service Framework for Older People (Standard 7.54–6; DoH 2001) and the Audit Commission (*Forget Me Not*, 2002), concerning the input of a specialist multi-disciplinary outreach team into care home settings. It is relevant to note that in the UK, despite the above guidelines, there is limited evaluation of the impact of the work of NHS community teams into care homes, with relatively few exceptions (Fossey *et al.* 2006; Moniz-Cook *et al.* 1998; Orrell *et al.* 2004; Proctor *et al.* 1999; Stevenson *et al.* 2006; Wood-Mitchell *et al.* 2007). In the international arena a number of researchers have conducted important controlled trials in this area (Bird *et al.* 2009; Cohen-Mansfield *et al.* 2007; Rovner *et al.* 1996; also see Cochrane review, Moniz-Cook *et al.* 2008). Related work has also been undertaken with people living in their own homes, with key studies undertaken by Marriott *et al.* (2000), Huang *et al.* (2003), Herbert *et al.* (2003), Teri McCurry, Logsdon and Gibbons. (2005) and Mittelman *et al.* (2007). It may be wishful thinking, but it seems evident by the dates of the above publications that there has been a surge in interest in providing better services for people with dementia over recent years. In support of this view, Esme Moniz-Cook (Hull, UK) has now received a large grant from the National Institute for Health Research, UK, to undertake two major randomised control trials (RCTs): one focused on challenging behaviour in care facilities and the other for 'people living at home'. Further, the Australian government has funded teams across Australia to use individualised psychological approaches in the treatment of challenging behaviours (Australian government 2007). It is hoped that with this higher level of interest from researchers and governments that we can start to establish a better evidence base for clinical work, and be able to train therapists to be competent in skills that have been shown to be effective.

Chapter 11

Concluding Comments

11.1: INTRODUCTION

This book has covered a range of topics over the previous ten chapters. Unfortunately, some important topics could not be addressed. This final chapter outlines three areas that could not be discussed in detail, but warrant some attention. These areas are: 'Working with carers' and 'Alternative models to CBT in the treatment of depression'; the latter theme only addresses depression due to the limited space available for discussion. The third area discussed is 'Improving Access to Psychological Therapies (IAPT)'. Following this, the final section presents a short passage reflecting on the nature of the book, and some observations on the topic of CBT with older people.

11.2: WORKING WITH CARERS

In the UK there is an increasing focus on the needs of carers, both informal and formal (CSIP/DoH 2005; National Dementia Strategy 2009). There is also a body of literature to draw upon examining their needs and stresses (Caress et al. 2009; Cossette and Levesque 1993; Seamark et al. 2004). One of the key sources of stress associated with caring concerns the lack of value assigned to the role of the carer. In recent years, Champion and Power's (1995) notion of 'role investment' has been used to help understand the nature of this stress. Discussing their model from a carer's perspective suggests that carers should avoid over-investing in the caring role at the expense of other important roles in their lives. Four domains have been associated with role investment: (1) the impact of the carer role on alternative roles and goals, (2) the investment of time and resources in the role, (3) the carer having realistic goals for the patient and themselves, and (4) appraisals of responsibility for the well-being of the patient. Within this framework, these domains have been linked to 'depressed' role investment (Barton *et al.* 2008). Barton believes that depressed mood may occur when adverse life events (i.e. a relative becoming ill) interact with dominant high value goals (e.g. enjoying one's job because of the social contacts it provides). This interaction can de-stabilise personal identity and devalue the self. Depression is predicted to be maintained when there is interference with alternative high value goals, or when there is inflated responsibility that maintains engagement with low value experiences in the carer role, or when carers become engaged in unattainable goals (e.g. to bring about their relative's full recovery). The above views form a helpful backdrop when developing carer interventions. The following section presents details of a few of the numerous studies in the area.

i. Types of carer interventions

Interventions take various forms. Psychotherapeutic approaches often use either a formal one-to-one therapy or a group format. Education and training aim to enhance skills, improve knowledge and attitudes (see Hepburn *et al.* 2005; Mittelman *et al.* 2004). In contrast, systems approaches utilise information sources (leaflets, drop-in-centres, programmes offered by local/ national societies) and respite resources to ease the strain on carers. It is relevant to note each of these interventions has a different goal. The formal therapeutic approaches tend to be used to tackle psychiatric disorders, such as depression and anxiety. The teaching methods enhance coping abilities, and help the carers to develop practical caring skills. The 'systems' methods provide organisational, respite, environmental, transport, and financial assistance to enable the carer to provide appropriate levels of support for the patient.

In recent years there have been a number of systematic reviews in the area (Cooper *et al.* 2007; Pinquart and Sorensen 2006; Sorensen, Pinquart and Duberstein 2002). Cooper's review examines anxiety in caregivers of people with dementia; her categorisation of the types of interventions is a helpful summary of the approaches used. She identified the following types of projects together with the number of trials in each category: *five* CBT (Akkerman and Ostwald 2004; Gendron *et al.* 1986, Gendron, Poitras and Dastoor 1996; Herbert *et al.* 2003; Wilkins *et al.* 1999); *four* coping strategy/professional support; *four* alternative placements; *three* behavioural interventions; *three* respite; *two* relaxation/yoga; *two* exercise; *one* group counselling; *one* information technology support. Her conclusion from the review was somewhat disappointing, with only Akkerman and Ostwald's CBT study showing significant effects in terms of anxiety.

ii. Empirical studies

Taken as a whole, the various systematic reviews undertaken highlight two main short-comings in the area: (i) the lack of good quality studies, and (ii) the heterogeneity of the interventions employed, making it difficult to determine the mechanisms of change. In the area of dementia, Akkerman and Ostwald (2004) showed that a nine-week CBT intervention reduced anxiety in family carers of people with dementia. Their approach also included training in relaxation when appropriate. Marriott *et al.*'s (2000) RCT of 14 families also demonstrated significant effects on measures of depression and psychiatric caseness for the carers, and improvements in 'activities of daily living' for the patients. Over the 14 weeks of this CBT study there were three sessions of caregiver education, six sessions of stress management, and five sessions of coping skills training. Moderate effects have also been observed by Buchanan (2004) in terms of family carers' self-reported anger and depression. It is noteworthy that there is a relatively healthy literature on the use of psychological treatments for carers of people with dementia (see Brodaty *et al.* 2003; Cooper *et al.* 2006; Mittelman *et al.* 2007; Peacock and Forbes 2003). However, the literature is less extensive in other areas. An exception to this observation is the well-described study undertaken by Secker and Brown (2005). They conducted a successful RCT study using a 12–14 week programme of CBT designed to alleviate strain and burden in carers of patients with Parkinson's disease. The content of the programme is summarised in Table 11.1. The positive effects were evident over a three-month follow-up period compared to controls. This study was modelled on the work of Marriott *et al.* (2000). Further, as one can see from Table 11.1, a number of the themes outlined in Champion and Power's (1995) investment framework are present in the treatment programme. For example, there was an emphasis on the carers stepping back and taking stock of their situations, creating time and space for themselves, seeking support from other sources, tackling unhelpful cognitions and rationalising guilt and other problematic emotions.

In Gallagher-Thompson and Steffens' (1994) controlled study, depressed family caregivers of frail, elderly relatives were randomly assigned to 20 sessions of either CBT or brief psychodynamic (PD) individual psychotherapy. At post-treatment, 71 per cent of the caregivers were no longer clinically depressed with no differences found between the two outpatient treatments. Of note, the results revealed evidence of therapy 'specificity' because there was an interaction between treatment modality and length of care-giving on symptom-oriented measures. Patients who had been caregivers for a shorter

Table 11.1: Modules used in the trial of CBT for Parkinson's carers

1. Education on Parkinson's and introduction to cognitive behavioural therapy:
Questions about Parkinson's disease were discussed and relevant information was given.
There was also a discussion about the therapy itself, and a review of the carer's goals and
expectations.

2. Accessing community resources and supports: In this module the carer's support
network was reviewed and information provided where necessary. The carer worked on how
to access and communicate effectively with available services.

3. Pleasant activity scheduling: This module consisted of (a) encouraging the carer to
make designated times for recreation without the person they cared for, and (b) designating
times to engage in enjoyable things with the person they cared for that did not involve normal
care duties.

4. Relaxation training: This module focused on practical strategies for the relief of anxiety
and tension.

5. Sleep improvement: This module covered sleep-preparation behaviour and also ways to
manage the sleep problems of the individual with Parkinson's disease.

6. Identifying and challenging negative thoughts and feelings: This module targeted
those carers with recurrent negative thinking patterns. This was most suitable for carers
presenting with depression, anxiety and persisent worry. Skills taught included identifying
and rating negative feelings, automatic thought recording, and rationalising guilt.

7. Challenging maladaptive rules and core beliefs: This was a more complex level of
CBT, which included teaching awareness of (a) rules and conditional assumptions around
caring, and (b) the restructuring of core schematic beliefs (for example, 'I am a bad carer',
and 'There is no future').

8. Review, planning for the future, and ending of treatment: This final module reviewed
all of the previous modules, and prepared the carer for ending therapy.

period showed improvement in the PD condition, whereas those who had
been caregivers for at least 44 months improved with CBT. These findings
suggest that patient-specific variables should be considered when choosing
treatment for clinically depressed family caregivers.

A helpful systematic review of the needs of carers looking after people
with physical problems was undertaken by Caress *et al.* (2009). Despite this
review focusing on caring for patients with chronic obstructive pulmonary
disease, the findings have broad applicability. From a CBT perspective, useful
work has also been undertaken by Kunik *et al.* (2001) and others, which is
reviewed by Laidlaw *et al.* (2003).

For readers interested in an introduction to working with carers of people with psychological difficulties, Molyneux *et al.*'s (2008) recent review provides a helpful overview; albeit from purely Irish perspective. They found a high prevalence of depression (21%) in their group of primary carers living in the community. They examined the predictors of carer well-being, and found that being a spouse was a protective factor, while the number of problematic behaviours and degree of functional impairment of the patients were negative predictors. Of note, the diagnosis did not affect carer depression or strain.

Finally, while it is evident that carers need support, it is demonstrable that not all forms of help are effective. Aakhus *et al.*'s (2009) small RCT showed that a single-session educational programme for caregivers of psychogeriatric inpatients resulted in increased distress. They accounted for this finding by suggesting that the knowledge given may have served to increase anxiety. Such an effect was previously observed by Graham, Ballard and Sham (1997), when they found that a higher degree of knowledge about dementia was associated with greater anxiety.

11.3: ALTERNATIVE MODELS TO CBT IN THE TREATMENT OF DEPRESSION

There are a host of different forms of therapy aimed at treating the mood disorders. NICE (2004) advocates using a stepped-care approach to the treatment of depression, suggesting that the brief and simpler treatments should be offered prior to any of the more intensive and invasive approaches in cases of mild to moderate depression. Thus for mild to moderate depression self-help programmes are suggested. For the more severe presentations cognitive therapy and interpersonal therapy (IPT) are recommended as first-line treatments, and psychoanalytic approaches are suggested for atypical, chronic presentations. The NICE guidelines are broadly in keeping with the conclusions of three systematic reviews conducted on the use of psychotherapies for older people (Mackin and Arean 2005; Scogin *et al.* 2005; Zalaquett and Stens 2006). These reviews only differ slightly to the general adult literature by placing greater emphasis on the potential benefits of reminiscence and life-review therapies (Gatz *et al.* 1998), and family and group therapies (Qualls 1999). The latter is generally considered a supportive treatment encouraging better social functioning (Pinquart and Sorensen 2001).

The various therapies target different aspects of depression in order to promote change. In Table 11.2, a number of evidence-based interventions are described for the treatment of depression in older people. Their inclusion

Table 11.2: Overview of evidence-based therapies for treatment of depression

Type of therapy	Mechanism of change	Suitability criteria and training	Evidence for older adults
CBT: The chaotic experience of depression is conceptualised, assessed and treated in terms of four inter-related features, aka the depressive cycle: depressogenic thoughts, behaviours, physical sensations and feelings. Particular attention is paid to the role of negative thinking and often to the core beliefs that underpin them.	The patient is socialised to the model. Once having developed an understanding of the depression in terms of the cycle, the patient is helped to re-evaluate her thoughts and dysfunctional belief systems. Behavioural and educational programmes are used to both disrupt problematic actions and facilitate new learning.	*Suitability*: Safran and Segal (1990) provided empirical evidence for ten suitability factors (see Chapter 5). *Training*: There are a large number of courses around the UK. The 'gold standard' courses are typically nine months long, part-time diploma/MSc programmes. The trainees receive weekly supervision and teaching.	A large number of quality studies, conducted by a number of different research groups.
IPT: People are social beings, and disruptions to people's social networks can both trigger and maintain depression. This model conceptualises the onset of depression in terms of losses, resulting from one of four sources: grief (death), life transitions, disputes, social skills deficits. The approach attempts to re-establish good social skills and networking that may have triggered and/or become disrupted as a result of the depression.	The onset of the depression is identified, and the subsequent changes to the patient's interpersonal network are assessed. The impact of the changes are acknowledged and 'mourned' where appropriate. Problem-solving techniques are then employed to re-establish or create a fulfilling and worth-enhancing social life (Hinrichsen and Clougherty 2006).	*Suitability*: No specific suitability criteria set. Originally designed specifically for unipolar depression, although currently used for a wider range of affective disorders. *Training*: Initial training involves a 3–4 day teaching programme, followed by a term of structured supervised work that provides 'Practitioner' status.	Moderate evidence, but from a small group of research centres.

Self-help: Self-help programmes are based on 'written materials' (books, leaflets), audio- or video-taped material or computer programs designed to meet therapeutic needs. The programs can be supported by either face-to-face or phone contact with a therapist, and may be delivered on an individual or group basis. The latter versions are usually termed 'guided self-help' programmes (Scogin *et al.* 1998).	These are usually based on CBT principles and include guidance on CBT change techniques (Floyd *et al.* 2006).	*Suitability*: NICE guidelines recommend use for mild to moderate depressive disorders. *Training*: None specified, although specific packages are named e.g. NICE support use of 'Beating the Blues' computer package.	Moderate evidence, a number of the key studies conducted in the older people area.
Psychoanalysis: Early negative experiences retard emotional development, resulting in the expression of immature impulses and desires. This produces conflicts between reality and the patient's ideals and standards. The resulting tensions, feelings of helplessness and depression invoke protective mechanisms (e.g. repression, projection, reaction formation). These protective mechanisms themselves tend to become dysfunctional, interfering with the person's decision-making abilities. Hence, the patient may perceive himself as acting maturely, although the emotional processing of the situation is that of a child.	The aim of every session is to put the patient in touch with as much of his true feelings as he can bear. This is done by careful inspection of the patient's past, promoting insight regarding the manner in which impulses and desires are impacting on attitudes, actions, goals and relationships.	*Suitability*: The therapist needs to judge: (i) the degree to which the patient is already in touch with his true feelings; (ii) the nature of the hidden feelings of which he is not aware; (iii) how close these feelings are to the surface; (iv) the degree of anxiety with which they are invested; (v) the patient's capacity to bear it. It is recommended for trauma, grief and adjustment disorders (Ardern 2002) *Training*: Due to the interpersonal stance of the therapist, it is necessary to undertake specialist training which usually involves personal psychoanalysis and the supervised treatment of a number of patients.	Evidence in terms of brief analytic form of the therapy. A small number of studies, conducted mainly by small number of research centres.

Table 11.2: Overview of evidence-based therapies for treatment of depression cont.

Type of therapy	Mechanism of change	Suitability criteria and training	Evidence for older adults
The evidence base mainly comes from brief psychoanalytic therapy (BDT) trials. BDT is generally limited to 15–20 sessions.	Main goal is to increase awareness and insight into the unconscious processes leading an individual to repeat past experiences and to institute corrective experiences through the interaction between client and therapist (Garner 2002).		
Life-review therapy: Sometimes referred to as reminiscence therapy, involves undertaking a structured evaluative approach of a patient's history. However, caution is needed as meta-analytic studies have failed to identify a unitary approach (Bohlmeijer *et al.* 2003).	Mechanisms are unclear, however life review often emphasises the need for past evaluation, with resolution of past conflicts. Knight (2004) suggests some similarities with grief work.	*Suitability*: Developmentally appropriate for older people with and without dementia. *Training*: Regular workshops from various sources throughout UK.	A small number of studies, requiring replication.

is based on the guidance suggested by NICE, and the reviews of effective treatments of older people provided by Scogin *et al.* (2005) and Mackin and Arean (2005). As one can see, the mechanisms of change differ markedly between the various methods, ranging from re-evaluating social networks to problem solving and promoting insight. Even so, they have all been shown to be effective in the treatment of geriatric depression. And of note, when the psychotherapeutic treatments have been compared head to head, there is often little evidence to suggest any one is better than the other (Wilson *et al.* 2008).

At one level, this may suggest that the psychotherapies share a generic mechanism of change. In the past (see James, Reichelt, Freeston and Barton 2007), I have argued that the generic process of change in all therapies is to (i) identify patients' problematic patterns of behaving and experiencing, and then to (ii) disrupt these problematic depressive patterns, making them more flexible and thus more adaptable to the person's life-style. Clearly, each of the different therapies focuses on different patterns to assess, monitor and target in order to achieve change. For example, in the case of IPT the focus of the therapeutic investigation is the patient's social network, while behavioural methods focus on the functions and consequences of the person's actions. It therefore seems that by working on, and successfully tackling, a single key feature of the depression (an element of the disorder), one can get a domino effect occurring. Hence, other aspects/elements that were contributing to the low mood (neuronal, chemical, cognitive, etc.) may change subsequently once the target feature has been appropriately dealt with.

Despite this notion of equivalence among the different therapies, it is important to stress that the quality of evidence regarding treatment effectiveness with respect to older people is poor, with only CBT interventions having been assessed well (Wilson *et al.*'s Cochrane Review, 2008). Hence, care needs to be taken when deciding on what treatment strategies to use, ensuring that one makes best use of the available evidence.

In relation to future developments, Ken Laidlaw and Bob Knight are currently working together on new frameworks that incorporate gerontological perspectives within mental health models (Laidlaw 2009). For example, the Selective Optimisation and Compensation perspective (Baltes and Baltes 1990) is being used with their patients to promote better adaptation to declining abilities. In this work, existing skills are identified and optimised through practice, and declining skills are compensated for. Further, the above researchers are using cultural belief systems, such as notions of wisdom, to counter negative age-related societal perspectives to do with 'deterioration' and 'frailty'.

In relation to the area of depression, over the last few years I have taken an interest in attempting to integrate cognitive psychology with CBT theory. There is a tradition of this within CBT with the work of Williams (1994), Teasdale (1994) and Brewin (1998) examining information processing issues in relation to negative affect. Some of these details have already been presented in Chapter 4. With respect to my own work, I have taken a keen interest in re-conceptualising the notion of schemas in mental illnesses. I suggest a revision of the concept of the schema as used in CBT, reconnecting its links with the memory literature and the manner in which information about life experiences is stored (see James 2008a, 2008b, 2008c). There are two aspects to the revision. The first, and perhaps least contentious, is the view that the diathesis-stress model leads one logically to the view that schemas are memories. This is because schemas are viewed as features that have been encoded in the past, are being stored, and may be activated at some future date in the presence of an appropriate cue. The second aspect of the revised perspective builds on clinical observations that inform us that once a person has been depressed, future episodes are likely to share *many* characteristics with the first episode. For example, in future episodes there will be characteristic cognitive themes, behavioural strategies, sensitivities relating to noise and sounds. For example, Mrs Smith's family can always tell when she is about to relapse into a depression, as she adopts a stooped body posture, becomes acutely sensitive to noise and the smell of cigarette smoke, and begins to withdraw from others. Mindful of this phenomenon, it is argued that multi-sensory information relating to the person's depression is stored as some form of unitary concept, and it is the multi-modal representation that is reactivated during subsequent episodes of depression. It is my view that this multi-modal representation should be called the schema. This view draws heavily on the cognitive psychology concept of schemas, which can be traced back to the work of Bartlett (1932), Minsky (1975) and Schank and Abelson (1977). This perspective has many similarities to the information processing models of Teasdale and Barnard's (1993) Interactive Cognitive Subsystems (ICS) and Power and Dalgleish's (1996) Schematic Propositional Associative Analogue Representation System (SPAARS).

In summary, the revised perspective differentiates between schemas and core beliefs, suggesting that a core belief is merely one component of a schema (i.e. the cognitive feature). Within this perspective, schemas are viewed as representations of a previous experience (i.e. memories) that are stored multi-modally, containing details about emotional, kinaesthetic, olfactory, sensory, physiological, neural and cognitive processes. Thus a person who has previously suffered from depression will have a stored representation of what it is like to be depressed. The more episodes of depression she experiences, the more familiar this state of 'being depressed' will be. As a consequence, there may be a lower threshold of activation for future depression and a more elaborate network of depression related information, including more activation points (Teasdale, 1994). Such features will make relapse more likely. The implications of such a perspective have been discussed in detail elsewhere (James 2008b; James *et al.* 2004).

11.4: IAPT: PROVISION OF MENTAL HEALTH SERVICES FOR OLDER PEOPLE

Securing Better Mental Health for Older Adults (DoH 2005) and its sister document *Everybody's Business* (CSIP/DoH 2005) set out to try to put mental health services for older people on a more equal footing to that of the services offered to their younger counterparts. Further, with the recent publication of the UK's Equality Bill, the public sector services will now have a duty to promote equality throughout the age ranges. This bill will have a significant impact in relation to how health and social care services are designed and commissioned (DoH 2009). As a consequence the government monies recently secured to improve access to psychological treatments (Improving Access to Psychological Therapies, IAPT 2006), will also be made available to older people and their carers.

The origins of IAPT lay in an economic argument put forward by Lord Layard who proposed that modern evidence-based psychotherapies should be used to treat the large numbers of people receiving incapacity benefit to assist them to return to work. It was suggested that this would require the training of 10,000 new therapists and the development of 250 services. The UK government have provided approximately £190 million in support of IAPT, and following the successful piloting of services in 2006 (Doncaster, Newham), the programme has been rolled out in England and Wales. Since its development, the remit of IAPT services has changed as well as their economic goals, which previously only targeted working aged adults. Indeed, IAPT commissioning is now able to support projects for: people with learning difficulties, offenders, black and minority communities and other groups, including older people. There have been a number of sites within the UK that have run IAPT projects for older people (e.g. Cheshire – Glynn-Williams 2008; Yorkshire – Hilton 2009; Derbyshire – Higginson 2009). It would be fair to say that most of them to date have struggled to get large numbers of older people to access the services that have been offered. Some of the reasons for the slow uptake are outlined in Table 11.3 (left-hand column), as well as some possible solutions (right column).

Table 11.3: Improving access to effective treatments for
older people – some problems and remedies

Common obstacles to accessing treatment	Potential solutions
1 Failure of services to work flexibly to accommodate the needs of older people.	– Services should ensure that clinics operate suitable opening hours, and that they are in places easily accessible both by public transport and to those with mobility difficulties.
2 Poor recognition and diagnosis of mental health problems in the elderly, and a masking of the problems when individuals have concurrent physical health difficulties. Sixty per cent of people over the age of 65 suffer from a long-standing physical illness (GHS 2001), and it is often the physical problems that receive the attention from medical practitioners when the person presents at the surgery.	– Working with medical practitioners, especially GPs, to improve their understanding of the benefits of IAPT. – Training staff to detect mental health problems, and to ask questions that seek the presence of the disorders. – Use specialist staff to raise awareness, and undertake specialist assessments. – Market the IAPT services in ways that encourage the participation of older people.
3 Social isolation of some elders compounded by a lack of transport facilities.	– Identify groups that are socially isolated (those in rural areas, high-rise flats), and provide weekly clinics in accessible centres.
4 The negative attitudes of clinicians regarding work undertaken with older people – attitudes may vary from a lack of confidence in skill base, to pessimism regarding possibilities of successful outcomes	– IAPT therapists should receive workshops on working with older people during their training to educate them about the benefits of psychotherapy for older people. – More older people should be trained as IAPT therapists. This would also ensure that the workforce reflected the wider community.
5 The lack of optimism of older people regarding the treatments of anxiety and depression. Obstacles that might arise from dysfunctional perspectives (e.g. 'My illness is a punishment for mistakes I made in my past').	– The use of suitable marketing, leaflets, brochures. Use of case examples in the material, which are culturally relevant to the different older people's groups (including ethnic minorities). – Offer to run education classes/road shows on mental health issues for relevant organisations (Age Concern, Alzheimer Society, etc.).
6 Support for therapists who may not be used to working with older people	– Many IAPT clinicians will require training and supervision in working with older people, at least initially.

Much of the above material has been drawn from the IAPT *Older People. Positive Practice Guide* (DoH 2009). This document provides a number of useful case examples of sites around the country that have run IAPT programmes for older people. A recent workshop on the topic organised by the national UK psychological society for older people (PSIGE) reviewed the progress of the work thus far. From the various presentations, a consensus began to develop concerning the lack of strategic planning of how the IAPT funding could best meet older people's needs. To date, existing programmes have tended to develop around local resources and clinicians' existing skill bases and interests. While this has some advantages in terms of being able to set up local services quickly, it has meant that the services offered do not necessarily meet the requirements of those most in need (DoH 2009). Indeed, a debate on this issue at PSIGE suggested that some clearer strategic thinking needed to be given about how best to target IAPT resources, because there was a danger that an important opportunity could be missed to develop better and more equitable services.

11.5: CONCLUDING COMMENTS AND REFLECTIONS

This book reflects my journey as a clinician over the last 20 years, from a trainee through to qualification, and it charts my move to working with older people in the late 1990s. My time at Newcastle Cognitive and Behavioural Therapies Centre (1992–1997) was significant, as here I was involved in research on competence and training. This was an exciting time for CBT too, as it was during this period of its development that it reached maturity, with seminal papers and 'classic' models emerging and gaining acceptance (Clark's model of panic; Salkovskis' model of OCD, etc.). Also many new CBT centres and courses started to be established across the country, and more and more therapists gained formal qualifications swelling the ranks of the British Association of Behavioural and Cognitive Psychotherapists (BABCP). In relation to the older people's specialty, national developments have been slow, although momentum has grown in recent years with the exciting work of Laidlaw and colleagues, and his links with Thompson and Gallagher-Thompson in the USA.

I think the above journey and the broader changes occurring in CBT over the last two decades has served to focus my mind on the importance of training, supervision and dissemination. This is reflected in this book in those sections where I have tried to provide guidelines and where I have attempted to summarise complex issues within tables. Clearly there is a danger here of making the complex appear overly simple; although the comprehensive referencing is intended to guide the reader to the key papers.

At the start of the book I stressed the importance of the acronym KISS (Keep It Simple and Slow), which evidently has potential benefits for both the patient and the therapist. However, in order to keep things 'simple', the therapist must have a very good understanding of exactly what he is doing such as: the mechanisms of change; an awareness of the technical skills underpinning questioning abilities, etc. It is my experience of working with trainees and some qualified therapists that the basic assumptions are often not fully appreciated. Such lacunas have always concerned me because these basic features are the bedrock on which the therapy is built. Further, without an understanding of them, one cannot adapt one's therapy appropriately because one may inadvertently violate fundamental assumptions. For example, when adapting therapy for people with dementia one needs to be clear about what abilities the patient needs to have in order to engage with the standard format. Furthermore, if adaptations are required we need to understand what changes start to make the therapy something other than CBT.

A further concern is the lack of attention paid to change strategies. I mentioned this issue in Chapter 5 (5.3ii), when I discussed getting stuck in 'an assessment-conceptualisation loop'. Clearly, effective therapy requires skilfully applied interventions, and it is the responsibility of therapists and trainers to ensure interventions are being used appropriately. In relation to interventions, I am also troubled by the lack of 'out of session practice' regarding the delivery of the methods. Some of the skills, particularly the change techniques, are complex processes (e.g. continua techniques, scaffolding, diary completion, etc.) and it is necessary to become a skilled practitioner in them before using them with patients. Too often I have witnessed poorly executed change strategies, which upon further investigation turned out to be the first or second time the therapist had ever used the methodology with a 'live' person in front of them.

Despite the above concerns, I think that in general this is an extremely exciting time for those of us working in the specialty of 'Older People's Services'. Owing to the demographic shifts with respect to ageing being witnessed in many parts of the world, our skills are becoming far more mainstream. As such, I believe our unique blending of neuro-biopsychosocial perspectives will increasingly be called upon by our colleagues. Further, the UK government's new Equality Bill will start to impact on the development of mental health services, and older people will now be able to assess services hitherto targeted more towards younger adults (e.g. IAPT). In order to utilise these new opportunities it will be necessary for therapists to be more systemic in their thinking and to develop strategies to enable and encourage take-up of services by older people. Such strategies would need to target older people and health professionals, as well as local and national organisations in society.

My final comment relates to working in my chosen area of dementia. As I have outlined in Chapters 2 and 10, I believe that CBT and its principles are important in delivering effective therapies to this group of people. However, because there has not been a tradition of applying formulation models in this area, treatment approaches have been rather unsophisticated – i.e. aromatherapy, music, light-box, dolls, animal therapy (NSF for Older People, DoH 2001; James and Fossey 2008). This lack of sophistication clearly needs to be addressed. Indeed, I believe that this group of people, particularly when displaying challenging behaviour, have the right to receive comprehensive formulation-led approaches. They deserve the same level of assessment, formulation, and evidence-based intervention that would be routinely offered to their younger counterparts. Is this asking too much?

Disorder-Specific Conceptual Models

This section examines a number of the disorder-specific conceptual frameworks used in CBT. The contents of these models are largely based on empirical investigations. Through the use of these frameworks both the therapist and patient are directed towards specific areas that are characteristic of each of the diagnostic disorders. The models are usually used alongside the generic ('hot-cross bun') cycle and can also be supplemented with details from the diathesis-stress framework (Chapter 6).

The reader will notice that the disorders are all anxiety based (i.e. panic, GAD, OCD and social phobia). This is because the frameworks generally used for depression were previously discussed in Chapter 6.

PANIC CYCLE

Clark (1986) considers the triggers in panic can be wide-ranging, both internal and environmental. He suggests a perceived fear of a panic attack makes the patient both hypervigilant and internally focused. The hypervigilance and internal focusing result in greater sensitivity to changes in physiology, and thus increase the probability of the onset of an attack. In the vicious cycle outlined in Figure AI.1, a possible trigger may be a slight change in bodily sensations, which is then perceived as threatening. This results in a state of apprehension, which leads to more focusing on the body. Any sensations are processed catastrophically and the patient feels unable to cope.

GENERALISED ANXIETY DISORDER (GAD)

GAD is characterised by excessive worry, and this tends to happen when the person holds negative beliefs about the nature of worry. In relation to Figure AI.2, these mainly occur at the Type 2 level (aka 'meta-cognitive belief' level). In such circumstances, a worry that hitherto has been triggered and processed relatively appropriately becomes problematic. Wells (1997) suggests there are two main categories of negative 'meta-cognitive' belief:

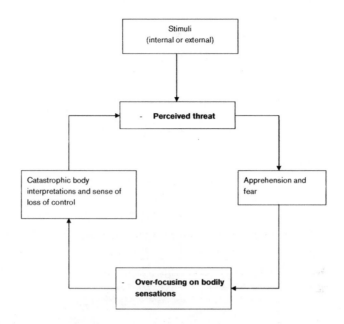

Figure AI.1: Conceptual framework for panic disorders

(a) perceptions that the worry is uncontrollable, and (b) a view that it is dangerous. He claims that people's ineffective responses to such beliefs leads to maintenance of the worry. For example, patients typically 'seek reassurance', or engage in 'thought avoidance and suppression' (Borkovec and Newman 1999).

OBSESSIVE COMPULSIVE DISORDER (OCD)

The triggers for OCD behaviour are normal everyday thoughts, intrusions and doubts, but when they occur in a patient they are imbued with particular significance. This is because the patient holds a set of beliefs regarding the meaning of the 'thoughts' and the degree of danger they represent (Wells 1997). These beliefs (aka meta-cognitive beliefs) take a number of forms, such as:

- *'Thought event fusion'* – the notion that having a negative thought about an event (e.g. a disastrous fire) increases the likelihood it will happen.

- *'Thought self-action fusion'* – having a thought that one will commit a negative act (e.g. kill someone) will increase its likelihood.

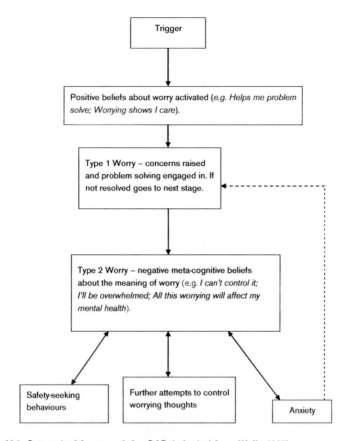

Figure AI.2: Conceptual framework for GAD (adapted from Wells 1997)

These thoughts lead to anxiety and distress. The person responds by engaging in rituals or strategies that she perceives will reduce the likelihood of the negative occurrences happening. Such rituals will initially reduce the level of anxiety, but result in excessive focus on the cognitions and thereby increasing the likelihood of further intrusions. There are a number of other important cognitions associated with OCD that serve to increase perceived levels of threat and responsibility (see Figure AI.3). These features need to be taken into account when treating patients (Westbrook *et al.* 2007, p.199). An account of the treatment of an older male with OCD is provided by Hirsh *et al.* (2006).

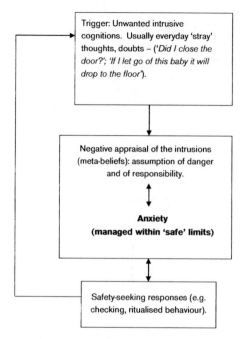

Figure AI.3: Conceptual framework for OCD

SOCIAL PHOBIA

Social phobia is an extreme form of social anxiety. When people with this disorder are in social situations, they perceive themselves to be in 'social danger' (Butler and Hackmann 2004). Assumptions are activated regarding rejection, humiliation, extreme negative social judgement (e.g. others think I'm odd or an idiot). Patients respond to these cognitions physiologically (anxiety symptoms, blushing, shaking, palpitations, tensing), and by engaging in safety-seeking behaviours (avoiding eye-contact, focusing on tasks rather than people, rushing to leave, etc.). Such responses increase the person's self-awareness and self-focus, resulting in them over-processing the situation and her reactions to it. Wells (1997) describes the excessive processing as 'processing the self as a social object'. By this he means that instead of engaging in normal interactions, the patient takes an external perspective, looking upon the self as something that requires monitoring and checking. Thus the person spends excessive time and energy processing her own performance. This makes the person appear 'odd', confirming one of the negative assumptions (see Figure AI.4).

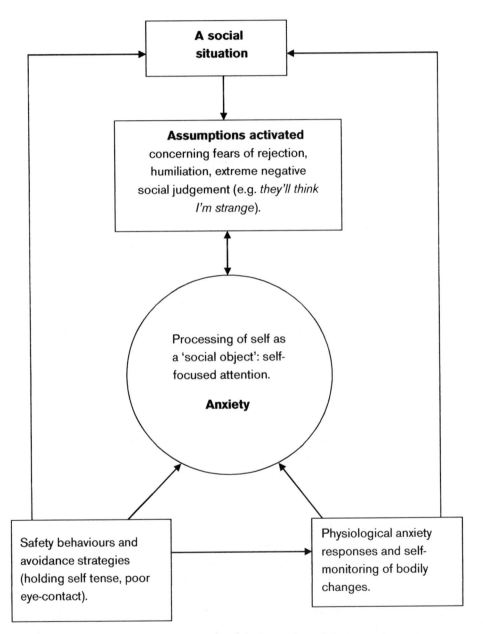

Figure AI.4: Conceptual framework for social phobia

CTS-R Training Manual for Promoting Therapeutic Competence

This section summarises the contents of a manual which was designed to aid training in the use of the CTS-R for both trainee therapists and raters of the scale. It is relevant to note that the use of the manual assumes that the raters are able to observe the trainee either as a co-therapist or via video equipment.

The manual informs by presenting examples of poor and good practices that have been witnessed when observing trainees' video-tapes. For each CTS-R item there are two sub-sections, one aimed at assisting therapists, and the other at helping raters to determine what they should be looking for while observing the trainee. The sub-sections are:

1. Examples of poor practice – the information highlights the common errors commited by trainees. The details are presented in the form of tables.

2. Examples of good practice – this sub-section illustrates the sorts of features that need to be present in order for the trainee to gain credit with respect to the CTS-R item.

LAYOUT OF THE MANUAL

Prior to providing the guidelines for good practice, a table of 'common problems' relating to each item is presented. For example, in terms of the 'agenda setting' the following problems are outlined:

• the item set was not associated with the overall goals of therapy

• the item was not set collaboratively.

Lists of these sorts of 'Examples of poor practice' are presented in tables with the aim of getting therapists to reflect and perform better on the items in the future.

Under each table are sets of questions, illustrating examples of good practice. This section is designed to help therapists see what a rater of the scale is looking-for when scoring the CTS-R. The contents of this section are also used to train raters in how to use the scale. Examples of such questions, relating to the agenda item, include:

- Did the therapist encourage the patient to participate in setting the agenda? (eg. Did you hear the therapist say something like – 'What would be useful for us to discuss today?').

- Did the therapist set an appropriate number of agenda items? (eg. Did you hear the therapist say something like – 'Do you think we'll manage to discuss all these features in the hour? Which ones are your priorities?').

As you can see, alongside each question, I have provided a therapist's statement (in italics). If a rater hears such statements during the session, the therapist will be awarded points on the CTS-R. Hence, this section can be extremely useful in helping therapists' improve their performance on the scale

ITEM 1 – AGENDA SETTING AND ADHERENCE

Some therapists seem to view the agenda as an unnecessary feature that has little bearing on the outcome of the therapy. This is an unfortunate perspective because a good agenda clarifies the topics and their relevance, and is an early opportunity to reinforce a collaborative style. When working with older people its use provides a helpful structure through which the patient can navigate the therapy. Its presence also reinforces the notion that the hour session requires a focused, goal-oriented approach. Table AII.1 presents some of the common problems I have observed when supervising trainee therapists working with older people.

a. Examples of poor practice

Table AII.1: Identifying examples of poor practice in Agenda Setting and Adherence

	Examples of poor practice	Comments
1	Agenda not set.	Typically the therapist either launches straight into the therapy, or tables an item so briefly that it serves no function.
2	Agenda not set collaboratively.	The therapist has a pre-set agenda and unilaterally tells the patient what topics are to be discussed. Such a situation fails to give patients an opportunity to contribute, and it socialises them to taking a passive role.
3	Failure to give rationale for undertaking the agenda. (NB: The rationale is mainly needed in the first few sessions during the socialisation process.)	It is important to reiterate to the patient the relevance of the agenda, and how its use will address her difficulties. Thus it is often helpful to remind the patient that this is her special time, and thus it's vital to cover issues that are relevant to her.
4	Too many items set.	Older people's lives are often complex, with lots of historical data, physical health issues, trans-generational events to consider. Hence, sometimes one finds that too many items can be tabled for discussion. The therapist must be realistic about both what is relevant and what can be achieved within the session. This may sometimes lead to a negotiation with the patient about selecting the topics that are most likely to move the therapy forward at this time.
5	The agenda not adhered to by therapist.	On occasions a good clear agenda is set, but the agreed plan is not carried out. There must be good reasons for such non-adherence. Otherwise the patient can become frustrated that the subjects they had previously identified as being important are not being discussed. Non-adherence also undermines the perceived relevance of the agenda-setting process
6	The agenda adhered to inflexibly.	On some occasions unforeseen topics will arise in therapy that require attention (e.g. abuse, risk, etc.) and need to be addressed immediately. Clearly, the original agenda should not be adhered to in such circumstances. However, it is relevant to formally state that owing to the importance of the 'emergent issue', the agenda is being altered. Also, it is helpful to say that the topics not covered in the session will be tabled for the next occasion.

b. Identifying good practice

Examples of the sorts of queries a CTS-R rater might have when making a judgement about the trainee's performance on this item are given below. Under each query is a statement/question demonstrating competence in relation to the query.

1. Do you think the trainee checked that the patient clearly understood why the agenda was important? Did you hear any of the following types of statements?

    • What benefits do you think we get from setting an agenda?

    • Do you think that these plans we've agreed will help us to cover the important issues?

2. Was the session set sensitively?

    • What would be the most helpful thing to discuss today?

3. Did the therapist set an appropriate number of agenda items?

    • What else would you like to put on the agenda?

    • That seems a lot for us to get through in an hour. Do you think we could review the items and see which ones would be the most helpful to discuss today?

4. Did the therapist set an agenda with clear, discrete and realistic goals?

    • Just to make sure I've understood what you want to discuss today. By the end of the session we'll have examined Y and looked at some alternative views for Y. And also set up a way of tackling X. Is there anything that I've missed out?

5. Was the patient encouraged to participate in setting the agenda?

    • What would you like to get from today's session?

6. Was the agenda set collaboratively?

    • We need to put some time aside for discussing X, and jointly give it some serious attention.

    • What is the most important thing to cover today? Are there any other things to include?

7. Did the agenda seem appropriate?

   • If we did discuss this item, how would it help improve your mood?

   • What would be most helpful to discuss today, keeping in mind the stage you're at in your therapy?

   • By discussing X, how will this help you move forward?

8. Were the items prioritised?

   • You have mentioned X, Y and Z. Which of these would you like to talk about first?

ITEM 2 – FEEDBACK

It is evident that the working memories of many older people, and people with affective disorders, are compromised (see Chapter 4). As such, their speed of processing and ability to integrate information is often affected. Therefore, it is extremely helpful if the therapist provides summaries at regular intervals. It is also particularly important to check that the person understands the contents of the session. Thompson *et al.* (2009) stress the value of written summaries both in terms of reminders and methods of consolidation.

a. Examples of poor practice

Table AII.2: Identifying examples of poor practice in relation to Feedback

	Examples of poor practice	Comments
1	Feedback given infrequently.	Therapists often fail to provide sufficient feedback. As a rule of thumb, a major summary should be given every ten minutes.
2	Feedback elicited infrequently.	Therapists often do not elicit feedback frequently enough. Sometimes they feel uncomfortable asking the patient to summarise what has been said, or her understanding of the current situation. Therapist may think that this process is too much like 'checking up' on the patient. However, if done sensitively, this feature often serves to increase collaboration between the two parties.

Table AII.2 Identifying examples of poor practice in relation
to Feedback

	Examples of poor practices	Comments
3	Not used either as a platform for advancement or as an aid to promoting insight.	Feedback and summaries help to consolidate key information that has been discussed. Relevant aspects of the discussion can be highlighted and put in a sequential order, facilitating patient reflection. In this sense the summaries are used as platforms to 'launch' further questions or enhance awareness.
4.	Information fed back incorrectly.	It is important that the feedback is accurate, otherwise it can lead to confusion or a perception by the patient of being manipulated.
5	Information fed back poorly (e.g. using jargon, or an inappropriate style).	Ideally, the feedback should take account of the patient's style of phrasing things, using relevant quotes as appropriate. This will demonstrate the therapist is listening and understanding, and values the patient's contribution. Jargon should be avoided, unless its goal is to either inject 'relevant' humour or mirror the patient's phraseology.
6	Major summary of session not provided.	At the end of the session it is useful to summarise the content of the therapy session, in relation to the overall goals and the point reached in relation to these goals.

b. Identifying good practice

Examples of the sorts of queries a CTS-R rater might have when making a judgement about the trainee's performance on this item are given below. Under each query is a statement/question demonstrating competence in relation to the query.

1. Was the patient encouraged to provide feedback throughout the session?

   • What do you remember from last week's session?

   • Could you tell me whether I've got that right?

   • Could you tell me the three most important issues we've discussed today?

   • What was the most/least helpful thing that we discussed today?

2. Do you think the feedback was frequent enough?

3. Do you think that the feedback improved the patient's understanding?

   • Just to summarise, at the beginning of the session we spoke about X and the effect it had on your mood. Then we discussed Y, and after that you made the connection between X and Y.

4. Did the therapist check out whether the content was appropriate for the patient?

   • Is there anything that I've said that didn't make sense?

5. Did the therapist chunk the salient pieces of information to provide a platform for new insight?

   • I think I have understood what you just said. Let me see if I can repeat back the main points, and then I'd like to ask a couple of questions arising from these points.

ITEM 3 – COLLABORATION

Like other patient groups, many older people need to be socialised to working in a collaborative style. Some people, particularly those who are used to receiving therapeutic services in medical settings, may find it difficult to adjust to the notion that they need to be active partners in the therapy. Constant reminders of the relevance of their contributions may be required, particularly in the early sessions. It is also important to remember to be discriminative when incorporating patient material into the therapy. This is because irrelevant or tangential contributions can destroy the flow of therapy, as well as its structure.

b. Examples of poor practice

Table AII.3: Identifying examples of poor practice in Collaboration

	Examples of poor practice	Comments
1	An overly didactic style is used.	In such circumstances, the therapist does not encourage the patient to be an active team-player, but adopts the role of an advisor, leader or a director.

Table AII.3: Identifying examples of poor practice in Collaboration

	Examples of poor practice	Comments
2	The style verges on collusion. (NB: A patient often needs to be operating outside of her comfort zone.)	On occasions difficult topics may need to be discussed that the patient is not entirely comfortable with. If these issues require exploration, it is important that the patient is guided to address them. When such issues arise, good collaboration can occur around the planning of how the issue can be discussed sensitively. An example of good collaboration would *not* be a joint decision to avoid discussing a sensitive issue.
3	A good therapeutic relationship does not necessarily imply effective teamwork.	Sometimes a good therapeutic relationship is mistaken for collaboration.
4	Collaboration should not always be led by the patient's immediate needs at the expense of the overall goals of therapy.	On occasions the patient can become overly dominant in the sessions, and the therapist may no longer be able to work effectively. As such, it is OK to question the patient's intentions when she suggests addressing a particular topic in therapy. Indeed, it is the therapist's role to ensure that the material discussed is goal driven and relevant to the therapeutic goals.

b. Identifying good practice

Examples of the sorts of queries a CTS-R rater might have, and also the statements one might hear from the therapist:

1. Was the patient encouraged to participate fully as a team member?

   • How might we get you to test that out?

   • Perhaps we could work out together an alternative way of looking at this issue.

   • Before agreeing that this is a suitable behavioural task, let's both examine the potential obstacles to doing it.

   • That's a difficult one. So let's put our heads together and try to think it through.

- Could you help me make sense of this?

- Let's look at this together.

- You're the expert with respect to your problem. So could you help me understand a bit more about this?

2. Was the therapist able to establish a collaborative relationship?

- You've now got your task for next week, so would you like *me* to do anything for next time?

3. Did the therapist give the patient sufficient space and time to think?

- Stop a second and give yourself a minute to think it through.

- It seems that we'll need to take some time with this issue, but I'm sure that together we can work this one out.

4. Did the therapist contribute to the session sufficiently and guide it appropriately (i.e. not overly acquiescent with respect to the patient's decisions)?

- I can see that you're keen to finish the treatment programme, but what might be the dangers of stopping the therapy too quickly?

5. When the patient tried to introduce unsuitable material into the session, was she gently quizzed about its relevance? If it was found to be inappropriate was it 'dropped' in a helpful manner?

- Before we get involved in a conversation about this topic, we know your time is precious, so can I just check out how that topic fits in with what you want to get out of today's session?

ITEM 4 – PACING AND EFFICIENT USE OF TIME

Sensory difficulties and slowed information processing may mean that the therapy progresses relatively slowly. With certain elders, this must be accepted, otherwise the patient will be outpaced and no longer an active participant in therapy. The therapist can further help the patient to keep pace by providing reminders of the stage of therapy achieved, as well as stating what aspects of therapy remain to be done or achieved.

a. Examples of poor practice

Table AII.4: Identifying examples of poor practice in Pacing and Efficient Use of Time

	Examples of poor practice	Comments
1	Insufficient sign-posts used to help pace the session.	To permit the patient to pace the therapy and her contributions, it is useful to inform her routinely about the time left in the session. It is also helpful to let the patient know what features of the therapy remain (e.g. OK, we've got 15 minutes left, we need to start thinking about how this information can be used to develop a good homework task).
2	Session not well time-managed.	The slowed processing common in many older people requires that the session is paced to their needs; outpacing is a common problem.
3	Rushed towards the end of the session.	Poorly managed sessions are often rushed at the end because the therapist attempts to summarise and squeeze in a homework task before the patient leaves. Rushing like this can often lead to confusion and the undoing of a whole sequence of good therapy.
4	Going over time with respect to the agreed length of the session.	Keeping to an hour (or agreed time period) is important as it permits the patient to pace her own thinking and contributions. It also provides a helpful 'structural feature' for the patient, who otherwise might start to routinely drop in key information just prior to the end of the session.

b. Identifying good practice

Examples of the sorts of queries a CTS-R rater might have, and also the statements one might hear from the therapist:

1. Was the pacing of the session adapted well to the needs of the patient (i.e. did the patient appear rushed)?

   • How much time should we spend on that item?

   • Have we spent too little time on this topic?

- Please tell me when you think we should move off this topic.

2. Was there any time during the session when the session moved too slowly/quickly?

   - Do you want me to go over this with another example?

   - I think I have gone through some of the material in today's session too quickly. I would be grateful for some feedback about this.

3. Do you think the session flowed well overall?

   - How could I have paced today's session better?

4. Was the therapist able to avoid unproductive digressions by the patient?

   - Do you mind stopping a second? You've given me lots of information already. Just to make sure I have understood completely, let's look at the major points you've made.

   - We may have strayed off the topic a little. Shall we get back and focus on the chief issues you've raised? I really don't want us to waste your valuable time.

5. Was there sufficient time left for the 'homework' assignment?

   - Now we have 20 minutes left before the end of the session. Is there anything you think we must cover before the end – keeping in mind that we will also need to set the weekly assignment?

ITEM 5 – INTERPERSONAL EFFECTIVENESS

It is helpful for all therapists to be aware of the dynamics set up between themselves and their patients. It is good to reflect on both one's feelings towards the patient and any perceived needs that may begin to emerge (e.g. desire not to fail her; need to pacify or punish her). When working with older people, trans-generational dynamics are common, and some of these may blur therapeutic boundaries. It is also important to engender hope and positivism in the sessions, as some trainee therapists can feel overwhelmed by the poor prognosis or complexity of people's presentations.

a. Examples of poor practice

Table AII.5: Identifying examples of poor practice in Interpersonal Effectiveness

	Examples of poor practice	Comments
1	Therapist unable to create a sense of warmth or mutual trust.	Some therapists seem unable to bond well with certain patients and/or particular diagnostic presentations. Such difficulties need to be addressed quickly via supervision and through reflection in order to determine the most appropriate action to take. Most difficulties of this nature can be addressed within supervision.
2	Maintaining a good relationship can be over-prioritised.	There is more to therapy than merely establishing a good relationship. Indeed, at times patients need be pushed and moved out of their comfort zones in order to engage with key material that they have avoided in the past.
3	The therapist is unable to recover from alliance ruptures (Westbrook *et al.* 2007, p.29).	Some therapists work competently when the therapy is going well, but find it difficult to work when there has been a disagreement in the session. Some therapists can react by becoming authoritarian, while others become passive.
4.	Therapist is scared to risk a loss of perceived trust, and thus will not engage fully in change strategies.	Change processes (role-plays, experiential exercises) may cause the patient to become uncomfortable. For this reason some therapists avoid using change methods with their patients, perceiving the tension that may result as a potential threat to the relationship.
5	Therapist unwilling or unable to deal with problematic dynamics.	Knight (2004) notes that therapists unused to working with older people often believe that older people cannot benefit from psychotherapy. Such beliefs may also be held by the patients themselves (aka nihilism). Dick *et al.* (1999) also discuss resistance, transference and counter-transference issues associated with the therapeutic relationship. The authors stress the importance of identifying and working through these dynamics, and warn against ignoring them because they are likely to undermine therapy if not attended to.

b. Identifying good practice

Examples of the sorts of queries a CTS-R rater might have, and also the statements one might hear from the therapist:

1. Was the therapist displaying appropriate empathy, understanding, warmth and genuiness?

   • You've made a great effort here.

   • Despite the difficulties, you did really well.

   • Many patients would feel the same way, but you have decided to do something positive about it.

2. Do you think he showed acceptance and liking of the individual, while remaining within professional boundaries?

   • I really admire what you have done so far. Well done!

   • Thank you very much for asking about my family – they're fine. *But* this is your precious time, and it's really important that we focus on you and your needs at the moment. So can we get back to our discussion about the homework task.

   • Shared laughter.

3. Did the therapist empathise with the patient's difficulties?

   • I can tell from your reaction that it was very upsetting for you.

   • I really understand that role-plays are difficult for you to do. However, I think you've just experienced how helpful they can be. Well done!

ITEM 6 – ELICITING APPROPRIATE EMOTIONAL EXPRESSION

Competent therapists are often good at working well with emotions. They are able to elicit them, working with them confidently at various levels of expression. They are also able to help their patients feel contained, and enable them to differentiate between the key emotional states. Some therapists find it difficult to work at an emotional level, preferring to operate at an intellectual level. This is perhaps because many clinicians feel more secure using logic – as there are fewer surprises using this approach. In contrast, when working with emotions situations can frequently shift quickly. For example, an 80-year-old woman who up until this time has presented in a very stoic fashion may suddenly become uncontrollably tearful; leaving both the therapist and her at a loss of what to do next.

a. Examples of poor practice

Table AII.6: Identifying examples of poor practice in Eliciting Appropriate Emotional Expression

Examples of poor practice	Comments
1 The emotional state is often not explicitly addressed in the session, even when the feelings are clearly evident.	Some therapists work too much in the cognitive domain. This can lead to overly intellectual forms of therapy. Problems can occur when both therapist and patient do not feel comfortable dealing with emotions. In such situations key emotional experiences can easily be avoided.
2 Emotions are not acknowledged, especially in situations where inconsistencies are evident (e.g. person talking about dreadful situations, yet smiling).	When emotions are expressed, they need to be acknowledged, and not ignored, by the therapist. Also, therapists should investigate when there are inconsistencies between the contents of the conversation and the appearance of the patient. For example, the 'stiff-upper lip' stance is often a barrier to progress in therapy.
3 Emotions are not being linked to the appropriate thoughts.	A common error is that the therapist fails to link the emotions with the thought content. This link is vital, as it serves to embed the CBT model within the therapy. The CBT model, via the content specificity hypothesis, links specific emotions with cognitive themes (*depression* – negative view of self, hopelessness for future, negative view of present; *anxiety* – fear for safety, chaotic environment, unpredictable future). Some therapists fail to recognise the centrality of this aspect of the therapy, and link inappropriate thoughts to their patients' emotional states (see Figure 2.1, Chapter 2).
4 Working with emotions that are cold.	The cognitive model suggests that NATs are associated with negative mood; as such the therapist needs to be able to elicit mood states routinely in the therapeutic arena. Therefore, it is problematic if the therapist is not prepared to elicit, and then work with, the negative moods (depression, anxiety, anger) in the session.

5	Therapist unable to raise the tone of a flat presentation.	Older people may be reticent at displaying emotions. Thus some patients will present with blunt affect. It is important that the therapist helps the person to become more emotionally articulate.
6.	Anger not addressed, or addressed inappropriately.	Many therapists find it difficult to deal with aggression and anger displayed by their patients. To help trainees prepare for such scenarios, it is helpful to role-play episodes, practising how to acknowledge, contain and deal with the issues underpinning the aggression.
7	In-session emotions neither elicited, nor well differentiated by therapists.	Some therapists fail to make use of emotional states displayed in therapy. For example, if a mood-state is evident it can be used to help the patient explore the experience of the mood, and how it differs from other mood states.

b. Identifying good practice

Examples of the sorts of queries a CTS-R rater might have, and also the statements one might hear from the therapist:

1. Did the therapist pay sufficient attention to the patient's emotions?

   - How did that make you feel?

   - How anxious did you get during the role-play?

   - What are the emotions you feel when speaking about these things?

   - You are relating a very distressing experience, but you are smiling. How do you understand this?

2. Did the therapist help the patient to differentiate between different emotions?

   - You say you felt upset. Was that anxiety or anger?

   - Besides guilt, what else did you feel following this event?

3. Did the therapist raise emotional topics in a sensitive manner?

   - I understand that you found the issues brought up in today's therapy session very difficult, especially as your own father died recently. So, if at any point you feel like you want to stop for a few seconds, let me know.

4.   Was there an optimal level of emotional arousal in the session?

   •   Our session seemed to lack energy today. How can we inject a bit more energy into it?

5.   Did the therapist motivate the patient appropriately?

   •   I always admire your hard work.

6.   Did the therapist empathise with the patient's emotions?

   •   I can see it's really difficult to talk about this issue.

7.   Was the therapist able to contain any emotional outbursts?

   •   I clearly upset you by what I've just said. Can we explore the reasons for this, because I feel uncomfortable ignoring your distress?

ITEM 7 – ELICITING KEY COGNITIONS

Working with relevant cognitions is often the most problematic part of CBT for patients. This is because: (i) the other features of the cycle are experiential, often can be reported easily as they happen, and are topics of conversation in everyday life (I feel this…, I'm doing this…, I've got tension in my shoulders, etc.); (ii) our minds are so busy that identifying specific thoughts associated with specific events is a difficult task. Further, like ice-bergs our beliefs are often hidden far below our levels of immediate perception. As such, it takes a good deal of work on the part of the therapist to socialise patients to work with cognitions. Too often insufficient time is spent helping patients understand the relevance of filtering out the relevant thoughts from the irrelevant ones. Sometimes, the latter problem can be masked by the use of well-constructed questioning, whereby skilful questions enable the person to provide details of what she was thinking. However, in truth, the patient doesn't really have an overview of how the information helps move the therapy forward. Typically, these are the patients who, when asked to explain the model of CBT, struggle to provide a coherent answer.

a. Examples of poor practice

Table AII.7: Identifying examples of poor practice in Eliciting Key Cognitions

	Examples of poor practice	Comments
1	The key cognitions are not linked to the formulation/ conceptualisation.	It is important that the cognitions identified and worked upon by the therapist are relevant to the diagnosis and the patient's presentation. On occasions one may find that the therapist gets confused (e.g. while treating panic, they get tangled up with cognitions related to anger). In such circumstances, when the therapist then attempts to fit the cognitions to the model both he and the patient may get confused.
2	The cognitions are not linked to appropriate emotions.	As above in Table AII.6, no.3.
3	Positive cognitions are not elicited.	Many patients, certainly older people, will have a history of coping well with negative life events. It is important to utilise those experiences and the actions and cognitions associated with them.
4	Too little attention paid to the groundwork required to work at the level of core beliefs.	Occasionally therapists use cognition-eliciting techniques (such as downward arrowing) without preparing the groundwork prior to belief activation (see section 7.5, Chapter 7). This can lead to major difficulties, owing to the high levels of affect associated with the elicitation of many of the core beliefs. A lot of preparation work is required (e.g. scheduling a debriefing period in the session prior to the homework task – see Chapter 7).
5	Core belief work engaged without adequate training or supervision.	Many therapists are able to expose core beliefs, but appear unsure how to work with them competently once they have been activated. A great deal of skill is required to work with this level of cognition, and such forms of therapy should not be undertaken without the appropriate training or supervision (James 2001b).
6	Cognitions from past not re-contextualised (leading to the potential for cognitive infection or re-infection).	Over their lives, patients will have had to make difficult decisions that had the potential for making them think negatively about themselves (e.g. leaving a relationship, giving up a baby, putting someone into care). However, the contexts and circumstances in which the decisions were made will have served to justify the difficult choices taken (e.g. I decided to leave my husband, but only because he beat me regularly). Unfortunately, therapists who do not reactivate the contexts in which the decisions were made may find that during therapy only the facts are recalled (i.e. divorce). Without the mitigating circumstances, these facts can then be used to *either* reinforce negative self-perceptions *or* become the focus of a new set of negative cognitions (e.g. As a Catholic, I should have stayed with him, so here's more proof I'm bad).

b. Identifying good practice

Examples of the sorts of queries a CTS-R rater might have, and also the statements one might hear from the therapist:

1. Was the therapist able to identify and elicit the appropriate cognitions?

    • What was going through your mind at the time?

    • What did you say to yourself when Y happened?

    • There seems to be a rule here that you are applying to yourself. What might the rule be?

    • A word that comes up often in these daily records is 'weak'. Is this how you see yourself in general?

    • If you didn't finish your homework on time, what would it say about you?

2. Was the therapist able to identify thinking biases and elicit hot cognitions?

    • Is that an example of an 'all-or-nothing' style of thinking?

    • By examining our list of biases, what type of bias was that an example of?

    • I can see that you are very upset. What are thinking about right now?

3. Was the thinking consistent with the emotions?

    • You say that you're depressed, but your thoughts are more consistent with anxiety. So if you wouldn't mind, could we examine what went through your head right at that moment?

4. Does the therapist adequately demonstrate to the patient how to identify key cognitions and biases?

    • Was that a depressing thought, or one that made you angry?

    • When I'm asking you to record your thoughts, I don't mean every single thing going through your head. No, I'm interested in those thoughts that are around when you feel depressed. Let's practise recording these types of thoughts on this diary sheet.

    • What would be a useful, perhaps more balanced, thing to say to yourself at this point?

ITEM 8 – ELICITING BEHAVIOURS

Obtaining a detailed description of patients' activities and actions is a crucial aspect of therapy. There is a rich body of work on functional analysis from the behavioural literature regarding this topic (Moniz-Cook *et al.* 2008). Therefore, it is somewhat surprising to see the poor quality of the behavioural analysis undertaken by some clinicians.

a. Examples of poor practice

Table AII.8: Identifying examples of poor practice in Eliciting Behaviours

	Examples of poor practice	Comments
1	Behaviours not elicited.	Some therapists pay too little attention to the behaviours in favour of the cognitions.
2	Insufficient attention is paid to interpersonal behaviours and supports.	Therapy can have a major impact on interpersonal relationships, changing the manner in which the patient views family and friends. Indeed, therapeutic work may reveal interpersonal patterns that require changing. This can present major difficulties for the patient because she may need to withdraw from social networks that were previously valued in some respects. For example, it could become apparent that supporting an alcoholic daughter might be having a major influence on the patient's mood. However, withdrawal from this relationship is likely to have implications on many levels, including physical contact with the grandchildren.
3	Inadequate investigation of safety-seeking behaviours (see Chapter 5).	If one views a disorder as a system, when one tries to change it there will be checks and balances trying to maintain it. Some of these features will be in the form of safety behaviours, and the therapist must ensure that the patient's own 'behavioural defence' system does not sabotage the therapy.
4	Behavioural analysis is not linked to the formulation.	The therapist needs to ensure that the behaviours investigated are in keeping with the formulation framework. Hence, one needs to be able to say why a certain behaviour is the focus of the therapy and how it fits in with the therapeutic rational. Thus, if the person is presenting with an obsessive compulsive disorder, it would be unusual to investigate his fear of public speaking.
5	Actions taken in the past are not re-contextualised, thus they are vulnerable to being assessed negatively.	As above in Table AII.7, no. 6. For example, a daughter feeling guilty for placing her father into a care home just prior to her dad's death. However, when recalling the story the daughter fails to recall the stress and pressures she was under at the time (family, financial, health, etc.), which meant she could not care for him in her home.

b. Identifying good practice

Examples of the sorts of queries a CTS-R rater might have, and also the statements one might hear from the therapist:

1. Did the therapist examine adequately the role that behavioural features played in the triggering and maintenance of the patient's problems?

   - Some people develop habits or rituals when they become stressed. What patterns, if any, have you noticed in relation to your behaviour?

2. Did the therapist help the patient discover the impact of her behaviours in terms of relevant emotional features?

   - When you felt fearful, did you *do* anything that reduced your level of fear?

   - After checking your pulse rate, following the panic attack, how did it make you feel?

3. Did the therapist obtain a good understanding of the behaviours?

   - If I had a camera and filmed you when you are feeling low, what would I see?

ITEM 9 – GUIDED DISCOVERY

Via the process of guided discovery, a therapist facilitates patients' gaining new levels of understanding through their own reasoning skills. Thus the therapist must avoid telling the patient what to do or how to think, rather he should help them to make the connections for themselves. This requires patience on the part of the therapist, and is particularly difficult when patients are being overly concrete or are poor at making their own links.

a. Examples of poor practice

Table AII.9: Identifying examples of poor practice in Guided Discovery

Examples of poor practice	Comments
1 Questioning style is tortuous and over-complicated.	Sometimes therapists' questions may contain more than one query or theme, which often serves to confuse the patient. Simple, non-abstract questions are usually the best (see Chapter 7).
2 Use of an interrogative style.	If question follows question follows question, the patients can feel they are on trial. Questions need to be interspersed with other forms of communication, including summaries, platforms, comments, explanations, analogies, etc.
3 Questions asked too rapidly.	Questioners must provide time for the patient to reflect and consider her response. If questions are asked too rapidly the patient's information processing system will soon be overloaded.
4 Questions are not used as a platform to further therapy.	Questions should have a purpose – hence there is often a line of questioning used to follow a theme. It is useful to inform the patient of the goal of the line of questioning so that she can provide relevant answers. For example, it is often useful to say something like: 'The next set of questions will help me to see how you have coped since you retired.'
5 Little use of circular questioning techniques (James and Morse 2007).	Circular forms of questioning permit the patient to take on other people's views and to re-examine her interpretations. Some therapists simply fail to use this very useful form of questioning style.
6 A general lack of awareness about questioning techniques.	Questions often form a major percentage of the communication of the therapist. However, studies show that therapists have relatively little awareness of the theory underpinning 'questioning styles' (James and Morse 2007). It is suggested that therapists should pay greater attention to the 'questioning' because this is one of the main tools of their trade.
7 Guided discovery only seen as questioning techniques, thus insufficient use is made of metaphor, analogy and self-disclosure.	Guided discovery involves helping patients to reappraise their experiences of their disorders through the use of many strategies, including the use of stories, self-disclosure techniques, provision of factual information, scaffolding, etc.

b. Identifying good practice

Examples of the sorts of queries a CTS-R rater might have, and also the statements one might hear from the therapist:

1. Were any questions asked in a manner that facilitated the patient's understanding?

    •   I wonder whether there were any other times in your life when you felt the same way?

    •   If you were speaking to a stranger, how would you deal with this situation?

    •   How does this relate to what you told me earlier – that is, you never feel comfortable about going for a drink with your dad?

    •   What is the common link between X and Y?

2. Did the questions lead to, or promote, change?

    •   You have this difficulty when you're with both John and Paul, but you never have it with Peter. Can you think of a reason for this?

    •   If you were giving advice to a colleague, what might you say to her?

    •   From what you've just said, in order to find out whether X will happen, you need to stop avoiding Y. Is that true?

3. Did the therapist use multiple means (questions, metaphor, appropriate self-disclosure) to promote discovery?

ITEM 10 – CONCEPTUAL INTEGRATION

The formulation forms the backbone of the therapy. Patients and therapists must have a shared understanding of the working formulations; this is not always evident. During therapy, the therapist will usually be moving between the formulation (e.g. the diathesis-stress conceptualisation) and mini-conceptual cycles (e.g. hot-cross bun framework). The patient must be fully aware of these types of conceptual models, and their differences, and also be able to work comfortably and confidently at either level.

a. Examples of poor practice

Table AII.10: Identifying examples of poor practice in Conceptual Integration

Examples of poor practice	Comments
1 Patients are not socialised adequately.	The CBT model requires that patients understand the nature of the therapy they are engaged in. If they do not, much of the material (diaries, monitoring sheets, homework tasks, questions) will not make sense to them. Hence, it is essential that if asked at any point in the therapy to describe the CBT model they are currently working with, they should be able to answer this query adequately. If they cannot do the latter, they have not been adequately socialised to the model.
2 Kitchen-sink formulations must be avoided.	Many formulations become unwieldy due to the amount of details they contain; having more information is not necessarily better. Good therapists often operate by the rule of parsimony, whereby they include only the essential details required to produce lasting change.
3 Insufficient attention is paid to the patient's conceptual model.	Patients enter therapy with their own conceptual view of their difficulties and change strategies. It is important that they are given the opportunity to voice these perspectives, because the perspectives may either hinder or facilitate the therapeutic work.
4 Insufficient attention is paid to information processing deficits and their influence on the patient's ability to engage in the therapy.	Cognitive deficits are apparent in the processing abilities of older people and also those with the affective disorders, psychoses, etc. Hence, it is important the problems associated with the patient's executive functioning, memory, attentional biases are all conceptualised within the patient's experience of her difficulties.
5 Obstacles to change are not fully conceptualised.	Obstacles to improvement can take the form of age, social status, class, education, financial security, race, accommodation, etc. Such features need to be discussed as part of the formulation.
6 Patient's coping skills insufficiently utilised.	The patient's previous methods of coping are not elicited and assessed regarding their appropriateness in current situation.

Table AII.10: Identifying examples of poor practice in Conceptual Integration *cont.*

	Examples of poor practice	Comments
7	Inappropriate use of schema formulations.	Schema formulations are not appropriate in many presentations (late onset presentations, panic, first-incident mild depression, etc.). Such formulations are very powerful, but are difficult to use (James 2001b). As such, they should be used with caution, and not by inexperienced therapists without supervision.
8	Conceptual models shared with patients are too complex.	Over time conceptual models of many of the CBT disorders have become more complex (GAD, social phobia, OCD). Many of them are now represented as dynamic box and arrow diagrams. Such complexity may help the therapist to understand what is going on, but caution is advised about sharing such complex diagrams with patients. Indeed, if presented with these forms of 'plumbing' diagrams, the patients may feel rather overwhelmed.

b. Identifying good practice

Examples of the sorts of queries a CTS-R rater might have, and also the statements one might hear from the therapist:

1. Has the therapist socialised the patient to the CT rationale?

   • Sometimes I have a tendency to confuse people, so would you be able to summarise what I've said, using the terms we use in CBT?

   • Let's see how the various things we have talked about hold together.

   • How does looking at your depression like this help you to make sense of your situation?

2. Does the therapist demonstrate a good understanding of generic CBT and a good understanding of the CBT rationale for the specific disorder?

   • Often when someone has OCD they experience a lot of anxiety; is this what you were feeling at that moment prior to checking the door? – *Patient: 'No, I didn't feel anxious'* – OK, but what if you weren't able to check the door, what emotion would you have experienced?

3. Does the patient have an adequate CBT understanding of the problem?

   - Using the CBT model, could you explain the link between the events, your thoughts and feelings?

4. Has the conceptualisation been truly integrated (i.e. has it been used to guide the therapy)?

   - Thinking about this negative cycle, what sorts of things could we do to break free of this unhelpful pattern?

5. Did the therapist make lateral and vertical links with respect to the patient's present difficulties?

   - What we have done so far is to look at the way your thoughts affect the way you feel and what you do. It would also be useful for us to look at some general rules and attitudes that are contained in these thoughts. The reason for doing this is for us to try to understand where the cognitions come from. Is this OK with you?

   - Let's look at previous times in your life when you have been depressed.

   - Describe the times in your life when you've felt good about yourself?

ITEM 11 – APPLICATION OF CHANGE METHODS

Many therapists simply do not employ effective change techniques that are available to them. That is, therapists do not use change techniques frequently enough, and tend to perform them poorly. One of the reasons for the low level of competence is that while negative beliefs can be elicited with relative ease, 'clinical change', particularly at the level of core belief, is difficult to achieve (Chapters 5 and 7).

a. Examples of poor practice

Table AII.11: Identifying examples of poor practice
in the Application of Change Methods

	Examples of poor practice	Comments
1	The therapy gets stuck in a circle of assessment (Chapter 5).	Therapists are usually quick at picking up assessment skills, but often find it more difficult to use change methodologies. When such circumstances exist, the patient can get stuck into a permanent cycle of questions and assessment procedures. Further, because change methods are not employed, despite a better understanding of the problems, the patient's status never improves.
2	Unclear about the goals of change.	The method must have a specified goal, which both the therapist and patient can work towards collaboratively. It is often good to specify the goal in concrete terms. The technique of goal attainment scaling is helpful is specifying one's goals and clarifying clinical change.
3	Realistic assessment of what can change/useful to think what one wants the patient to be thinking when she leaves the session.	The goal needs to be realistic and achievable. In order to clarify what one is trying to achieve with a given method, it is useful to think about what *ideally* you would want the patient to be thinking by the end of the technique. For example, consider a woman who perceives herself to be evil because of her frequent abusive thoughts. At the end of the re-evaluation exercise, I might want her to move from 'I'm evil' to 'If I was really evil, I wouldn't get so upset about having these unpleasant thoughts'. Having clarified one's aim, one can judge whether this is feasible, and tailor one's methods more precisely.
4	Therapist fails to check whether the patient has the abilities (e.g. cognitive, sensory, intellectual) to use the technique effectively.	Prior to setting certain 'change processes' some simple sensory and physical checks may need to be made. At the simplest level this may be asking whether the patients have their spectacles and/ or hearing device with them. Some checks may require the assistance of a medical advisor prior to conducting the physical task.

| 5 | A failure to take account of the impact of change. | Change brings about re-conceptualisation, and thus patients may need time to deal with the changes to their world-view. The therapist needs to be careful about moving on to a new topic too quickly. For example, therapy may highlight major problems within a marriage. One would need to handle such a situation with care, and be wary of the patient making any impulsive decisions about their relationship as a consequence of an insightful session. |
| 6 | Poor skills in change techniques (continua/responsibility pie charts) Westbrook *et al.* 2007, p.239). | Sometimes therapists will attempt complex change methods without having spent time practising the techniques previously. On such occasions one often observes them becoming confused, which results in therapeutic ruptures and patient confusion. With complex strategies, it is important, and ethical, for the therapists to have practised (role-played) the techniques before subjecting their patients to them. |

b. Identifying good practice

Examples of the sorts of queries a CTS-R rater might have, and also the statements one might hear from the therapist:

1. Were change methods employed effectively?

2. Has the therapist ensured that the patient understands the rationale underpinning the method?

   • What are the benefits of thinking in this way…and are there any problems?

   • How else could you have seen this situation? Are there alternative views?

   • What would you say to your best friend?

   • When have you had the same experience in the past and reacted differently?

   • Would other people have the same opinion of you, and if 'not' why so?

   • What are the disadvantages of thinking that way? What are the advantages?

3. Prior to using the techniques were the learning goals clearly established?

   • Do you understand the things we are going to be testing out during this assignment?

4. Were the learning goals achieved?

   • How has doing this assignment helped you start to reassess the situation?

5. Were too many/few techniques used in the session?

6. Were the techniques suitable and appropriate for the patient (i.e. neither too complicated nor too demanding)?

   • In what way is this a useful test of the hypothesis?

   • On a scale of 1–10, how confident are you to try and do this yourself during the week?

7. Was the technique consistent with the formulation?

   • How does this outcome help to clarify the formulation?

   • Can we test out this assumption in this session? What might you try and do differently to see whether your predictions are right?

8. Where necessary, was a competent explanation of the rationale of the technique given?

   • Let's go through the reasoning behind this assignment one more time?

   • What useful things will you learn from doing this?

9. Were there valuable opportunities missed when appropriate techniques could have been administered?

ITEM 12 – HOMEWORK SETTING

When working with older people, the potential obstacles that may prevent the completion of the assignment need to be investigated. For example, there may be issues to do with physical health, mobility, sensory deficits, finance, lack of transport, etc. As such, Laidlaw and Thompson (2008) suggest that the tasks should be set up as 'no-lose' scenarios. This is usually done by preparing the patient prior to undertaking the assignment for all possible eventualities, including non-completion. Helpful statements relating to this scenario could be 'Even if you don't manage to get out of the house at all next week, what useful lessons can we learn from this fact?' 'And what information about your experience of "not getting out" would it be useful to bring along to the next session?'

Unfortunately, owing to poor time management or a failure to appreciate their importance, many homework assignments are rushed, poorly conceived and planned – and thus unsurprisingly poorly conducted by patients.

a. Examples of poor practice

Table AII.12: Identifying examples of poor practice in Homework Setting

	Examples of poor practice	Comments
1	All the items specified in Table AII.11 (Application of Change Methods) are appropriate.	As above in Table AII.11.
2	Failing to put the homework task on the agenda of the next session.	In order to highlight the key role of the task in the therapeutic process, it is important that the previous homework is discussed in detail, and the lessons learned reflected upon in relation to setting the new assignment.
3	The inappropriate use of prefabricated tasks (Laidlaw and Thompson 2008).	The task should develop as a product of the session, it should not be determined by the therapist prior to the start of the session (i.e. prefabricated). When prefabricated tasks are used, the assignment setting can make the therapy disjointed and the momentum of the therapy can be lost. Such a problem is more common among novice rather than experienced therapists.
4	Too little time left to prepare homework task.	Therapists sometimes do not leave sufficient time to conduct a well-planned homework task. Then, because the task is so rushed, it is often not explained well, and the patient ends up being confused. Further, there is less chance she will carry out the task successfully, which can further undermine the patient's self-esteem. This problem can be overcome by routinely setting the task within the main body of the session (Tompkins 2004). Such a process is often preferred, as it is a more natural and developmental process.

Table AII.12: Identifying examples of poor practice in Homework Setting *cont.*

Examples of poor practice	Comments
5 Potential obstacles are not adequately identified, and a 'learning-scenario' is not programmed into the task.	In the 'real world' there are many potential obstacles to conducting the task. It is helpful to spend time anticipating such problems and problem-solving around them.
	Laidlaw and Thompson (2008) suggest care when giving written homework, due to the fact some older people can be self-conscious about the quality of their writing and their spelling. They recommend that this issue is checked out prior to the assignment and a sample of handwriting viewed in-session to try to dispel any fears of criticism.
	One can also plan what the fall-back strategies are. For example, if the task can't be completed fully, what can be learned by the patient from the partial completion of the task?

b. Identifying good practice

Examples of the sorts of queries a CTS-R rater might have, and also the statements one might hear from the therapist:

1. Did the therapist adequately explain the rationale underpinning the assignment?

   • To make sure we're in agreement about the goals of the task, shall we go through the relevance of the assignment one more time?

2. Did the therapist check that the patient was confident about conducting the task correctly?

   • What are your greatest fears about doing this?

   • How nervous do you think you'll get just before you do it?

   • What emotions are you likely to experience?

   • How confident are you that you'll be able to do it?

3. Did the patient see the relevance of the assignment?

   • Do you think anything useful will be learned from doing this?

   • Is the task going to be a helpful thing to do…and in what way?

4. Was the assignment adequately planned within the session?

   • Before doing such assignments, I like to think through the steps and goals involved. Here are some of the steps that we've agreed are important. Have we:

     ° thought through the relevance of the assignment

     ° checked through anticipated level of arousal

     ° planned what needs to be done carefully, and are aware of potential obstacles

     ° practised the behaviour, before you put yourself in the difficult situation

     ° prior to actually doing the task, been able to relate either success or failure to a change in perspective?

   • Can you think of any other important steps and goals?

5. Were the obstacles to conducting the plan discussed?

   • What are going to be the difficulties in doing this?

   • How are you going to overcome the problems that will arise?

   • If you wake up on the day you've planned to take your first steps out of the house, and it's pouring with rain, what are you going to do? Good, so you've got a coat, and what will you wear on your feet? (NB: It is often these small details that prevent an anxious person carrying out assignment tasks.)

6. Did the therapist set the most appropriate homework task?

   • In what ways do you think this assignment is relevant to what we've just been talking about?

   • Will the task help test out the key hypotheses? Could we change it in any way so that it would be even more helpful?

   • How is this homework consistent with the ideas that we've spoken about in the session?

7. Will the patient learn something useful from engaging in this task?

   • What is the most useful thing you could learn from doing this?

References

Aakhus, E., Engedal, K. Aspelund, T., and Selbaek, G. (2009). 'Single session educational programme for caregivers of psychogeriatric in-patients – results from a randomised controlled pilot study'. *International Journal of Geriatric Psychiatry*, 24, 269–274.

Adler, A. (1927). *The Practice and Theory of Individual Psychology*. New York: Harcourt Brace.

Adshead, F., Day Cody, D. and Pitt, B. (1992). 'BASDEC: a novel screening instrument for depression in elderly medical inpatients'. *British Medical Journal*, 305, 397.

Akkerman, R. and Ostwald, S.K. (2004). 'Reducing anxiety in Alzheimer's disease family caregivers: effectiveness of a nine-week cognitive behavioural intervention'. *American Journal of Alzheimer's Disease and Other Disorders*, 19(2), 117–123.

Alexopoulos, G.S. (2005). 'Depression in the elderly'. *Lancet*, 365 (9475), 1961–1970.

Alexopoulos, G.S., Abrams, R.C., Young, R.C. and Shamoian, C.A. (1988). 'Cornell scale for depression in dementia'. *Biological Psychiatry*, 23, 271–284.

Andrews, G. (1996). 'Talk that works: the rise of cognitive behaviour therapy'. *British Medical Journal*, 7071 (313), 1501–1502.

Anderson, L., Lewis, G., Araya, R., Elgie, R., *et al.* (2004). 'Self-help books for depression: how can practitioners and patients make the right choice'. *British Journal of General Practice*, 55, 387–392.

Anderson, T., Watson, M. and Davidson, R. (2008). 'The use of cognitive behaviour therapy techniques for anxiety and depression in hospice patients: a feasibility study'. *Palliative Medicine*, 22, 814–821.

Ardern, M. (2002). 'Psychodynamic therapy'. In J. Hepple, J. Pearce and P. Wilkinson (Eds) *Psychological Therapies for Older People*. Hove: Brunner-Routledge.

Armstrong, P. and Freeston, M. (2006). 'Conceptualising and formulating cognitive therapy supervision'. In N. Tarrier (Ed), *Case Formulation in Cognitive Behaviour Therapy*. London: Routledge.

Audit Commission (2002). *Forget Me Not 2002*. www.audit-commission.gov.uk

Australian Government (2007). *Dementia Management Advisory Service: Operational Guidelines*. Canberra: Department of Health and Ageing.

Ayers, C., Sorrell, J., Thorp, S. and Wetherell, J. (2007). 'Evidence based psychological treatments for late-life anxiety.' *Psychology and Aging*, 22(1), 8–17.

BABCP (2008). *Use of the ICS in Clinical Practice: Symposium*. Edinburgh University (July, 2008).

Baddeley, A.D. (1983). 'Working memory', *Philosophical Transactions of the Royal Society, Series B*, 302, 311–324.

Ballard, C. and Waite, J. (2006). 'Atypical antipsychotics for aggression and psychosis in Alzheimer's disease'. *Cochrane Database of Systematic Reviews*. Issue 1, article no. CD003476.

Ballard, C., O'Brien, J., Reichelt, K. and Perry, E. (2002). 'Aromatherapy as a safe and effective treatment for the management of agitation in severe dementia: the results of a double-blind, placebo controlled trial on Melissa'. *The Journal of Clinical Psychiatry*, 63(7), 553–558.

Baltes P.B., and Baltes, M. (1990). 'Psychological perspectives on successful ageing: the model of selective optimisation with compensation'. In P. Baltes and M. Baltes (Eds) *Successful Aging: Perspectives from the Behavioral Sciences*. Cambridge: Cambrdge University Press.

Barber, J. and De Rubeis, R.J. (1989). 'On second thought: where the action is in cognitive therapy for depression'. *Cognitive Therapy and Research*, 13, 441–457.

Bartlett, F.J. (1932). *Remembering*. Cambridge, UK: Cambridge University Press.

Barton, S., Armstrong, P., Freeston, M. and Twaddle, V. (2008). 'Early intervention for adults at high risk of recurrent/chronic depression'. Cognitive model and clinical case series. *Behaviour and Cognitive Psychotherapy*, 36, 263–282.

Beck, A.T. (1976). *Cognitive Therapy and the Emotional Disorders*. New York: International University Press.

Beck, A.T., Epstein, N., Harrison, R.P. and Emery, G. (1983). *Development of the Sociotropy – Autonomy Scale: A Measure of Personality Factors in Psychopathology*. Philadelphia, PA: Center for Cognitive Therapy, University of Pensylvania Medical School.

Beck, C., Ortigara, A., Mercer, S. and Shue, V. (1999). 'Enabling and empowering certified nursing assistants for Quality Dementia Care'. *International Journal of Geriatric Psychiatry*, 14, 197–212.

Beck, A.T. and Steer, R. (1993). *Beck Anxiety Inventory Manual*. San Antonio: The Psychological Corporation.

Beck, A.T., Steer, R., Ball, R. and Ranieri, W. (1996). 'Comparison of Beck depression inventories-IA and –II in psychiatric outpatients'. *Journal Personality Assessment*, 67, 588–597.

Beck, A.T., Ward, C.H., Mendelson, M., Mock, J. and Erbaugh, J. (1961). 'An inventory for measuring depression'. *Archives of General Psychiatry*, 4, 561–571.

Beck, A.T., Weissman, A., Lester, D. and Trexler, L. (1974). 'The measurement of pessimism: the hopelessness scale'. *Journal of Consulting and Clinical Psychology*, 42(6), 861–865.

Beutler, L.E. and Crago, M. (1991). *Psychotherapy Research: International Programmatic Studies*. Washington, DC: American Psychological Association.

Bieling, P.J. and Kuyken, W. (2003). 'Is cognitive case formulation science or science fiction?' *Clinical Psychology: Science and Practice*, 10(1), 52–69.

Bird, M., Llewellyn-Jones, R.H. and Korten, A. (2009). 'An evaluation of the effectiveness of a case-specific approach to challenging behaviour associate with dementia'. *Aging and Mental Health*, 13(1), 73–83.

Bird, M, Lelwellyn-Jones, R.H., Korten, A. and Smithers, H. (2007). 'A controlled trial of a predominantly psychosocial approach to BPSD: treating causality'. *International Psychogeriatrics*, 19(5), 874–891.

Blackburn, I.M and Davidson, K. (1995). *Cognitive Therapy for Depression and Anxiety*. (2nd ed) Oxford: Blackwell Scientific Publications.

Blackburn, I.M., James, I.A. and Flitcroft, A. (2006). 'Case formulation in depression'. In N. Tarrier (Ed) *Case Formulation*. London: Routledge

Blackburn, I.M., James, IA., Milne, D.L., Baker, C.. Standart, S., Garland, A. and Reichelt, F. (2001). 'The revised cognitive therapy scale (CTS-R): psychometric properties'. *Behavioural and Cognitive Psychotherapy*, 29(4), 431–447.

Blake, D.D., Weathers, F., Nagy, L., Kaloupek, D. *et al.* (1995). 'The development of a clinician-administered PTSD scale'. *Journal of Traumatic Stress*, 8, 75–90.

Bohlmeijer, E., Smit F. and Cuipers, P. (2003). 'Effects of reminiscence and life review on late-life depression: a meta-analysis'. *International Journal of Geriatric Psychiatry*, 18, 1088–1094.

Bordin, E,S. (1994). 'Theory and research on the therapeutic working alliance: New Directions'. In A. O. Horvath and L. S. Greenberg (Eds)*The Working Alliance: Theory, Research, and Practice*. New York: Wiley.

Borkovec, T. and Newman, M. (1999). 'Worry and generalized anxiety disorder'. In P. Salkovskis (Ed) *Comprehensive Clinical Psychology*, 6 Oxford: Elsevier.

Brewin, C.R. (1998). 'Intrusive memories, depression, and PTSD'. *The Psychologist*, 11, 281–283.

Brodaty, H., Green, A. and Koschera, A. (2003). 'Meta-analysis of psychosocial interventions for caregivers of people with dementia'. *Journal of American Geriatric Society*, 51, 657–664.

Buchanan, J. (2004). 'Generalization of the effects of a cognitive-behavioral intervention for family caregivers of individuals with dementia'. *Dissertation Abstracts International: Section B: The Sciences and Engineering*, 65, US.

Burns, A., Lawlor, B. and Craig, S. (2004). *Assessment Scales in Old Age Psychiatry* (2nd ed). London: Informa Healthcare.

Burns, D. (1980). *Feeling Good*. New York: New American Library.

Butler, G. (1998). 'Clinical Formulation'. In A. Bellack and M. Hersen (Eds) *Comprehensive Clinical Psychology*. New York: Perganon.

Butler, G. and Hackmann A. (2004). 'Social anxiety'. In J. Bennett-Levy, G. Butler, M. Fennell, A. Hackmann, M. Mueller and D. Westbrook (Eds) *Oxford Guide to Behavioural Experiments In Cognitive Therapy*. Oxford: Oxford University Press.

Buysse, D.J., Reynolds, C., Monk, T.H., Berman, S. and Kupfer, D. (1989). 'The Pittsburgh Sleep Quality Index: a new instrument for psychiatric practice and research'. *Psychiatric Research*, 28, 193–213.

Calder, F. (2000). *The Development of a Client Completed Suitability Measure for Short-term Cognitive Therapy*. In part fulfilment of Doctorate in Clinical Psychology, School of Health, University of Teesside, UK

Caress, A.L., Luker, K.A., Chalmers, K.I., and Salmon, M.P. (2009). 'A review of the information and support needs of family carers of patients with chronic obstructive pulmonary disease'. *Journal of Clinical Nursing*, 18, 479–491.

Carey, T.A. and Mullan, R.J. (2004). 'What is Socratic questioning?' *Psychotherapy: Theory, Research Practice, Training*, 41, 217–226.

Cassens, G., Wolfe, L. and Zola, M. (1990). 'The neuropsychology of depressions'. *Journal of Neuropsychiatry and Clinical Neurosciences*, 2(2), 202–213.

Champion, L.A. and Power, M.J. (1995). 'Social and cognitive approaches to depression: towards a new synthesis'. *British Journal of Clinical Psychology*, 34, 485–503.

Charlesworth, G. and Reichelt, F.K. (2004). 'Keeping conceptualisations simple: examples with family carers of people with dementia'. *Behaviour and Cognitive Psychotherapy*, 32, 401–409.

Clark, D.M. (1986). 'A cognitive approach to panic'. *Behaviour Research and Therapy*, 24, 461–470.

Cohen-Mansfield, J. (2000a). 'Use of patient characteristics to determine nonpharmacologic interventions for behavioural and psychological symptoms of dementia'. *International Psychogeriatrics*, 12(1), 373–386.

Cohen-Mansfield, J. (2000b). 'Nonpharmalogical management of behavioural problems in persons with dementia: the TREA model'. *Alzheimer Care Quarterly*, 1, 22–34.

Cohen-Mansfield, J., Libin, A. and Marx M. (2007). 'Nonpharmacological treatment of agitation: a controlled trial of systematic individualized intervention'. *Journal of Gerontology: Medical Sciences*, 62A,(8), 906–918.

Cole, K. and Vaughan, F. (2005). 'Brief cognitive-behavioural therapy for depression associated with Parkinson's disease: a literature review'. *Parkinsonism and Related Disorders*, 11, 269–276.

Cook, A.J. (1998). 'Cognitive-behavioural pain management for elderly nursing home residents'. *Journal of Gerontology*, 53B(1), 51–59.

Cook, J.M. and O'Donnell, C. (2005). 'Assessment and psychological treatment of posttraumatic stress disorder in older adults'. *Journal of Geriatric Psychiatry and Neurology*, 18, 61–71.

Coon, D.W. and Gallagher-Thompson, L. (2002). 'Encouraging homework completion among older adults in therapy'. *JCLP/In session: Psychotherapy in Practice*, 58, 549–563.

Coon, D.W. and Thompson, L.W. (2003). 'The relationship between homework compliance and treatment outcomes among older adult outpatients with mild-to-moderate depression'. *American Journal of Geriatric Psychiatry*, 11(1), 53–61.

Coon, D. W., Thompson, L. W., and Gallagher-Thompson, D. (2007). 'Adapting homework for an older adult client with cognitive impairment'. *Cognitive and Behavioral Practice*, 14(3), 252–260.

Cooper, C., Balamurali, T., Selwood, A. and Livingston, G. (2007). 'A systematic review of the treatment of anxiety in caregivers of people with dementia.' *International Psychogeriatrics*, 28, 1-21.

Cooper, C., Katona, C., Orrell, M. and Livingston, G. (2006). 'Coping strategies and anxiety in caregivers of people with Alzheimer's disease: the LASER-AD study.' *Journal of Affective Disorders*, 90(1), 15-20.

Cossette, S. and Levesque, L. (1993). 'Caregiving tasks as predictors of mental health of wife caregivers of men with chronic obstructive pulmonary disease.' *Research in Nursing and Health*, 16(4), 251-263.

CSIP/DoH (2005). *Everybody's Business: Integrated Mental Health Services for Older Adults. A Service Developmental Guide.* Department of Health.

Cuijpers, P. (1998). 'Psychological outreach programmes for the depressed elderly: a meta-analysis of effects and dropout'. *International Journal of Geriatric Psychiatry*, 13(1), 41–48.

Cully, J.A., and Stanley, M. (2008). 'Assessment and treatment of anxiety in later life'. In K. Laidlaw and B. Knight (eds) *Handbook of Emotional Disorders in Later Life: Assessment and Treatment.* Oxford: Oxford University Press.

Cummings, J.L., Mega, M., Gray, K., Rosenberg-Thompson, S. *et al.* (1994). 'The neuropsychiatric inventory: comprehensive assessment of psychopathology in dementia'. *Neurology*, 44, 2308–2314.

Davison, G.C. (2000). 'Stepped care: doing more with less?' *Journal of Consulting and Clinical Psychology*, 68(4), 580–585.

DoH (2001). *National Service Framework for Older People.* DOH, PO Box 777, London SE1 6XH. Fax: 0623 724524

DoH (2005). *Securing Better Mental Health for Older Adults,* London: Department of Health.

DoH (2009). *Older People. Positive Practice Guide: IAPT.* DOH, PO Box 777, London SE1 6XH. Fax: 0623 724524

Dick, L., Gallagher-Thompson, D. and Thompson, L. (1996). 'Cognitive-behavioural therapy'. In R.T. Woods (Ed). *Handbook of the Clinical Psychology of Ageing.* Chichester: Wiley and Sons.

Dick, L., Gallagher-Thompson, D. and Thompson L. (1999). 'Cognitive-behavioural therapy: the theory of cognitive-behavioural therapy'. In R.T. Woods (Ed). *Handbook of the Clinical Psychology of Ageing.* Chichester: Wiley and Sons.

Di Nardo, P., Moras, K., Barlow, D., Rapee, R. and Brown, T. (1993). 'Reliability of DSM-III-K anxiety disorder categories using Anxiety Disorders Interview Schedule-Revised (ADIS-R)'. *Archives of General Psychiatry*, 50, 251–256.

Doubleday, E.K., King, P. and Papageorgiou, C. (2002). 'Relationship between fluid intelligence and ability to benefit from cognitive-behavioural therapy in older adults: a preliminary investigation'. *British Journal of Clinical Psychology*, 41(4), 423–428.

Duberstein, P. and Heisel, M. (2008) 'Assessment and Treatment of Suicidal Behaviour in Later Life' In K. Laidlow and B. Knight (eds) *Handbook of Emotional Disorders in Later Life: Assessment and Treatment.* Oxford: Oxford University Press.

Drevets, W.C. and Raichle, M.E. (1995). *Positron Emission Tomographic Imaging Studies of Human Emotional Disorders.* Cambridge, Mass: MIT Press.

Edelstein, B.A., Woodhead, E., Segal, D., Heisel, M. *et al.* (2008). 'Older adult psychological assessment: current instrument status and related considerations'. *Clinical Gerontologist*, 31(3), 1–35.

Eells, T., Kendjelic, E. and Lucas, C. (1998). 'What's in a case formulation: development and use of a content coding manual'. *Journal of Psychotherapy Practice and Research*, 7, 144–153.

Elliott, C. and Kirby-Lassen, M. (1998). *Why Can't I Get What I Want?* Palo Alto, CA: Davies Black Publishing.

Elliot, R. (1998). 'The neurological profile in unipolar depression'. *Trends in Cognitive Sciences*, 2, 447–484.

Emerson, E. (1998). 'Working with people with challenging behaviour'. In E. Emerson, C. Hatton, J. Bromley, and A. Caine (Eds) *Clinical Psychology and People with Intellectual Disabilities.* Chichester: John Wiley and Sons.

Feil, N. and de Klerk-Rubein, V. (2002) *The Validation Breakthrough: Simple Techniques for Communicating with People with Alzheimer's type Dementia.* Baltimore: Health Professions Press.

Flitcroft, A., James, I.A. and Freeston, M. (2007). 'Determining what is important in a good formulation'. *Behavioural Cognitive Psychotherapy,* 35, 325–333.

Floyd, M. (1999). 'Cognitive therapy for depression: a comparison of individual psychotherapy and bibliotherapy for depressed older adults'. *Dissertation Abstracts International,* 58(9–B), 5081.

Floyd, M., Rohen, N., Shackelford, J.A.M., Hubbard, K.L., *et al.* (2006). 'Two-year follow-up of bibliotherapy and individual cognitive therapy for depressed older adults'. *Behavior Modification,* 30(3), 281–294.

Floyd, M., Scogin, F., McKendree-Smith, N.L., Floyd, D.L. and Rokke, P.D. (2004). 'Cognitive therapy for depression: a comparison of individual psychotherapy and bibliotherapy for depressed older adults'. *Behavior Modification,* 28(2), 297–318.

Folstein, M.F., Folstein, S. and McHugh, P. (1975). 'Mini mental state: a practical method for grading the cognitive state of patients for the clinician.' *Journal of Psychiatric Research,* 12, 189-198.

Fossey, J., Ballard, C., Juszczak, E., James, I. *et al.* (2006). 'Effect of enhanced psychosocial care on antipsychotic use in nursing home residents with severe dementia: cluster randomised trial'. *British Medical Journal,* 332, 756–8.

Fossey, J. and James, I.A. (2008). *Evidence-based Approaches for Improving Dementia Care in Care Homes.* Alzheimer's Society: London.

Fothergill, C. and Kuyken, W. (2002). *Reliability of cognitive case formulation using the J.S. Beck Case Conceptualisation diagram.* Manuscript submitted for publication (see Kuyken, Padesky and Dudley, 2009).

Fry, P. (1986). *Depression, Stress and Adaptations with the Elderly. Psychological Assessment and Intervention.* Bethesda, MD: Aspen.

Gallacher, J. (2004). 'Hearing, cognitive impairment and aging: a critical review'. *Reviews in Clinical Gerontology,* 14, 199–209.

Gallagher, D. and Thompson, L.W. (1981). *Depression in the Elderly: A Behavioral Treatment Manual.* Los Angeles: University of Southern California Press.

Gallagher-Thompson, D. and Steffens, A.M. (1994). 'Comparative effects of cognitive behavioural and brief psychodynamic psychotherapies for depressed family caregivers'. *Journal of Consulting and Clinical Psychology,* 62, 543–549.

Gallagher-Thompson, D. and Thompson, L. (1996). 'Applying cognitive-behavioural therapy to the psychological problems of later life.' In S.H. Zarit and B.G. Knight (Eds) Guide to Psychotherapy and Aging: Effective Clinical Interventions in a Life-stage Context. Washington, DC: American Psychological Association.

Gallagher-Thompson, D. and Thompson, L.W. (2009). *Treating Late Life Depression: A Cognitive-Behavioural Approach, A Therapist Guide,* New York, NY: Oxford University Press.

Garner, J. (2002). 'Psychodynamic work with older people'. *Advances in Psychiatric Treatment,* 8, 128–137.

Garner, J. (2008). 'Psychodynamic psychotherapy'. In R. Jacoby, C. Oppenheimer, T. Dening and A. Thomas (Eds) *Oxford Textbook of Old Age Psychiatry.* Oxford: Oxford Press.

Gatz, M., Fiske, A., Fox, L., Kaskie, B. et al. (1998). 'Empirically validated psychological treatments for older adults.' *Journal of Mental Health and Aging,* 4, 9-46.

Gazzaniga, M.S, Ivry, R.B. and Mangun, G.R. (2002). *Cognitive Neuroscience: The Biology of the Mind.* New York; London: Norton.

Gendron, C., Poitras, L. and Dastoor, D.P. (1996). 'Cognitive-behavioural group intervention for spouse caregivers: findings and clinical considerations'. *Clinical Gerontol,* 17(1), 3–19.

Gendron, C., Poitras, L., Engels, M., Dastoor, D. Sirota, S., Barza, S., Davis, J. and Levine, N. (1986). 'Skills training with supporters of the demented'. *Journal of American Geriatric Society,* 30(12), 875–880.

GHS (2001). *General Household Survey.* Stationary Office. SSD Project Support Branch.

Gilbert, P. (1998). 'What is shame? Some core issues and controversies.' In P. Gilbert and B. Andrews Shame: *Interpersonal Behaviour, Psychopathology and Culture.* New York: Oxford University Press.

Gilbert, P. (2003). 'Evolution, social roles and the differences in shame and guilt'. *Social Research,* 70, 401–426.

Glantz, M. (1989). 'Cognitive therapy with the elderly'. In A. Freeman, K. Simon, L. Beutler and H. Arkowitz (Eds) *Comprehensive Handbook of Cognitive Therapy.* New York: Plenum Press.

Glynn-Williams, R. (2008). 'Improving access to psychological therapies for older people in the Wirral PSIGE Newsletter'. *British Psychological Society,* 104, 14–20.

Graham, C., Balllard, C. and Sham, P. (1997). 'Carers' knowledge of dementia, their coping strategies and morbidity'. *International Journal of Geriatric Psychiatry,* 12, 931–936.

Graves, M.E. and Braaten, S. (1996). 'Scaffolded reading experiences. Bridges to success'. *Preventing School Failure*, 40, 169–173.

Greenberger, D. and Padesky, C. (1995). *Clinician's Guide to Mind Over Mood*. New York: Guilford Press.

Hamilton, M. (1959). 'The assessment of anxiety states by rating'. *British Journal of Medical Psychology*, 32, 50–55.

Hamilton, M. (1960). 'A rating scale for depression'. *Journal of Neurology, Neurosurgery and Psychiatry*, 23, 56–62.

Harper, D. and Moss, D. (2003). 'A different kind of chemistry? Reformulating formulation'. *Clinical Psychology Forum*, 25, 6–10.

Hartman-Stein, P. E. (2005). 'An impressive step in identifying evidence-based psychotherapies for geriatric depression'. *Clinical Psychology: Science and Practice*, 12(3), 238–241.

Heason, S. (2005). 'Talking therapy as a psychological intervention for people with dementia: a literature review'. *PSIGE Newsletter, British Psychological Society*, 89, 22–29.

Hébert, R., Lévesque, L., Vézina, J., Lavoie, J.P., Ducharme, F., Gendron, C., Préville, M., Voyer, L., Dubois, M.F., (2003) Efficacy of Psychoeducative Group Program for Caregivers of Demented Persons Living at Home: A Randomized Controlled Trial.

Henry, L. and Williams, R. (1997). 'Problems in conceptualisation with cognitive therapy: an illustrative case study'. *Clinical Psychology and Psychotherapy*, 4, 201–213

Hepburn, K.W., Lewis, M., Narayan, S., Center, B. *et al.* (2005). 'Partners in caregiving: a psychoeducation program affecting dementia family caregivers' distress and caregiving outlook'. *Clinical Gerontologist*, 29(1), 53–68.

Hepple, J., Wilkinson, P. and Pearce, J. (2002). 'Psychological therapies with older people'. In J. Hepple, J. Pearce amd P. Wilkinson (Eds) *Psychological Therapies with Older People*. Hove: Bruner-Routledge.

Higginson, G. (unpublished) 'Using autobiographical narrative history and ICS model with depressed individuals in the early stages of dementia. As part fulfilment of MSc. in Cognitive Behavioural Psychotherapy'. Univeristy of Derby (2005).

Higginson, G. (2009). 'IAPT meets the dementia strategy: CBT with a shame and compassion focus supporting the early diagnosis of vascular dementia. Older People's Symposium'. *BABCP Conference*, Exeter University (July).

Hilton, C. (2009). 'The East Riding of Yorkshire Improving Access to Psychological Therapies pathfinder project – struggles in relation to the inclusion of older people'. *PSIGE Newsletter*, 106, 26–30.

Hinrichsen, G.A. and Clougherty, K.F. (2006). *Interpersonal Psychotherapy for Depressed Older Adults*. Washington DC: American Psychological Association.

Hirsh, A., O'Brien, K., Geffken, G.R., Adkins, J. *et al.* (2006). 'Cognitive-behavioral treatment for obsessive-compulsive disorder in an elderly male with concurrent medical constraints'. *American Journal of Geriatric Psychiatry*, 14(4), 380–381.

Holland, R. (2009). 'Assessing competences against the cognitive behaviour therapy framework'. *CBT Today*, 39(1), 12–13.

Hollon, S.D. and Kendall, P. (1980). 'Cognitive self-statements in depression: development of an automatic thoughts questionnaire'. *Cognitive Therapy and Research*, 4, 383–395.

Holsworth, N. and Paxton, R. (1999). *Managing Anxiety and Depression*. London: Mental Health Foundation.

Howard, R., Ballard, C., O'Brien, J. and Burns, A. (2001). 'Guidelines for the management of agitation in dementia'. *International Journal of Geriatric Psychiatry*, 16, 714–17.

Huang, H., Shyu, Y., Chen, M., Chens, S. and Lin, L. (2003). 'A pilot study on a home-based caregiver training program for improving caregiver self-efficacy and decreasing the behavioural problems of elders with dementia in Taiwan'. *International Journal of Geriatric Psychiatry*, 18, 337–345.

IAPT (2006). www.scmh.org.uk/pdfs/layard+lecture+scmh+120905.doc

Ingram, R.E., Kendall, P.C., Siegle, G., Guarino, J. and McLaughlin, S.C. (1995). 'Psychometric properties of the Positive Automatic Thoughts Questionnaire'. *Psychological Assessment*, 7, 495–507.

James, I.A. (1999). 'Using a cognitive rationale to conceptualise anxiety in people with dementia'. *Behavioural and Cognitive Psychotherapy*, 27(4), 345–351.

James, I. (2001a). 'Cognitive therapy formulations and interventions for treating distress in dementia'. In C. Ballard, J. O'Brien, I. James, and A. Swann (Eds) *Managing Behavioural and Psychological Symptoms in People with Dementia*. Oxford: Oxford University Press.

James, I.A. (2001b). 'Schema therapy: the next generation, but should it carry a health warning?' *Behavioural and Cognitive Psychotherapy*, 29(4), 401–407.

James, I.A. (2001c). 'Therapeutic implications of the Interactive Cognitive Sub-systems (ICS) model for people with dementia'. *Psychology Special Interest Group for Older People (PSIGE) Newsletter*, BPS 77, 32–36.

James, I.A. (2001d). The anger triad and its use with people with severe dementia'. *Psychology Special Interest Group for Older People (PSIGE) Newsletter*, BPS 76, 45–47.

James, I.A. (2003). 'Working with older people: implications for schema theory'. *Clinical Psychology and Psychotherapy*, 10, 133–143.

James, I.A. (2008a). 'Stuff and nonsense in the treatment of older people: essential reading for the over 45s'. *Behaviour and Cognitive Psychotherapy*, 36(6), 735–747.

James, I.A. (2008b). 'Total recall: treating chronic mental illness as a memory'. *Journal of Rational Emotive Behaviour Therapy and Cognitive Behavior Therapy*, 26(4), 276–285.

James, I.A. (2008c). 'Schema therapy in older people'. In K. Laidlaw and B. Knight (Eds) *Handbook of Emotional Disorders in Later Life: Assessment and Treatment*. Oxford: Oxford University Press.

James, I.A. (in press) *Challenging Behaviour: A Practitioner's Guide*. London: Jessica Kingsley Publishers.

James, I. A. and Barton, S. (2004). 'Changing core beliefs: the use of continua'. *Behaviour and Cognitive Psychotherapy*, 32, 431–442.

James, I.A., Blackburn, I.M., Milne, D. and Freeston, M. (2005). 'Supervision Training Assessment Rating Scale (STARS) for assessing competence in CBT supervision'. Doctorate in Clinical Psychology, University of Newcastle upon Tyne.

James, I.A., Blackburn, I.M., Milne, D. and Reichelt, F.K. (2001). 'Moderators of trainee therapists' competence in cognitive therapy'. *British Journal of Clinical Psychology*, 40, 131–141.

James, I.A., Blackburn, I-M., Reichelt, F.K. (2000). 'Manual to the Revised Cognitive therapy scale'. Doctorate in Clinical Psychology, University of Newcastle upon Tyne.

James, I.A. and Fossey, J. (2008). 'Non-pharmacological intervention in care homes'. In R. Jacoby, C. Oppenheimer, T. Dening and A. Thomas (Eds) *Oxford Textbook of Old Age Psychiatry*. Oxford: Oxford Press.

James, I.A., Kendell, K. and Reichelt, F.K. (1999). 'Conceptualisations of self-worth in older people'. *Behavioural and Cognitive Psychotherapy*, 27(3), 285–290.

James, I.A., Mackenzie, L., Stephenson, M. and Roe. P. (2006). 'Dealing with challenging behaviour through an analysis of need: the Colombo approach'. In M. Marshall (Ed) *On the Move: Walking not Wandering*. London: Hawker Press.

James, I. A., Milne, D. and Morse, R. (2008). 'Micro-skills of clinical supervision: scaffolding skills'. *Journal of Cognitive Psychotherapy: An International Quarterly*, 22(1), 29–36.

James, I.A., Milne, D., Morse, R. and Blackburn, I.M. (2007). 'Conducting successful supervision: novel elements towards an integrative approach'. *Behavioural and Cognitive Psychotherapy*, 35(2), 191–200.

James, I.A. and Morse, R. (2007). 'The use of questioning in cognitive behaviour therapy: Identification of question type, function and structure'. *Behavioural and Cognitive Psychotherapy*, 35, 507–511.

James, I.A., Morse, R. and Howarth, A. (2010). 'The science and art of asking questions in cognitive therapy'. *Behavioural and Cognitive Psychotherapy*, 38(1),83–94.

James, I.A., Powell, I. and Kendell, K. (2003a). 'The castle and the know-it-all – access to the inner circle'. *Journal of Dementia Care*, 11(4), 24–26.

James, I.A., Powell, I. and Kendell, K. (2003b). 'A cognitive perspective on training in care homes'. *Journal of Dementia Care*,11(3), 22–24.

James, I.A., Powell, I. and Reichelt, K. (2001). 'Cognitive therapy for carers: distinguishing fact from fiction'. *Journal of Dementia Care*, 9(6), 24–26.

James, I.A., Reichelt, F.K., Carlsson, P. and McAnaney, A. (2008). 'Cognitive behaviour therapy and executive functioning in depression'. *Journal of Cognitive Psychotherapy: An International Quarterly*, 22(3), 210–218.

James, I.A., Reichelt, F.K., Freeston, M. and Barton, S. (2007). 'Schema as memories: Implications for treatment'. *Journal of Cognitive Psychotherapy: An International Quarterly*, 21(1), 51–57.

James, I.A. and Sabin, N. (2002). 'Safety seeking behaviours: conceptualising a person's reaction to the experience of cognitive confusion'. *Dementia: The International Journal of Social Research and Practice*, 1(1), 37–46.

James, I.A., Southam, L. and Blackburn, I.M. (2004). 'Schemas revisited'. *Clinical Psychology and Psychotherapy*, 11, 369–377.

James, I.A. and Stephenson, M. (2007). 'Behaviour that challenges us: the Newcastle support model'. *Journal of Dementia Care*, 15(5), 19–22.

James, I.A., Wood-Mitchell, A., Waterworth, A.M., Mackenzie, L. and Cunningham, J. (2006). 'Lying to people with dementia: developing ethical guidelines for care settings'. *International Journal of Geriatric Psychiatry*, 21, 800–801.

Kazantzis, N., Deane, F., and Ronan K. and L'Abate (2005). *Using Homework Assignments in Cognitive Behaviour Therapy*. New York: Routledge.

Kennedy, E. and Mackenzie, L. (2007). 'Understanding Thomas: needs born of fear and frustration'. *Journal of Dementia Care*, 15, 20–23.

Kipling, T., Bailey, M. and Charlesworth, G. (1999). 'The feasibility of a cognitive behavioural therapy group for men with mild/moderate cognitive impairment'. *Behavioural and Cognitive Psychotherapy*, 27, 189–193.

Kitwood, T. (1997). *Dementia Reconsidered*. Buckingham: Open University Press.

Kneebone, I. (2006). 'Behavioural and cognitive therapies with older people: a selected biography'. *PSIGE Newsletter, British Psychological Society*, 96, 46–49.

Knight, B. (2004). *Psychotherapy with Older Adults* (3rd Edition). Thousand Oaks: Sage.

Koder, D.A. (1998). 'Treatment of anxiety in the cognitively impaired elderly: can cognitive behaviour therapy help?' *International Psychogeriatric*, 10(2), 173–182.

Koder, D., Brodaty, H. and Anstey, K. (1996). 'Cognitive therapy for depression in the elderly'. *International Journal of Geriatric Psychiatry*, 11, 97–107.

Kogan, J.N., Edelstein, B. and McKee, D. (2000). 'Assessment of anxiety in older adults: current status'. *Journal of Anxiety Disorders*, 14, 109–132.

Krupnik, J.L., Sotsky, S.M., Simmens, S., Moyer, J. *et al.* (1996). 'The role of the therapeutic alliance in psychotherapy and pharmacotherapy outcome in the National Institute of Mental Health Treatment of Depression Collaborative Research Program'. *Journal of Consulting and Clinical Psychology*, 64, 532–539.

Kunik, M.E., Braun, U., Stanley, K. *et al.* (2001). 'One session cognitive behavioural therapy for elderly patients with COPD'. *Psychological Medicine*, 31, 717–723.

Kupfer, D. J. (2005). 'The pharmacological management of depression'. *Dialogues in Clinical Neuroscience*, 7(3), 191–205.

Kupfer, D., Horner, M., Brent, D., Lewis, D. et al. (2008). *Oxford American Handbook of Psychiatry*. New York: Oxford Press.

Kuyken, W., Padesky, C. and Dudley, R. (2009). *Collaborative Case Conceptualisation: Working Effectively with Clients in Cognitive Behaviour Therapy*. New York: Guildford.

Laidlaw, K. (2008). 'Cognitive behaviour therapy for depression in Parkinson's disease'. In K. Laidlaw and B. Knight (Eds) *Handbook of Emotional Disorders in Later Life: Assessment and Treatment*. Oxford: Oxford University Press.

Laidlaw, K. (2009). Cognitive behaviour therapy for older people (Keynote). BABCP conference, Exeter University (July 2009).

Laidlaw, K., Davidson, K., Toner, H., Jackson, G. *et al.* (2008). 'A randomised controlled trial of cognitive behaviour therapy vs treatment as usual in the treatment of mild to moderate late life depression'. *International Journal of Geriatric Psychiatry*, 23(8), 843–850.

Laidlaw, K. and Knight, B. (2008). *Handbook of Emotional Disorders in Later Life: Assessment and Treatment*. Oxford: Oxford University Press.

Laidlaw, K. and Thompson, L. (2008). 'Cognitive behaviour therapy with depressed older people'. In K. Laidlaw and B. Knight (Eds) *Handbook of Emotional Disorders in Later Life: Assessment and Treatment*. Oxford: Oxford University Press.

Laidlaw, K., Thompson, L., Dick-Siskin, L. and Gallagher-Thompson, D. (2003). *Cognitive Therapy with Older People*. Chichester: John Wiley.

Laidlaw, K., Thompson, L.W. and Gallagher-Thompson, D. (2004). 'Comprehensive conceptualisation of cognitive behaviour therapy for late life depression'. *Behavioural and Cognitive Psychotherapy*, 32, 389–399.

Landreville, P. (1998). 'Cognitive bibliotherapy for depression in older adults with a disability'. *Clinical Gerontologist*, 19(3), 69–75.

Landreville, P. and Bissonette, L. (1997). 'Effects of cognitive bibliotherapy for depressed older adults with a disability'. *Clinical Gerontologist*, 17, 35–55.

Lazarus, L. and Sadavoy, J. (1996). 'Individual psychotherapy'. In J. Sadavoy, L. Lazarus, L. Jarvik *et al.* (Eds), *Comprehensive Review of Geriatric Psychiatry*, 2nd ed. Washington DC. American Psychiatric Press.

Leeming, D., Boyle, M. and Macdonald, J. (2009). 'Accounting for psychological problems: how user-friendly are psychological formulations?' *Clinical Psychology Forum*, 200, 12–17.

Lewinsohn, P., Munoz, R. and Youngren, M. (1992). *Control Your Depression*. London: Simon and Schuster Books.

Lincoln, N. B. and Flannaghan, T. (2003). 'Cognitive behavioral psychotherapy for depression following stroke: a randomized controlled trial'. *Stroke*, 34(1), 111–115.

Livingston, G., Johnston, K., Katona, C., Paton, J. and Lyketsos, C. (2005). 'Systematic review of psychological approaches to the management of neuropsychiatric symptoms of dementia'. *American Journal of Psychiatry*, 162(11), 1996–2021.

Logsdon, R.S., McCurry, S. and Teri, L. (2008). 'Assessment and treatment of dementia-related affective disturbances'. In K. Laidlaw and B. Knight (Eds) *Handbook of Emotional Disorders in Later Life: Assessment and Treatment*. Oxford: Oxford University Press.

McGee, D., Del Vento, A. and Bavelas, J. (2005). 'An interactional model of questions as therapeutic interventions'. *Journal of Marital and Family Therapy*, 31, 371–384.

Mackin, R.S. and Arean, P.A. (2005). 'Evidence-based psychotherapeutic interventions for geriatric depression'. *Psychiatric Clinics of North America*, 28, 805–820.

McGinn, L. and Young, J. (1996). 'Schema-focused therapy'. In P.M. Salkovskis (Ed) *Frontiers of Cognitive Therapy*. New York: John Wiley.

Marks, I. and Mathews, A. (1979). 'Brief standardised self-rating for phobic patients'. *Behaviour Research and Therapy*, 17, 263–267.

Marmar, C.R., Gaston, L., Gallagher, D. and Thomson, L.W. (1989). 'Alliance and outcome in late-life depression'. *The Journal of Nervous and Mental Disease*, 177, 464–472.

Marriott, A., Donaldson, C., Tarrier, N. and Burns, A. (2000). 'Effectiveness of cognitive-behavioural family intervention in reducing the burden of care in carers of patients with Alzheimer's disease'. *British Journal of Psychiatry*, 176, 557–562.

Matthews, H. and Wilkinson, P. (unpublished). *Staying Well After Depression with Group Cognitive Therapy Participant Treatment Manual* (email: Philip.Wilkinson@psych.ox.ac.uk).

Melzack, R. and Wall, P. (1996). *The Challenge of Pain*. London: Penguin Science.

Meyer, T.J., Miller, M., Metzger, R. and Borkovec, T.D. (1990). 'Development and validation of the Penn State Worry Questionnaire'. *Behaviour Research and Therapy*, 28(6), 487–495.

Miller, M.D. (2009). *Clinician's Guide to Interpersonal Psychotherapy in Later Life: Helping Cognitively Impaired or Depressed Elders and Their Caregivers*. New York, NY: Oxford University Press.

Milne, D. (2008). *Evidence-Based Clinical Supervision: Principles and Practice*. Chichester: BPS Blackwell

Minsky, M.L. (1975). 'A framework for representing knowledge'. In P.H. Winston (Ed) *The Psychology of Computer Vision*. New York: McGraw Hill.

Mintz, J., Steuer, J. and Jarvik, L. (1981). 'Psychotherapy with depressed elderly patients'. Research considerations. *Journal of Consulting and Clinical Psychology*, 49(4), 542–548.

Mittelman, M., Roth, D., Clay, O. and Haley, W. (2007). 'Preserving the health of Alzheimer's caregivers: impact of a spouse caregiver intervention'. *American Journal of Geriatric Psychiatry*, 15, 780–789.

Mittelman, M.S., Roth, D., Haley, W. and Zarit, S. (2004). 'Effects of caregiver intervention on negative caregiver appraisals of behaviour problems in patients with alzheimer's disease: results of a randomised trial'. *Journal of Gerontology*, 59B(1), 27–34.

Mohlman, J., Gorenstein, E.E., Kleber, M., de Jesus, M. *et al.* (2003). 'Standard and enhanced cognitive-behavior therapy for late-life generalized anxiety disorder: two pilot investigations'. *American Journal of Geriatric Psychiatry*, 11(1), 24–32.

Mohlman, J. and Gorman, J.M. (2005). 'The role of executive functioning in CBT: a pilot study with anxious older adults'. *Behaviour Research and Therapy*, 43(4), 447–465.

Molyneux, G., McCarthy, M., McEniff., M., Cryan, M. and Conroy, R. (2008). 'Prevalence and predictors of carer burden and depression in carers of patients referred to an old age psychiatric service'. *Journal of the American Geriatrics Society*, 28, 237–247.

Moniz-Cook, E., Agar, S., Silver, M., Woods, R. *et al.* (1998). 'Can staff training reduce carer stress and behavioural disturbance in the elderly mentally ill?' *International Journal of Geriatric Psychiatry*, 13, 149–158.

Moniz-Cook, E., Walker, A., De Vught, M., Verhey, F. and James, I. (2008). 'Functional analysis-based interventions for challenging behaviour in dementia – (Cochrane Review)' In *The Cochrane Database of Systematic Reviews*, Issue 1. Art. No.: CD006929. DOI: 10.1002/14651858.CD006929.

Montgomery, S.A. and Asberg, M. (1979). 'A new depression scale designed to be sensitive to change'. *British Journal of Psychiatry*, 134, 382–389.

Morin, C.M. (1994). 'Dysfunctional beliefs and attitudes about sleep: preliminary scale development and National Dementia Strategy, Department of Health (2009). 'Living well with dementia: a National Dementia Srategy'. (www.dh.gov.uk/en/socialcare/deliveringadultsocialcare/olderpeople/nationaldementiastrategy/index.htm)

National Dementia Strategy, Department of Health (2009) 'Living with dementia: a National Dementia Strategy'. Available at www.dh.gov.uk/en/socialcare/deliveringadultsocialcare/olderpeople/nationaldementiastrategy/index.html

NICE (2004). 'Depression: management of depression in primary and secondary care – Clinical guideline 23' (www.nice.org.uk/CG023).

Orpwood, R. and Chadd, J. (2007). 'Exploring the use of technology to improve the quality of life of people with dementia'. *Les Cahiers de la Fondation Mederic Alzheimer*, 3, 84–91.

Orrell, M. and Hancock, G., Hoe, J., Woods, B., Livingston, G. and Challis, D. (2004). 'A cluster randomized controlled trial to reduce unmet needs of people with dementia living in residential care'. *International Journal of Geriatric Psychiatry*, 20, 1273–1293.

Overholser, J.C. (1993). 'Elements of the Socratic method: I systematic questioning'. *Psychotherapy*, 30, 67–74.

Pachana, N., Byrne, G., Siddle, H., Koloski, N. *et al.* (2006). 'Development and validation of the Geriatric Anxiety Inventory'. *International Geriatrics*, Online, Jun 29, 1–12.

Padesky, C. (1993). 'Socratic questioning: changing minds or guiding discovery'. *Keynote Address, European Congress of Behavioural and Cognitive Psychotherapies*, London, 24 September.

Padesky, C.A. (1994). 'Schema change processes in cognitive therapy'. *Clinical Psychology and Psychotherapy*, 1, 267–278.

Padesky, C. and Greenberger, D. (1995). *Clinician's Guide to Mind Over Mood*. New York: Guilford.

Peacock, S., and Forbes, D. (2003). 'Interventions for caregivers of persons with dementia: a systematic review'. *Canadian Journal of Nursing Research*, 35(4), 88–107.

Perris, C. (2000). 'Personality-related disorders of interpersonal behaviour: a developmental-constructivist cognitive psychotherapy approach to treatment based on attachment theory'. *Clinical Psychology and Psychotherapy*, 7, 97–117.

Persons, J., Mooney, K. and Padesky, C. (1995). 'Interrater reliability of cognitive-behavioural case formulations'. *Cognitive Therapy and Research*, 19, 21–34.

Persons, J. and Tompkins, M. (1997). 'Cognitive-behavioural case formulation'. In T. Eells (Eds) *Handbook of Psychotherapy Case Formulation*. New York: Guilford Press.

Pinquart, M., Duberstein, P. and Lyness, J. (2006). 'Treatments for later-life depressive conditions: a meta-analytic comparison of pharmacotherapy and psychotherapy'. *American Journal of Psychiatry*, 163, 1493–1501.

Pinquart, M., Duberstein, P. R., and Lyness, J. M. (2007). 'Effects of psychotherapy and other behavioral interventions on clinically depressed older adults: a meta-analysis'. *Aging and Mental Health*, 11(6), 645–657.

Pinquart M., and Sorensen, S. (2001). 'How effective are psychotherapeutic and other psychosocial interventions with older adults? A meta-analysis'. *Journal Mental Health Aging*, 7, 207–243.

Pinqart, M. and Sorensen S. (2006). 'Helping caregivers of persons with dementia: which interventions work and how large are their effects?' *International Psychogeriatrics*, 18(4) 577–595.

Power, M.J. and Dalgleish, T. (1996). 'Two routes to emotions: some implications of multi-level theories of emotion for therapeutic practice'. *Behavioural and Cognitive Psychotherapy*, 27(2), 129–142.

Proctor, R., Burns, A., Powell, H., Tarrier, N., Faragher, B., Richardson, G., Davies, L. and South, B. (1999). 'Behavioural management in nursing and residential homes: a randomized controlled trial'. *Lancet*, 354, 26–29.

Qualls, S.H. (1999). 'Family therapy with older clients'. *Journal Clinical Psychology*, 55, 977–990.

Rabbitt, P. (2006). 'Tales of the unexpected: 25 years of cognitive gerontology', *Psychologist*, 19(11), 674–676.

Radloff, L. (1977). 'The CES-D Scale: a self report depression scale for research in the general population.' *Applied Psychological Measurement*, 1, 385–401.

Ranzijn, R. (2002). 'Towards a positive psychology of ageing: potentials and barriers'. *Australian Psychologist*, 37(4), 79–85.

Reason, J.T. (1988). 'Stress and cognitive failure'. In S. Fisher and J. Reason (Eds) *Handbook of Life Stress, Cognition and Health*. New York: Wiley.

Roth, A.D. and Pilling, S. (2007). *The Competences Required to Deliver Effective Cognitive and Behavioural Therapy for People with Depression and with Anxiety Disorders*. London: Department of Health (ref:8666).

Rovner, B., Steele, C., Shmuely, Y. and Folstein, M. (1996). 'A randomised trial of dementia care in nursing homes.' *Journal of the American Geriatric Society*, 44(1), 7-13.

Rybarczyk, B. Gallagher-Thompson, D., Rodman, J., Zeiss, A. *et al.* (1992). 'Applying cognitive-behavioural psychotherapy to the chronically ill elderly: treatment issues and case illustration'. *International Psychogeriatrics*, 4, 127–140.

Safran, J.D. and Segal, Z.V. (1990). *Interpersonal Processes in Cognitive Therapy*. New York: Basic Books.

Salthouse, T.A. (2000). 'Steps towards the explanation of adult age differences in cognition'. In T.J. Perfect and E.A. Maylor (Eds) *Models of Cognitive Aging*. Oxford, Oxford University Press.

Schaie, K.W. (2008). 'A lifespan developmental perspective of psychological ageing'. In K. Laidlaw and B. Knight (Eds) *Handbook of Emotional Disorders in Later Life: Assessment and Treatment*. Oxford: Oxford University Press.

Schank, R.C. and Abelson, R. (1977). *Scripts, plans, goals and understanding*. Hillsdale, NJ: Lawrence Erlbaum Assoc. Inc.

Scholey, K.A., and Woods, B.T. (2003). 'A series of brief cognitive therapy interventions with people experiencing both dementia and depression: a description of techniques and common themes'. *Clinical Psychology and Psychotherapy*, 10(3), 175–185.

Scogin, F., Hamblin, D. and Beutler, L. (1987). 'Bibliotherapy for depressed older adults: a self-help alternative'. *Gerontologist*, 27, 383–387.

Scogin, F., Jamison, C., Floyd, M. and Chaplin, W. F. (1998). 'Measuring learning in depression treatment: a cognitive bibliotherapy test'. *Cognitive Therapy and Research*, 22(5), 475–482.

Scogin, F., Jamison, C. and Gochneaur, K. (1989). 'Comparative efficacy of cognitive and behavioural bibliotherapy for mildly and moderately depressed older adults'. *Journal of Consulting and Clinical Psychology*, 57, 403–407.

Scogin, F., Welsh, D., Hanson, A., Stump, J., and Coates, A. (2005). 'Evidence-based psychotherapies for depression in older adults'. *Clinical Psychology: Science and Practice*, 12(3), 222–237.

Seamark, D.A., Blake, S., Seamark, C. and Halpin, D. (2004). 'Living with severe chronic obstructive pulmonary disease (COPD): perceptions of patients and their carers. An interpretative phenomenological analysis'. *Palliative Medicine*, 18, 619–625.

Secker, D. and Brown, R.G. (2005). 'Cognitive behavioural therapy (CBT) for carers of patients with Parkinson's disease: a preliminary randomised control trial'. *Journal of Neurological Neurosurgery and Psychiatry*, 76, 491–497.

Segal, Z.V. and Williams, J.M. and Teasdale, J.D. (2002). *Mindfulness-Based Cognitive Therapy for Depression*. Guildford: Wiley.

Sink, K., Holden, K. and Yaffe, K. (2005). 'Pharmacological treatment of neuropsychiatric symptoms of dementia: a review of the evidence.' *Journal of American Medical Association*, 293(5), 596-608.

Sinoff, G., Ore, L., Zlotogorsky, D. and Tamir, A (1999). 'Short Anxiety Screening Test–a brief instrument for detecting anxiety in the elderly'. *International Journal of Geriatric Psychiatry*, 14(12) 1062–71.

Smith, A. (2004). 'Clinical uses of mindfulness training in older people'. *Behavioural and Cognitive Psychotherapy*, 32(4) 385–388.

Smith, A., Graham, L. and Senthinathan, S. (2007). 'Mindfulness-based cognitive therapy for recurring depression in older people: A qualitative study'. *Aging and Mental Health*, 11(3), 346–357.

Sorensen, S., Pinquart, M. and Duberstein, P. (2002). 'How effective are interventions with caregivers? An updated meta-analysis'. *Gerontologist*, 42(3), 356–372.

Spector, A., Thorgrimsen, L., Woods, B., Royan, L., Davies, S., Butterworth, M. and Orrell, M. (2003). 'Efficacy of an evidence-based cognitive stimulation programme for people with dementia: randomised controlled trial'. *British Journal of Psychiatry*,183, 248–254.

Sperry, L., Gudeman, J., Blackwell, B. and Faulkner, L. (1992). *Psychiatric Case Formulations*. Washington DC: American Psychiatric Press.

Speilberger, C.D., Gorsuch, R., Lushene, R., Vagg, P. and Jacobs, G. (1983). *Manual for the State-Trait Anxiety Inventory (STAI)*. PaloAlto, CA: Consulting Psychologists Press.

Spira, A. and Edelstein, B. (2006). 'Behavioral interventions for agitation in older adults with dementia: an evaluative review'. *International Psychogeriatrics*, 18(2), 195–225.

Stanley, M. A., Hopko, D. R., Diefenbach, G. J., Bourland, S. L. *et al*. (2003). 'Cognitive-behavior therapy for late-life generalized anxiety disorder in primary care: Preliminary findings'. *American Journal of Geriatric Psychiatry*, 11(1), 92–96.

Stevenson, G.S., Ewing, H., Herschell, J. and Keith, D. (2006). 'An enhanced assessment and support team (EAST) for dementing elders – review of a Scottish regional initiative'. *Journal of Mental Health*, 15(2), 251–258.

Swales, P., Solfvin, J. and Sheikh, J. (1996). 'Cognitive-behavioural therapy in older panic disorder patients'. *American Journal of Geriatric Psychiatry*, 4, 46–60.

Tarrier, N. and Calam, R. (2002). 'New developments in cognitive-behavioural case formulation. Epidemiological, systemic and social context: an integrative approach'. *Behavioural and Cognitive Psychotherapy*, 30, 311–328.

Teasdale, J.D. (1994). 'Emotions and two kinds of meaning. Cognitive therapy and applied cognitive science'. *Behaviour Research and Therapy*, 31, 339–354.

Teasdale, J.D. and Barnard, P. (1993). *Affect Cognition and Change: Remodelling Depressive Thought*. Hove: Erlbaum.

Teri, L. (1994). 'Behavioural treatment of depression in patients with dementia'. *Alzheimer Disease and Associated Disorders*, 8, 66–74.

Teri, L. and Logsdon, R.G. (1991). 'Identifying pleasant activities for Alzheimer's disease patients: the pleasant event schedule-AD.' *The Gerontologist*, 31, 124-127.

Teri, L, Logsdon, R. and Uomoto, J. (1991). *Treatment of Depression in Patients with Alzheimer's Disease. Therapist Manual*. Seattle: University of Washington School of Medicine.

Teri, L., McCurry, S., Logsdon, R. and Gibbons, L. (2005). 'Training community consultants to help family members improve dementia care: a randomised controlled trial'. *Gerontologist*, 45, 802–811.

Teri, L., and Gallagher-Thompson, D. (1991). 'Cognitive-behavioural interventions for treatment of depression in Alzheimer's patients'. *Gerontologist*, 31(3) 413–416.

Teri, L., McKenzie, G. and LaFazia, D. (2005). 'Psychosocial treatment of depression in older adults with dementia'. *Clinical Psychology: Science and practice*, 12(3), 303–316.

Thompson, L.W., Dick-Siskin, L., Coon, D., Powers, D. and Gallagher-Thompson, D. (2009). 'Treating late life depression: a cognitive-behavioral workbook (Treatment that works)'. New York, NY: Oxford University Press.

Thompson, L.W., Gallagher-Thompson, D., Laidlaw, K. and Dick, L.P. (2000). 'Cognitive-behaviour therapy for late life depression'. *A Therapist Manual. UK Version*. Edinburgh: University of Edinburgh, Department of Psychiatry.

Thompson, L., Gallagher-Thompson, D., and Dick, L. (1996). *Cognitive-Behavioural Therapy For Late Life Depression: A Therapists Manual*. Clinical Center and Psychology Service of the VA Palo Alto Health Care System and Stanford University.

Tompkins, M. (2004). *Using Homework in Psychotherapy. Strategies, Guidelines and Forms*. London: The Guilford Press.

Tversky, A. and Kahneman, D. (1973). 'Availability: a heuristic for judging frequency and probability'. *Cognitive Psychology, 5*, 207–232.

Ungar, M. (2006). 'Resilence across cultures'. *British Journal of Social Work*, 38(2), 218–235.

Verkaik, R., van Weert, J. and Francke, A. (2005). 'The effects of psychosocial methods on depressed, aggressive and apathetic behaviours of people with dementia: a systematic review'. *International Journal of Geriatric Psychiatry*, 20, 301–314.

Vygotsky, L.S. (1978). *Mind in Society: The Development of Higher Psychological Processes*. Cambridge, MA: Harvard University Press.

Walker, D.A. and Clarke, M. (2001). 'Cognitive behavioural psychotherapy: a comparison between younger and older adults in two inner city mental health teams'. *Aging and Mental Health*, 5(2) 197–199.

Watkins, E. and Brown, R. G. (2002). 'Rumination and executive function in depression: an experimental study'. *Journal of Neurology, Neurosurgery and Psychiatry*, 72(3), 400–402.

Weissman, A. and Beck, A.T. (1978). 'Development and validation of the Dysfunctional Attitude Scale: a preliminary investigation'. Paper presented at the meeting of the American Educational Research Association, Toronto, Ontario, Canada.

Wells, A. (1997). *Cognitive Therapy of Anxiety Disorders: A Practice Manual and Conceptual Guide*. Chichester: John Wiley.

Wenzlaff, R. and Bates, D. (2000). 'The relative efficacy of concentration and suppression strategies of mental control'. *Personality and Social Psychology Bulletin*, 26, 1200–1212.

West, R.J. (1996). 'An application of prefrontal cortex function theory to cognitive aging'. *Psychological Bulletin*. 120, 272–292.

Westbrook, D., Kennerley, H. and Kirk, J. (2007). *An Introduction to Cognitive Behaviour Therapy: Skills and Applications*. London: Sage Publications.

Wetherell, J.L., Gatz, M. and Craske, M.G. (2003). 'Treatment of generalized anxiety disorder in older adults'. *Journal of Consulting and Clinical Psychology*, 71(1), 31–40.

Whisman, M.A. (1993). 'Mediators and moderators of change in cognitive therapy of depression'. *Psychological Bulletin*, 114, 248–265.

Wilkins, S., Castle, S., Heck, E. *et al.* (1999). 'Immune function, mood, and perceived burden among caregivers participating in a psychoeducational intervention'. *Psychiatric Services*, 50(6), 747–749.

Wilkinson, P. (2008). 'Cognitive behaviour therapy'. In R. Jacoby, C. Oppenheimer, T. Dening, A. and Thomas (Eds) *Oxford Textbook of Old Age Psychiatry*. Oxford: Oxford Press.

Wilkinson, P., Alder, N., Juszczak, E., Matthews, H. *et al.* (2009). 'A pilot randomised controlled trial of a brief cognitive behavioural group intervention to reduce recurrence rates in late life depression'. *International Journal of Geriatric Psychiatry*, 24(1), 68–75.

Williams, C. (2001). *Overcoming Depression: A Five Areas Approach*. London: Arnold.

Williams, J.M. (1992). The *Psychological Treatment of Depression: A Guide to the Theory and Practice of Cognitive Behaviour Therapy*. London: Routledge.

Williams, J.M. (1994). 'Interacting cognitive subsystems and unvoiced murmurs: a review of affect, cognition and change by Teasdale and Barnard'. *Cognition and Emotion*, 8(6), 571–579.

Wilson, K.C.M., Mottram, P. G. and Vassilas, C. A. (2008). 'Psychotherapeutic treatments for older depressed people'. *Cochrane Database of Systematic Reviews, 1.*

Wisocki, P.A., Handen, B. and Morse, C. (1986). 'The worry scale as a measure of anxiety among homebound and community active elderly'. *The Behaviour Therapist*, 9, 9–95.

Wood-Mitchell, A., Mackenzie, L., Stephenson, M. and James, I.A. (2007). 'Treating challenging behaviour in care settings: audit of a community service using the neuropsychiatric inventory'. *PSIGE Newsletter, British Psychological Society*, 101, 19–23.

Yesavage, J.A., Brink, T., Rose, T., Lum, O. *et al.* (1983). 'Development and validation of a geriatric depression screening scale: a preliminary report'. *Journal of Psychiatric Research*, 17, 37–49.

Young, J. and Beck, A. T. (1980). *Cognitive Therapy Scale Rating Manual*. Unpublished manuscript, University of Pennsylvania, Philadelphia, PA.

Young, J. and Beck, A. T. (1988). *Cognitive Therapy Scale*. Unpublished manuscript, University of Pennsylvania, Philadelphia, PA.

Young, J.E. (1994). *Cognitive Therapy for Personality Disorders: A Schema-focused Approach*. Florida: Professional Resource Press.

Young, J.E., Klosko, J.S. and Weishaar, M. (2003). *Schema Therapy: A Practitioner's Guide*. New York: Guilford.

Zalaquett, C.P. and Stens, A. (2006). 'Psychosocial treatments for major depression and dysthymia in older adults: a review of the research literature'. *Journal of Counselling Development*, 84(2) 192–201.

Zarit, S. and Knight, B. (1996). *A Guide to Psychotherapy and Aging*. Washington, DC: American Psychological Association.

Subject Index

Author Index